THE
SIMPSONS

THE
SIMPSONS

An Uncensored, Unauthorized History

JOHN ORTVED

Faber and Faber, Inc.

An affiliate of Farrar, Straus and Giroux

New York

Faber and Faber, Inc.
An affiliate of Farrar, Straus and Giroux
18 West 18th Street, New York 10011

Grateful acknowledgment is made to the following for permission to reprint material: Judith Brennan; Joe Morgenstern; Sean Mitchell; David Owen; Eric Spitznagel and *The Believer*; and WHYY, Inc.

Library of Congress Cataloging-in-Publication Data
Ortved, John, 1980–
    The Simpsons : an uncensored, unauthorized history / John Ortved. — 1st ed.
        p.   cm.
    Includes bibliographical references and index.
    ISBN 978-0-86547-988-3 (hardcover : alk. paper)
    1. Simpsons (Television program)   I. Title.

PN1992.77.S58O78 2009
791.45'72—dc22

2009015216

www.fsgbooks.com

10   9   8   7   6   5   4   3   2   1

For Stella, who let me watch TV
And for my mother, who didn't

Contents

Foreword

BY DOUGLAS COUPLAND

Here it is, two decades later. I never thought that as I aged I would develop Groundskeeper Willie Eyebrow Syndrome (GWES), and yet nature has cruelly slotted me with it. And here it is, two decades later, and I still can't go near cafeteria food without thinking of Bart Simpson's corrupt lunch lady and her massive cartons of beef hearts on the rear loading dock. And finally, here it is, two decades later, and despite my urbane demeanor and general support for worthy causes, I can't help but wonder how cozy Mr. Burns's pair of loafers made of former gophers would feel.

I remember back at the start of the kraziness, back when Fox was a plucky young network with a gleam in its eye, with the amusing-but-doomed *Tracey Ullman Show* operating at the tent pole of its aspiring avant-garde sitcom regime. I remember in that show seeing an amusing animation clip in which a very badly drawn and animated Matt Groening character barfed into a dish of mints in a doctor's waiting room. (I think that's what it was; my brain cells may well now have the neuro equivalent of GWES.) I remember thinking to myself, *Man, I can't believe they showed barfing on TV—that was so transgressive. Thank you, Fox, for opening new doors through which satire may enter.*

And so the Simpsons have been barfing into dishes of mints for more than two decades. Actually, to be technically correct, it's the *Family Guy* characters who do the avant-garde barfing these days. But the Simpsons did open that door, and in so doing have created a self-sustaining mythology of archetypes and stories that unite mankind far better than NATO, Esperanto, or metric. During book tours I used to hand out cards and ask people to write down the name of their favorite Simpsons character and then hand it in at the end of the reading. Surprisingly, it wasn't Bart or Homer or the big kahunas that were the favorites—it was the peripheral characters that were beloved: Duff Man with his *Ooh yeah!* and his tendency to refer to himself in the third person; Selma, the beloved chain-smoking lesbian hag; or (possibly the most obscure character of all) alcoholic marketing cipher Lindsay Nagle.

The larger goal of asking people to write down the names of their favorite character was simply to create a nice mood in the room, and it always worked. You can find people in just about any mood, and after a bit of *Simpsons* banter, a more cheerful psychic homeostasis emerges. I remember in a Quebec hardware store, a teenage girl at the end of an aisle holding up a blue feather duster and saying to her friend, *"C'est Marge Simpson."* Now that's world peace in action.

I suppose having GWES is simply a subset of a larger condition called growing old. I look in the mirror and am daily insulted by myself, and yet the Simpsons remain as young and fresh as always—except for the earlier episodes, which aren't as well drawn as in later episodes, the ones in which Homer sounds funny, and which are too weird to watch repeatedly. (Fans know what I mean.) I like the fact that we don't know where Springfield is. I like the fact that you still never really know where an episode is going to take you—to Capitol City, to Epcot, to Winnipeg, or to a dash of mints filled with barf.

You may be entering this book with ambivalence—maybe it's not a good thing to see how the show comes into being; maybe it's best not to see the beef hearts being turned into lunch. But maybe you'll come away from the book fortified and more eager than ever to turn the TiVo to Fox on Sunday nights. Forget Disneyland. Sunday night at eight is the happiest place on earth. *Ooh yeah!*

Preface

If you bought this book to learn something about comedy or its work-ings, I suggest you return it and put the money toward a copy of *Freaks and Geeks* on DVD. Comedy can't really be explained with words, and Judd Apatow's brilliant and short-lived series sheds more light on the subject than I could ever hope to.

In a remarkable scene from the episode "Dead Dogs and Gym Teach-ers," Bill Haverchuk, a young teenager and perhaps the geekiest of geeks, comes home to an empty house after another humiliating day at school (he is fatherless; his mother, who works as a waitress, is dating the gym coach he loathes). Making himself a cheese sandwich, he sits down in front of the television. Immersed in Garry Shandling and the loneliness that will define his adolescent life, Bill begins to laugh. He laughs so hard the food falls from his mouth. The Who's "I'm One" plays over the action. His face scrunches into apoplectic expressions of joy. It's a deeply poignant moment, representing not only the alienation and indignities many of us suffered as high school losers, but our search for solace, and comedy's ability to save us.

The series is Apatow's finest work, and the touchstone in his path to becoming the James L. Brooks for my generation—developing thought-ful comedy blockbusters with fully realized and deeply flawed charac-ters. Brent Forrester, who has worked with Apatow, told me that the scene was based on Judd's personal experience, which I can believe. But really, it could be any of us.

I'm stealing from George Meyer here, but I like to laugh more than the average person. I'm not sure where it fits on my list, but it's up there. I and those of us who love comedy feel as though it is essential because, as one of James L. Brooks's associates put it, "Funny helps you live through the pain." I can remember countless weekend evenings, long past the time I should have been going to parties or on dates, spent alone or with a single friend, eating pizza and watching *The Simpsons*, *Spaceballs*, *Saturday Night Live*, or *Waiting for Guffman*. And I loved it, not because I didn't know there was another world that I was missing but because this really was the next best thing; if I couldn't laugh with others, I would laugh by myself.

Humor's import has been debated for centuries. Countless critics, from Aristotle to George Saunders, have qualified, augmented, and tried to define its role: humor challenges society's conventions and institutions, explains them, or even reinforces them; it brings high men low and social criminals to justice, or can be a conduit for truth; it can be an expression of man's most base and vulgar instincts, the most sophisticated of human reactions, or a challenge to authority.

And yet, for all these abounding opinions, comedy remains a tricky animal to trap. "The problem of writing about comedy," Conan O'Brien told me, "it's like trying to hold a gas, the tighter you squeeze, the more it dissipates." I agree with Conan, and E. B. White, who said that humor "can be dissected as a frog can, but the thing dies in the process . . . and the innards are discouraging to any but the pure scientific mind."

I don't think what follows offers a solution to the quandary, but my chosen format, the oral history, is my way around it. I didn't want to write about comedy, about why *The Simpsons* is funny; that's not only futile, it's boring. I believe that the most accurate insights are derived from well-told stories, which are hopefully what follows this preface. Comedy is too personal, far-reaching, and complex for me to even attempt to tell you anything about it.

If you want to know about ancient Greek society, you can read a textbook and come away well informed, if a little bored. Another option would be to read the myths. They won't tell you everything, but listening to the stories of Homer, Hesiod, Aeschylus, and Herodotus will fill your head with the dress, wars, economies, and sexual mores that founded Western culture. They may inspire you to read more, even to see history, literature, and art with a new eye. The point is that there are truths in those myths, and they are fascinating. If there's more to be found underneath the dizzying array of *Simpsons* anecdotes that follow, I'm certainly glad, but the joy for me isn't in exploring those larger concepts. It's writing about all those horny Greek gods as they toy with humans, start wars, and turn peasant girls into magical bears. The goal is to tell the story of *The Simpsons*, or more to the point, to let the story tell itself.

And this isn't the whole story. Far from it. One thing I've accepted as a journalist is that the truth, if it exists, is highly elusive. All we have to go on are stories, people's versions of events. Numbers lie. So do humans. But even more complex is that truths differ. Two witnesses to the same event will never have the same story. I have to believe there are truths in myths, because I believe, from the Bible to the 9/11 Commission Report, stories are what we have to work with. There are facts: I wrote this book; Ali beat Foreman; the tiger attacked Roy. But the minute you go deeper, as soon as you look into how these things happened, or what *really* happened, you run up against eyewitness accounts, biographies, police reports, and videotapes—all of these will be, unequivocally, someone's version of events.

The best way for me to acknowledge and address this problem, especially when my topic was as contentious, bitchy, and riddled with vendettas as *The Simpsons*, was to tell it as an oral history. The lack of cooperation from Jim Brooks and the current *Simpsons* staff made this approach even more logical, and even necessary. The fact that these were individuals' stories is underscored by the narrative coming straight from their mouths. With the exception of gaps filled in by secondary research, some minimal editorial comments, and information conveyed from unattributed sources, I think I've managed to do that. There were a host of reasons I wanted this history to be an oral one, not least of which was how much smarter my interview subjects are than I. But this was the major one. Objectivity is horseshit. Let's hear the good stuff.

THE
SIMPSONS

Introduction: "Hi, Everybody!"

In August 1992, at the Republican National Convention in Houston, George H. Bush made a commitment to strengthen traditional values, promising to make families "a lot more like the Waltons and a lot less like the Simpsons." A few days later, before the opening credits rolled on the sitcom's weekly episode, *The Simpsons* issued its response. Seated in front of the television, the family watched Bush's remarks. "Hey! We're just like the Waltons," said Bart. "We're praying for an end to the Depression, too." While the immediacy of the response was unique, it was vintage *Simpsons*: tongue-in-cheek, subversive satire, skewering both the president's cartoonish political antics and the culture that embraced them. Five months later, Bill Clinton moved into the White House. The Waltons were out; the Simpsons were in.

Back in the late eighties, when *The Simpsons* premiered on Fox, comedically speaking prime-time television was somewhat lacking. Despite some bright spots like *Cheers* and the cheerfully crude *Roseanne*, the sitcom roost was ruled by didactic, saccharine family fare: *The Cosby Show*, *Full House*, *Growing Pains*, *Golden Girls*, *Family Ties*, and *Family Matters*. Of the latter, Tom Shales piously declared in *The Washington Post*, "A decent human being would have a hard time not smiling."

It was on this sad entertainment landscape that, in December of 1989, *The Simpsons* launched its offensive. Prime time had not seen an animated sitcom since *The Flintstones*, and the Christmas special that debuted the series made clear that Springfield and Bedrock were separated by more than just a few millennia. "Couldn't be better . . . not only exquisitely weird but also as smart and witty as television gets," raved the *Los Angeles Times*. "Why would anyone want to go back to *Growing Pains*?" asked *USA Today*. They were neither human beings nor the least bit decent, but the rich characters, subversive themes, and layered humor resounded deeply with both child and adult audiences demanding more from their entertainment.

What followed is one of the most astounding successes in television history. *The Simpsons* went on to be a ratings and syndication winner for twenty years and has grossed sums of money measuring in the billions for Fox. It has garnered twenty-three Emmys and a Peabody Award, and it beat out *Mary Tyler Moore*, *Seinfeld*, and the *CBS Evening News with Walter Cronkite* to be named *Time* magazine's best television series of all time: "Dazzlingly intelligent and unapologetically vulgar, *The Simpsons* have surpassed the humor, topicality and, yes, humanity of past TV greats." (*Time* also named Bart one of the one hundred most influential people of the twentieth century. "[Bart] embodies a century of popular culture and is one of the richest characters in it. One thinks of Chekhov, Céline, Lenny Bruce," the writer cooed.) Most tellingly, it is the longest-running sitcom ever.

Such lofty significance was never the goal of Matt Groening, who, with writing aspirations, moved to Los Angeles in 1977, immersing himself in the punk rock scene and working stiff jobs to pay the rent. He recorded his disgust with LA in the comic strip *Life in Hell*, which transposed Groening's dissatisfaction, beefs, and whimsical cynicism into the thoughts and speeches of a wordy, deeply cynical one-eared rabbit named Binky, his illegitimate son Bongo, and a gay couple—who may or may not be identical twins—named Jeff and Akbar. It found its way into the *LA Reader* and then *LA Weekly*, and in 1986, caught the attention of James L. Brooks, legendary writer/producer of *Taxi* and *The Mary Tyler Moore Show*, and writer/director of *Terms of Endearment*. Brooks was looking for a cartoon short to place before commercials on *The Tracey Ullman Show*, which he was producing at the behest of Barry Diller for the struggling Fox network. Groening came up with an idea for a cartoon family, based on his own, called the Simpsons.

Fox was the new kid on the block and was taking daily beatings in the ratings. Rupert Murdoch had successfully wooed Diller to Fox in 1986, and he'd bet on the right pony. Diller launched some of television's first reality programming—*Cops* and *America's Most Wanted*—while taking the sitcom in lewd new directions with *Married . . . with Children*. While Fox lost approximately $50 million its first year,[1] it caught a break in 1988, when the writers in Hollywood went on strike, forcing the major networks (who were bound to the union) to play reruns against first-run shows on the union-free Fox.

The network began turning a profit, but Diller still didn't have his monster hit. When Brooks approached him with the idea of making *The Simpsons* into its own series, Diller bit. "It's not often I've had the experience of watching something great and praying that the next minute doesn't dash it," Diller told *Newsweek*. "And not only having that not happen, but saying at the end: 'This is the real thing! This is the one that can crack the slab for us.' "

When it premiered, the show was both a hit and a lightning rod for criticism. Principals around the country banned Bart Simpson T-shirts, with their slogan "Underachiever and proud of it." Conservatives bristled at a cartoon family portraying such dysfunction and distrust of institutions (police, church, teachers—all are suspect in Springfield), living under the shadow of a dangerous nuclear power plant. Barbara Bush called it "the dumbest thing I had ever seen." After Marge Simpson wrote her a letter, she apologized.

But the Bushes had missed the bus. By the summer of 1990, the Simpsons were *everywhere*. It was Bartmania; America had fallen in love with Homer, Lisa, Marge, Maggie, but especially the spiky-haired, underachieving, authority-challenging Bart. He made the cover of *Time*, *Newsweek*, and *Rolling Stone*.

Fox struck a deal with Mattel and talking Bart dolls began disappearing from department store shelves. Bart Simpson T-shirts were selling at the rate of a million per day in North America.[2] His catchphrases, like "I'm Bart Simpson, who the hell are you?" and "Don't have a cow, man," became such staples of early nineties lexicon that their overuse would eventually be parodied on the show. *The Simp-*

sons Sing the Blues reached number four on the *Billboard* charts, and bootleg merchandise became as ubiquitous as the real thing. Black Bart T-shirts became a popular phenomenon in African-American communities, with Bart's catchphrases altered to "Watch it, mon!" and, without irony, "It's a black thing, you must understand!"

What is so striking about the early episodes is how sweet, and at times intimately dramatic, they were. "The question was: could you make cartoon characters that looked this weird and grotesque and actually make you feel some real emotion," Groening has said. The creators achieved this, at least in part through the real-life problems the Simpsons faced: Homer lived in fear of losing his job; he had trouble connecting to his daughter. In later years, to keep the writing interesting, the characters became more exaggerated, as did their situations (Homer went to space; Maggie killed a man; the family created an international incident with Australia).

Animation opened up a whole new world to the creative staff. Not only could they take their characters anywhere, physically and emotionally, but there were no adorable actors to become tangled up in pubescence, no live studio audience to dictate jokes (even when *Seinfeld* appeared a year later, certainly a step forward for the sitcom, viewers were still being told when to laugh), and the cartoon format meant that the humor could be riskier than would have been possible otherwise.

In addition, because of Brooks's unparalleled clout, *The Simpsons* was the only show on television where network executives were forbidden from giving notes. For comedy writers, it was the land of Milk and Honey. Originally, those writers worked under the guidance of Sam Simon, a TV sitcom veteran and producing partner of Brooks's, who assembled what became one of the most hallowed staffs in television's history. Simon would eventually depart from the show, after one too many confrontations with his fellow producers, especially Matt Groening. Still, many of the original, great writers of *The Simpsons* credit Simon as the show's true architect.

And as Bartmania cooled off, and the show moved toward becoming a full-fledged institution, with its fourth, fifth, and sixth seasons, the show's quality miraculously refused to drop. Fox's merchandising explosion had ultimately been deceiving; *The Simpsons* had struck a chord that reverberated deeper than a mass-market logo on a T-shirt. It got funnier, smarter, richer in allusion and parody. They changed animation studios from Klasky-Csupo to Film Roman in the fourth season, updating the rudimentary look with slicker designs and a more varied palette. The writers increasingly filled the show with sly popular culture references and filmic parodies (Hitchcock and Kubrick were recurring favorites). Chat rooms, websites, and newsgroups overflowed with *Simpsons* conversations. Even the conservatives eventually came around. "It's possibly the most intelligent, funny, and even politically satisfying TV show ever," wrote the *National Review* in 2000. "*The Simpsons* celebrates many . . . of the best conservative principles: the primacy of family, skepticism about political authority . . . Springfield residents pray and attend church every Sunday."

The Simpsons spawned imitators and opened doors for new avenues of animated comedy. Directly or indirectly, they sired *Beavis and Butt-Head, King of the Hill, Futurama, Family Guy,* Adult Swim, and *South Park,* which, nearly a decade after Bart's boastful underachieving, managed to regenerate a familiar cacophony of ratings, merchandise, and controversy (the latter perhaps deservedly: so far Bart's greatest sin was sawing the head off the statue of the town's founder; in season 9 on *South Park,* Cartman tried to exterminate the Jews). While there have been few successes—for every *King of the Hill,* there is a *Fish Police* and a *Critic*—the show inspired a new genre of television, the prime-time animated comedy.

The Simpsons became both a celebration of buffoonery and a polished incisor, descending into America's overweight midsection. And yet it was impossible for the show to keep producing comedy at the level it had for the first five or six seasons. Around Season 9, it hit a point where the characters and situations became so exaggerated, the comedy so dispensable, and the show so unmoored from its origins that even the most die-hard fans had trouble finding positive things to say. As seasons accelerated past the double digits, fans who'd come of age with the series found fewer reasons to tune in and fewer areas of interest for this history,* yet the show plowed for-

---

*This book is much more concerned with the show's conception, development, and institutionalization into the pop canon. If you're really interested in what was going on in season 16, go on the Internet.

ward. And while today it tends to go more topical, and the jokes come off a little "easy," millions of viewers still look to *The Simpsons* for profound misunderstandings of our often incomprehensible postmodern world. *The Simpsons* provides answers. Or as Homer might say, "It's funny because it's true."

After twenty years, the residents of Springfield no longer merely hold mirrors to our way of life; they have ingrained themselves into it. *The Simpsons* has been so influential that it is difficult to find a strain of television comedy that does not contain its bloodline. And yet its footprint is so much larger than this. Homer's signature "Doh!" has been added to the *Oxford English Dictionary*. The characters have graced every magazine cover from *Spy* to *Rolling Stone*. *Psychology Today* published an article in 2003 using Marge and Homer to investigate sexual behavior between married couples. And in 2009 the Simpsons joined Frank Sinatra, Rachel Carson, and Mickey Mouse when the United States Postal Service issued stamps featuring the family. There's a Simpsons course at Berkeley (for credit), not to mention the hundreds of academic articles with *The Simpsons* as their subject. Next to pornography, no single subject may have as many websites and blogs dedicated to its veneration. It has permeated our vernacular, the way we tell jokes, understand humor, and tell our stories, particularly those of us who came of age with the show.

It is rare to find someone young enough to have tuned in for *Saved by the Bell* and *Beverly Hills 90210* and old enough to remember the fall of the Berlin Wall whose sense of humor and understanding of comedy are not somewhat structured by *The Simpsons* and peppered with its content. And while I believe that generation was most deeply touched, the show's influence is much broader. *The Simpsons* was immediately popular with young children, teenagers, college students, and many adults as well.

Although the marketing and merchandise onslaught that accompanied the first seasons would provide physical evidence of the show's beloved status, its true acceptance came with the level of interest and commitment of its fans. People went nuts for it: kids never missed it; those who never watched TV were watching it. After the initial thirteen episodes ran, Fox reran them and reran them again. Yet people kept watching. The show had impact. And while the wave of Bartmania soon rolled back, the force of the show's influence never broke, and, in fact, aided by syndication and the Internet, grew exponentially.

The viewers it attracted with Bart's sass in the first years matured and grew along with the show's humor, developing their voice, comedic timing, and interpretative and critical faculties with *The Simpsons* (among other influences). The comedy that originated in *The Simpsons'* writers room had a prime role in shaping and developing a massive and international audience. The size and depth of that influence cannot be measured quantitatively, but listen to the way any of your friends, or your kids' friends, tell jokes. As unpleasant as it sounds, examine the things that make you laugh in current television shows, in films, or on the Web. The connection won't be far away.

The Simpsons' writers went on to run other shows, like *Frasier*; *King of the Hill*; *3rd Rock from the Sun*; *Sabrina, the Teenage Witch*; and *The Office* ("Every writer's assistant I've ever worked with has gotten a big TV writing job," Mike Reiss, one of the show's veteran producers, once boasted[3]). And those of us within that age range ideal to absorb its lessons in humor are now writing for *The Daily Show with Jon Stewart*, *The Colbert Report*, *Hannah Montana*, *Late Night with Conan O'Brien*, and *Saturday Night Live*. And that's just the influence within television comedies. We of *The Simpsons* generation are becoming lawyers and lawmakers, executives and enemies of the state. So what? What could it possibly matter if the guy interviewing you, or presenting a talk to your ethics seminar, watched *The Simpsons* when he was twelve?

It probably doesn't, superficially, but chances are that part of his narrative, the way he tells his own story, whether in a barroom or a boardroom, is influenced by *The Simpsons*.

It may seem like a leap to place such weight on a silly TV series, but *The Simpsons* is one of the longest-lasting and most pervasive forces in our popular culture, which has a profound effect on how we live. What our society says, collectively, is absorbed, reflected, and influenced by our popular culture. The terrorist attacks of 2001, interest rates, and architecture certainly affect all of our lives today, but that doesn't mean that Fox News, blogs, Paris Hilton's sex tape, and Marc Jacobs's designs don't as well. The point is that elements of our popular culture, like television and YouTube, do affect how we think, act, and speak, just as Shakespeare's plays did during his time.

Many television series have survived, and many more have been funny, but *The Simpsons* remains the most powerful, lasting, and resonant entertainment force television has ever seen. Not many people reference *Home Improvement* in casual conversation, or write scholarly essays on *Cheers*. *Roseanne* and *Frasier* were both hilarious, intelligent shows, and for the most part, their ratings drowned *The Simpsons*—yet they have very little cultural influence. *The Simpsons*, by contrast, has entrenched itself so far into our culture that its content has seeped right into the popular vernacular and ingrained itself into our imaginations.

We, as a culture, speak Simpsons.

ONE

The Matt Groening Show

In which evil grade-school teachers destroy masterworks . . . punk rock brings together *Life in Hell*'s bunnies and *Maus*'s mice . . . Matt Groening becomes the Casanova of the *LA Reader* . . . and Deborah Kaplan becomes the Bennett Cerf of alternative comics.

The Simpsons did not spring out of one man's brain, fully formed, like a hilarious Athena. Its inception was a process, and it has more than one parent (as well as stepparents, grandparents, creepy uncles, and ungrateful children—I'm looking at you, *Family Guy*), but its most direct progenitor is Matt Groening's comic strip *Life in Hell,* which, by the late 1980, was being syndicated in alternative weeklies all over the country, earning him success and cult celebrity status.

But before *The Simpsons,* before *Life in Hell,* before any of the fame or money or angst-ridden bunnies, there was a little boy with an imaginary TV show, hosted by its creator, Matt Groening. He even recorded a theme song.

MATT GROENING, creator, *The Simpsons* (on NPR's *Fresh Air*, 2003): [Singing] First you hear a mighty cheer, then you know that Groening's here. Then a streak of color flashes on the ground. You know it's not a train or a comet or a plane. You know it must be Matt Groening, cool guy . . . Matt Groening. Matt Groening. Matt Groening. Not a coward, superpowered Matt Groening, coolest guy there is in town, coolest guy around.

Considering that *The Simpsons* paterfamilias would name the animated family after his own (father Homer, mother Marge, sisters

Lisa and Maggie), it would indeed be a nice touch to this story if he had grown up in a town named Springfield, but he didn't. Born February 15, 1954, he grew up in Portland, the middle child of five children in a house so close to the Portland Zoo that, as a little boy, Matt would go to sleep at night to the sound of roaring lions.[1] Playing in the grizzly bear ghetto and the abandoned zoo's caves and swimming pools,[2] Groening does seem to have had an idyllic childhood, especially for someone with creative ambitions. As Groening told *Playboy* in 1990, his father was a cartoonist, filmmaker, and writer who showed by example that one could put food on the table and succeed using one's creative faculties.

Writing stories, drawing cartoons, playing in worlds of his own imagination in the family basement, Groening was a fine student but constantly in trouble at Ainsworth Elementary School because his attentions were elsewhere. "I have to write 'I must remember to be quiet in class' 500 times and hand it in tomorrow" is an exemplary entry in Groening's diary, which he kept from an early age. "The Boy Scouts are alright if you don't have much to do, or you like to pretend to be in the army, and you enjoy saluting the flag a lot," reads another one.[3]

MATT GROENING (to *The New York Times*, October 7, 1990): When I was in fourth grade, I read a World War II prisoner-of-war book, I said, "Yeah, this is like my grade school. There's guards, and you can't do anything."

MARGARET GROENING, Matt's mother (to *The Seattle Times*, August 19, 1990): Actually, he did well in school—he was popular and got good grades . . . although he doesn't particularly want anyone to know that.

MATT GROENING (to the *Los Angeles Times*, April 29, 1990): You are what you are basically despite school. I think there's a lot of unnecessary misery in education. I certainly felt it. Just the idea of punishing a kid for drawing stacks of cartoons, or ripping them up and throwing them away. Some of the stuff was senseless and immature, but other stuff was really creative, and I was amazed that there was no differentiation between the good stuff and the bad stuff, or very little.

Lincoln High School (class of '73) was less rigid, but Groening still felt the constraints of conservative suburban culture, especially when contrasted with the radical and antiestablishment sentiments of the sixties burgeoning all around him. Groening was a mix of the straitlaced and rebellious. He was elected student body president, but under the banner of a tongue-in-cheek group called Teens for Decency (a parody of a local Christian group). His campaign slogan: "If you're against decency, then what are you for?"[4]

In high school, Groening would also discover his lifelong passion for alternative music and would continue drawing his cartoons. One story from Matt's teenage years involved Matt telling a girl with whom he was infatuated that it was his plan to have a career as a cartoonist. The girl rejected him because she believed she was going to have a very big life, saying something along the lines of, "Maybe if you were like Garry Trudeau or somebody." Never short on ego, even then, apparently Matt told her, "I'm going to be bigger than Garry Trudeau."

For college, Groening applied to only two schools: Harvard (which said no) and Evergreen College. The latter was a newly formed progressive state-funded college in Washington, where there are no grades or exams.

MATT GROENING (to *The Seattle Times*, September 28, 2003): [Evergreen] was condemned in the Legislature by conservative Republicans as being a haven for hippies, poets and revolutionaries . . . The main square was made out of red bricks, and there was some suspicion as to why we had a red square.

While the school remains a progressive, liberal feel-goodery, it is also regularly ranked among the West's best liberal arts colleges.[5] Its funding as a state school has been a topic of debate in Washington's state legislature, especially among Republicans. "We went into one dormitory and the smell of marijuana was everywhere. And there were a bunch of people watching *The Simpsons*, whatever that means," said youth and media expert representative Gene Goldsmith, after visiting the school in 1995. "And there were two girls sitting in there necking, kissing—two lesbians."[6] While it's unknown how rampant lesbianism was at Evergreen during Groening's time there, he did indeed attend a hippie college at the height of hippiedom.

Studying literature and philosophy, Groening decided he wanted to be a writer. That, combined with his studies of Kierkegaard and Nietzsche in the gloom of rainy Olympia, Washington, was a recipe for moodiness.[7]

LYNDA BARRY, cartoonist and friend (to the *Los Angeles Times Magazine*, April 29, 1990): Matt was like this guy who was a kind of straight guy at a hippie college, but so militantly straight that he was hipper than the hippies. He was the opposite of that song "The Poetry Man"; his sensibility was that life is not a haiku. Even though he's not "The Poetry Man," he's a guy with real strong feelings.

At one point, one of Matt Groening's writing teachers, Mark Levensky, drew a simple formula on the blackboard to show Groening what the basic plot structure was for all his short stories and asked him if he felt his writing was worthwhile. Groening has said that that question has "haunted" him ever since.[8] The ghosts of his writing failures would return in *The Simpsons* writing room—where Matt's writing was ridiculed—and linger like Banquo.

A place like Evergreen, with all its liberal pretensions, was hardly safe from Groening's scorn—he delighted in sending up the school once he took the reins of Evergreen's student newspaper, the *Cooper Point Journal*. He sensationalized the paper, getting political with his attacks on the state legislature, as well as lampooning the school's countercultural piety.[9] Groening added a cartoon page to the *Journal*, where he and his friend Lynda Barry (of *Ernie Pook's Comeek* fame) showed their work. Professors would post his cartoons, yet the school's most ardently liberal students were indignant. When Groening made fun of communes, a petition was circulated: "Dear Mr. Groening: Communal struggles are not funny!"[10] While Groening enjoyed annoying people with his antics, he could also be affected by their reactions. Of his days at the paper, Groening's friend Steve Willis remembered how he would find Groening, his head cradled in his hands, repeating to himself, "I didn't mean for it to come out this way."[11]

In 1977, a freshly graduated twenty-three-year-old Groening headed to Los Angeles. He lived with his girlfriend, Lynda Weinman, worked on his writing, and paid the rent with a series of dead-end jobs. Matt's initiation to LA was, in a word, hellish. As he later told *Playboy*, "*Life in Hell* was inspired by my move to Los Angeles in 1977. I got here on a Friday night in August; it was about a hundred and two degrees; my car broke down in the fast lane of the Holly-wood Freeway while I was listening to a drunken deejay who was giving his last program on a local rock station and bitterly denouncing the station's management. And then I had a series of lousy jobs."[12]

These included being a writer/chauffeur to an ancient director, writing slogans for horror movies at an ad agency, landscaping at a sewage treatment plant, and working at a copy shop.[13] His interest in music drew him to the punk scene, and he got a job at the Whisky a Go Go, where he got to wait on Elvis Costello, as well as Licorice Pizza, the record shop across the street. In addition to selling records, Licorice Pizza also sold drug paraphernalia, including coke vials. Because the store sold the caps separately from the vials, Matt would have to count them out one by one. It was great fun for him to take his time counting out hundreds of coke vials while the cus-tomer, ramped up on cocaine, waited impatiently.[14]

At this point, Groening was already drawing *Life in Hell*, which he photocopied and sent to his friends, or sold for $2 a pop at Licorice Pizza.[15] Groening attacked the institutions the angsty twentysomethings found most repellent and conformist: school, work, and love.

A typical strip asked, "Is there a *Life in Hell* philosophy?" The answers were as follows: "Your days are numbered." "It's later than you think." "We're all doomed." "Have a nice day."

Originally, Binky the bunny (Groening's mouthpiece) was conde-scending and preachy, but Groening altered him to be more of a vic-tim with forces working against him, like Reaganite social values, the religious right, commercialism, teachers, and bosses. The car-toons reeked of depression, death, and fear, but there was fun to be had, ironies and insights in the commentary that people related to. A classic strip has Binky bound and gagged in an empty room. Two eyes peer in through a slit in the room's only door and a menacing voice intones, "Are you ready to embrace family values yet?"

MATT GROENING (to the *Portland Oregonian*, March 25, 1990): The more horrible things I did to that rabbit, the more people liked it.

"Today 'hell' is such an ingrained part of the American lexicon that it's hard to remember a time when it was considered unprintable on a par with the 'f' word," wrote Paul Andrews in *The Seattle Times*. But Groening's comic reconstituted the meaning of "Hell," taking a word from the Bible and throwing it in the face of the Me Decade and all its emptiness, with the word's new countercultural undertones. "'Life in Hell' was every ex-campus protester's, every Boomer idealist's, conception of what adult existence in the '80s had turned out to be."[16]

Life in Hell was first published in 1978 by Leonard Koren's *Wet* magazine, an alternative, artsy periodical centered on the concept of "gourmet bathing."

GARY PANTER, cartoonist, friend of Matt Groening: Leonard Koren showed me *Life in Hell* for the first time. He was really impressed with it and I was too. And I'm under the impression that Matt was working at a copy shop because he made really fancy minicomics, with lots of pages and color changes and foldins and all kinds of stuff. His drawings were really ambitious, but also very simple and beautifully designed. It has clarity, which is what you need to communicate visually with comics. He's a great writer, and he understands human psychology, so he can be very effective in whatever medium he's using.

One thing Matt was always mentioning was to make the drawing funny to start with. If the drawing is funny, then the ball's already rolling. There has to be some way to invite people into your comic. He also said he was surrounded by really good drawers in high school, and he felt he didn't want to compete with them, so he made his work simple.

But simplicity in comics is a really powerful thing. If you pick up certain comics like Dick Tracy or Krazy Kat, they may be the greatest comics ever made, but it takes you a minute to adjust to their vocabulary. Comics these days are really much more simple.

In high school, the animals Matt had drawn for his friends had been unrecognizable, except for his rabbits. Groening also liked it that there is a distinguished history of rabbits in pop culture—"Peter Rabbit, Bugs Bunny, Rabbit Redux—the John Updike stuff—Crusader Rabbit," he told *Playboy*.

JAMES VOWELL, editor in chief, *LA Reader*: I was the founding editor of the *LA Reader* back in 1978. Very shortly after we got the first issue out, maybe in the next week or two, Matt called me, probably in November of 1978. He was looking for writing and editing jobs in LA. And we just got to talking.

JANE LEVINE, former publisher, *LA Reader*: Matt came in with these silly cartoons with the rabbits with one ear. And showed them to James. I was the publisher; I was the money person. James was the editor. Matt leaves. James comes out of his office and says, "That guy is gonna be famous someday." And I look at these flipping rabbits, you know, and go, "Whatever, James." But I've since learned that James was right about a lot of people, not only Matt.

JAMES VOWELL: The first story of his that got published was in something like February 9th or 10th, 1979. It was a very interesting story about how people put the signs up on Sunset Boulevard and how they painted them; he covered the whole scene.

He kept doing minor assignments over the next few months and then the publisher hired Matt as our distribution manager. Free newspapers, you have to go out to find places to put the racks; you have to make deals with merchants. So he went all around LA, he did some of the delivery himself.

He was a full-time employee, writing more features. Very shortly after that, maybe within six months or so, I was able to convince Jane Levine to let him be my assistant editor. He was my assistant editor at the *LA Reader* for two or three years.

The *Reader*, which was even smaller (and more alternative) than its competitor, the *LA Weekly*, gave Groening an income, a forum for his writing, and an official entrée into the underground music and arts scenes.

GARY PANTER: Punk rock was happening, so there were shows all the time. And Matt and me and everybody went to these shows. And a lot of the same bands would play, they became very famous, and it was really creative. Punk rock in LA was a lot of people out of art school, doing creative things, making publications and clothing and music and so on. We were part of that. And the idea that we could get things into the *LA Reader* and then have them be blowing down the street, weeks later, seemed like some sort of interesting accomplishment, to impact the landscape somehow. And I think Matt and I were both interested in doing that. We were both interested in entering into culture somehow. It's interesting if the individual can have an effect in culture, that's an interesting problem.

Matt fell in love with the punk scene that was blooming in LA. He reviewed unknown bands in the *Reader*, then a week after the review had been published would check in with the record store, only to find that they hadn't sold a single copy. "So," Matt told NPR, "I wasn't that good as a rock critic."

JANE LEVINE: Oh, God, it [*LA Reader*] was so cool. It was an alternative weekly, as if the *Village Voice* had a baby. It was very small, but it always had incredibly high standards of literary journalism and, these are such difficult words, hipness and alternativeness. In '78, the calendar section of the *LA Times* was an amazing fat arts and entertainment section, but the line hadn't blurred between mainstream and alternative journalism to the extent that it has now.

   So when we wrote about punk rock in Chinatown it wasn't something that everybody was writing about. And we wrote about the city as a city, as a place to live, and not about the industry. And James Vowell collected this amazing group of writers and illustrators like Matt, but also like Gary Panter, Steve Erikson, the crazy Richard Meltzer, Richard Gehr—these really, really great writers

Known as the "father of punk comics," Gary Panter went on to be a seminal figure in the new-wave comics movement, with his drawings published in *The New Yorker*, *Time*, and *Rolling Stone*. He designed the set for *Pee-wee's Playhouse*, for which he won three Emmys. His

work has been displayed, alongside that of Jack Kirby and Will Eisner, in the "Masters of American Comics" exhibition. Steve Erickson went on to be a hugely successful surrealist author. His novels, like *Rubicon Beach*, have won him acclaim from the National Endowment for the Arts, as well as a Guggenheim Fellowship. Richard Meltzer is a seminal rock critic and the author of fifteen books, including a collection of his writing, *A Whore Just Like the Rest*. Gehr was an editor and columnist at *Spin* and has written for *The New York Times*, *Rolling Stone*, and *The Village Voice*. He also wrote *The Phish Book*, in collaboration with the jam band.

JANE LEVINE: It was also this totally fun time in LA. The late seventies, early eighties. Punk rock. X. The band X. And it was just like all those romanticized stories about how this little group of us did this thing and hung out together. You know, worked a million hours a week, and the hours that we weren't working, we hung out together.

It was this little tiny office. The circulation director and the publisher were in the same office. I told him I felt like I'd found another member of my family. Another sibling. Just the ease of talking to each other.

Levine and Groening began a relationship that would last several years. She would leave the *Reader* in 1983 but continue to work with alternative weeklies until 2004, when she stepped down as publisher of the *Chicago Reader*. "I think got out of alternative newspapers when the getting was good. It's so hard now," she says.

JANE LEVINE: He made me insane, just generally fomented dissent. He saw the world with malicious frivolity. And I was earnest. You know, I was the evil boss in the *Work in Hell* strips. He was the guy who brought his copy not after deadline but like nine seconds before the thing was going to the printer.

JAMES VOWELL: [Matt was] just a great guy. Hardworking. Give him anything to do and he'd work on it. Ask him to do a certain story and within a few hours, or a day, he'd do a bunch of interviewing; he'd pull it together. Very careful. Very conscientious. He was *so* much fun to be around—turn around and there's a joke. In fact, what I learned from

Matt is how to tell jokes. He even explained to me what a joke is: a joke is what somebody doesn't expect.

On Tuesday night we'd go up to Hollywood where the typesetter had his operation and pick up stuff to proof. Often we got hungry and went off and had supper and proofread. Matt was always trying to sell *Life in Hell* as an idea to me for a weekly cartoon in the paper. And he'd draw these little pictures on paper napkins, just ballpoint pen stuff, and occasionally I'd say, "Matt, why don't you make that chin a little smaller." I was trying to edit his cartoons, but he didn't need me to edit his cartoons, I guarantee you.

In April 1980, we published the first weekly newspaper version of *Life in Hell*.

GARY PANTER: Matt's earliest comics were about language. That was the major theme of his early minicomics, and I think it went into *Life in Hell*. He did a whole series of *Life in Hell* called "Forbidden Words." Before I met him, I thought, Oh, this guy seems very critical and tough, because he would just name all these words that were overused in culture and forbid them from being used again [these included "ambience," "bummer," and "boogie"].

Groening's cartoon was popular at the *Reader,* but the strip really caught on once Matt hooked up with Deborah Kaplan, the tiny paper's ad sales representative and his future wife (and ex-wife).

MATT GROENING (to the *Los Angeles Times Magazine*, April 29, 1990): Everyone I know goes, "Well, if *I* had a Deborah, I could be a success too." And they're right.

DEBORAH GROENING, Matt Groening's ex-wife: I came to the *Reader* in 1981 and I got a job as a sales rep. One of the things I discovered was that Matt's cartoon was a major selling point when I was going around town. My beat was Melrose, which at the time was where all the fashion, music, sort of the hip street.

I would look through the archives and bring the coolest issues, [including] one that Matt wrote, a cover story called "Hipness and Stupidity."

When I met [Matt], he was on Valentino Place, formerly Mary Pickford's apartment building, next to Paramount Studios, in a really seedy part of Hollywood. [Matt's neighborhood was so bad, Deborah would not visit after dark.][17] I mean, he was hunting for quarters in his ugly orange shag carpeting. He had checks, $10, $15 checks that were, like, three years old, from some paper somewhere. So we made an amazing team. You know? Because I really appreciated the artistic aesthetic, but I had a natural instinct for business so—it was really kind of an amazing ride for around ten years.

JAMES VOWELL: The thing about *Life in Hell* was people really related to it. People don't know what *Life in Hell* means, in terms of the title. The real meaning of *Hell* is LA. It was really life in LA Hell. So it connected with the people.

ART SPIEGELMAN, Pulitzer Prize–winning cartoonist, *Maus*: *Life in Hell* was neither mainstream nor underground, and at that point, that was unusual. There was the stuff that was totally unpublishable, outside the margins, and there was stuff like *Cathy*. There wasn't yet a zone that wasn't either of those things, that had its own voice and personality, that was interesting. It always struck me that he was a good writer; it didn't feel like it was necessarily meant for *Raw* [Spiegelman's magazine], because it wasn't that visual, finally.

GARY PANTER: He drove around in his car, in his Volkswagen Squareback or whatever it was, with it piled full of *Readers*. And people kept breaking into it all the time, because they thought there must be something valuable in there. And he would lie on the floor [of his apartment] and pennies would fall out of his pockets. So when I went over to his apartment, I always felt like he had a lot of extra money because there was this change on the ground. And then I realized, from looking at his environment, mainly what he was doing there was lying in bed and reading everything under the sun. Also, he was writing novels—that was a main project.

And we were both interested in Frank Zappa. I think that idea that Frank Zappa [had], of giving reading lists to young people—if you give a young person the right reading list, a lot happens—I think you see that really built into Matt's work. [*Life in Hell*, for all its dark humor, gave its readers something philosophical to chew on.]

DEBORAH GROENING: Jane Levine, she was my mentor. We were sort of all young and beautiful, and we were kind of aware that we were at the hub of the scene in the eighties in Los Angeles. And so, for example, Jeff Spurrier, who did the listings, and his girlfriend, Ann Summa, who did the photography for the *Reader*—we would all go to the same events. You know there was Raymond Pettibon, a punk artist, and he would have a show and people would go there. There was Steve Samniock, who was like one of the hipster organizers, and he would have something called "Steve's House of Fine Art." Now I realize it was like a renaissance, a burgeoning scene in LA that compared to New York in its sophistication.

The young, urban professionals—which we were, you know, highly educated, disposable income, all that stuff—turned to us and trusted our *Reader*. But also it was sort of a reaction to the hippies, so we were more cynical. Matt's strip really represented that sort of "We're wise. We're not gullible. We don't think the world's going to change so easily."

And so we wanted to become part of the establishment to make the changes happen. So it was sort of this thing, plus of course there was the extreme like punk and new wave music and all this stuff. And then of course it was the same way in fashion, restaurants, so my clients were like l.a. Eyeworks, Vertigo, Industrial Revolution, Grow-Design, all these really fabulous stores on Melrose. Melrose was *it*.

JANE LEVINE: Everybody was working so hard. And Matt was working really hard alongside of us. But did Matt work harder than James or, you know, ten other people? No. But he worked really hard. You know the way I mentioned him coming in with a column nine seconds before it had to go the printer? It wasn't like he was screwing off. He was busy.

RANDY MICHAEL SIGNOR, editor, the *LA Reader* (to *The Seattle Times*, August 19, 1990): Matt didn't particularly have a reputation for discipline. We'd have to call his answering machine and yell into it, "Can you hear! Wake up! Call in!"

DEBORAH GROENING: One day, Matt wrote a strip called "Isn't It About Time You Quit Your Lousy Job?" By that time it was 1984 or '83. And I was like, "Yeah!" You know? Because I realized I always wanted to sort of start my own business, and I realized I actually could do it because I've got a lot of confidence, and also I had learned I was the best salesperson there. I became sales manager, and I made the *Reader* kind of survive. Then I decided I would be an artist's rep.

And Matt was going to be one of my artists.

Matt would defer to Deborah in all matters of business, telling *Playboy* that if it hadn't been for her, he never would have made it big. They put out the book *Love Is Hell* for the Christmas rush of 1984. It sold twenty thousand copies.

JAMES VOWELL: Deborah Kaplan was a major driver in Matt's early history, mainly because they were married, and they wanted to get things going, and she was more business-oriented. In terms of getting it syndicated originally, that was Matt; *Life in Hell* was already well on the way when they [got together].

JANE LEVINE: I don't think Deborah gets the credit she deserves for Matt's success. I mean, Matt's talent is undeniable. Are there other people that talented? I don't know. But Deborah was really the one who got other papers to run *Life in Hell* and started making calendars and greeting cards and all that sort of stuff. I don't know what role she played in getting him on *Tracey Ullman*. But I really think she was the push to make him successful. Obviously she wasn't the push to make him creative. He just was. But I'm not sure he would have ever made himself the popular success he was without Deborah.

DEBORAH GROENING: The first thing I did was I started to organize Matt and syndicate his strip, and we created a company called Acme Features Syndicate (a reference to the Warner Bros. cartoons, where all the cartoons are branded Acme).

And it was a blast. I did *all* the business, and Matt just got to be the artist, the struggling artist. And it was a very romantic time for everybody at the *Reader*, and, you know, it was just a really amazing time.

So what we did was, we made deals every time we got [Matt's strip syndicated in] a new paper. I went to the Association of Alternative Newsweeklies convention and I created a publicity package. I created a product line [there were *Life in Hell* mugs, calendars, greeting cards, T-shirts, and books], but these papers that were only giving him $15 for his weekly strip, so I negotiated free ads [for the merchandise]. And then I used those ads to capitalize on this audience that loved him.

And I got them in all these papers, I got quarter-page ads, which I otherwise never could have afforded. Eventually I quit the *Reader*, I went on unemployment, and I ran the business in my kitchen. And every time I'd get a new paper syndicated, I would negotiate ads, which started this feedback loop. The more papers I got the strip in, the more we did this mail-order business. And then I thought, Why not retail?

There were places like the Soap Plant and Oz—it was like a precursor to Urban Outfitters and Anthropologie. There were a lot of concept stores starting, so I got this idea that these products could be distributed there. George DiCaprio, who is the father of Leonardo DiCaprio, was at the time a cartoonist, but mostly a promoter of underground cartoonists. He became our distributor. And then I did a calendar, a 1986 calendar. We had these events [at Oz, Book Soup, l.a. Eyeworks] that were technically book signings but they were really just happenings. [In Polaroids from these book signings, one can see a young Matt Groening looking svelte and handsome—more alternative artist than Comic Book Guy— before he began to cultivate his signature, paunchier look of Hawaiian shirts and baggy pants.]

Matt was an amazing creative talent, and I got to—I wouldn't say "exploit" it, but I got to make him famous, really.

JAMES VOWELL: I actually helped Matt publish some of his *Life in Hell* books. I probably helped publish the first three, four, or five of them

DEBORAH GROENING: We were cooking. That year *Playboy* called the book "Coffee Table Book of the Month." We were starting to get incredible press. And then what happened is Pantheon came along. They found an article in *Saturday Review* about the *Love Is Hell* book, and they were intrigued.

ART SPIEGELMAN: It was around the time Françoise and I were hanging with Matt and his wife, Deborah. It was well into the time where I'd been signed up for a book with Pantheon, which was eventually *Maus*, but it seemed to be churning along forever. And at that point Matt had already put out some self-published "Life Is Hell" kind of books, and was wondering if this would be a good idea, to work with a publisher. He was kind of skittish about it, I think. And I said, "Well, these people have been great. Every other publisher in America seems to have turned down *Maus*, and although Pantheon turned it down as well, they did take it on a back-door, secondary submission from the art director. And the people up in the office seem swell." So they were interested, and I kind of showed it around at Pantheon, which had a very minimal relationship with visual books at the time. So it was really a matter of "Hey, did you see this?" There really wasn't any reason for them to leap on it at that point, except they liked it. Matt wasn't a household name.

DEBORAH GROENING: Meanwhile, things were happening right and left. Finally, in 1986, Matt got into *The Village Voice*, which was a huge goal of his. And we got in more and more papers. We ended up being in 200 newspapers (now it's more than 250) that all had from 50,000 to 500,000 readership. So there were like literally millions of fans.

And we had these rep networks, and we negotiated to retain the non-book rights, so we had gift stores, novelty stores, comic book stores. And it was amazing when I got the call from Pantheon. Then he was asked to do a computer drawing, a poster, for Apple Computers and it was just really exciting.

Maneuvering to ensure that they retained the rights to *Life in Hell* merchandise was a smart and practical move, but more important, it was a decision that would foreshadow the Groenings' insistence, when *The Simpsons* came along, that they do the same thing.

DEBORAH GROENING: We started getting requests to license on other things, like calendars and so forth. And *then* we did a line of greeting cards for Paper & Graphics, which was the groovy card company at the time, so we were really diversifying.

Between Groening's creativity and Kaplan's industriousness, they had managed to create a *Life in Hell* cottage industry. They moved to Venice Beach and there was no more digging in the carpets for spare change. Matt and Deborah would marry in 1987, handing over the management of their business to Pantheon (a part of Random House) in 1989 when Deborah became pregnant with their first child. Their union would last until 1999, when Deborah would file for divorce, citing irreconcilable differences. She retained custody of their two children, Homer and Abe. She has become a licensed therapist and is using her considerable means to build a foundation for troubled families.

JAMES VOWELL: I actually wrote the original business plan for Matt's publishing operation, probably in 1987 or '88—I still have a copy of it on my bookshelf at home. He was just trying to raise a little money to expand his operations. And on the last page on the business plan it talks about how "This may not go forward because Matt is talking with people at Fox Television about doing some cartoons for *The Tracey Ullman Show*."

TWO

The King of Comedy

In which we meet James L. Brooks, Stalin, Hitler, and Rupert Murdoch . . . a billionaire tyrant is mocked by Brandon Tartikoff . . . Jim Brooks establishes Yaddo in La-La Land . . . and the real Wayland Smithers is universally feared and mocked.

If he were a little dumber, he'd be a lot happier.

—Shirley MacLaine

In 1987, as much as it was anyone's, Hollywood belonged to James L. Brooks. An unprecedented string of successes writing and producing for television in the seventies and eighties that included *The Mary Tyler Moore Show*, *Rhoda*, *Lou Grant*, and *Taxi* had proved he was a force. *Terms of Endearment* in 1983, which he produced, wrote, and directed, taking Oscars for each one, had made him a juggernaut. In 1987, he cemented his position among Hollywood's elite with *Broadcast News*, starring longtime friend and collaborator Albert Brooks, another smash hit with critics and at the box office. Brooks's ability to take the foibles, neuroses, and failings that make us human, and translate them into believable and beloved characters on screen would continue to entrance moviegoers with *Big*, *The War of the Roses*, and *Say Anything*, all of which he produced before the eighties were done. Whereas his sitcoms had projected heart and wit, his ability in films to draw laughter from the most tragic and awkward moments, and to infuse humor with the most dramatic poignancy, earned him the nickname "the Dark Prince of Comedy."[1] And yet, while his film career was rocketing forward in 1987, it was on *The Tracey Ullman Show*, a television program he was producing for Fox, that Brooks would lend his genius to a dysfunctional cartoon family who, more than anything, would make his fortune, his name, and his legacy.

GAVIN POLONE, former agent for Conan O'Brien, *Simpsons* writers; executive producer, *Curb Your Enthusiasm*: He was the very top of the ladder. And in a weird way he was probably the writer held in the greatest respect back in the late eighties. [He] still [had] that track record that he had going back through *Mary Tyler Moore* and all the other shows that he'd done. But keep in mind that he was at the pinnacle of his movie career, too. I would just say, in terms of the people behind the camera of movies and TV, [at the time] he was not only the most successful but the most respected.

Brooks did not have an easy time growing up in North Bergen, New Jersey. His father, Edward, whom Brooks has described as "a drinking man," abandoned the family when Brooks's mother was pregnant with him, later sending his wife, Deborah Brooks, a postcard that read, "If it's a boy, name him Jim."[2]

Edward Brooks reappeared sporadically over the next decade, before finally disappearing when Jim was twelve, leaving the boy to be raised by Deborah and his sister, Diane, who was eight years his senior. (The Brooks family was Jewish, and their name was originally Bernstein—a fact Jim discovered when he went to visit his grandparents and saw the name on their doorbell.[3] Brooks Sr. had changed the name and originally told Jim that they were Irish.) There was very little money; Deborah worked as a saleswoman at a children's clothing store. Brooks has said that as a boy he would wake up in the middle of the night, terrified that his father had not sent the money the family would need to get through that week.[4]

If there is a driving force to Jim Brooks, an event that informs his sensibilities as a writer, it is in his own unhappy childhood. "He loves funny," one friend told me, "because funny makes you live through the pain." Or, as Jim told the *Los Angeles Times* in 1993, "In my mind, if you write a comedy where human beings experience pain, you're just being realistic." Later, when critics praised the early *Simpsons* episodes for the real emotions found in their silly, cartoon world, they were praising the key contribution of James L. Brooks.

POLLY PLATT, production designer, *Terms of Endearment* (to the *Los Angeles Times*, 1993): Jim feels it's his lot in life to be unhappy and to suffer.

JAMES L. BROOKS (to *The New York Times*, April 8, 1984): I'm very competitive about unhappy childhoods. But I'm not the champ. The champ is a girl I know who comes from a family of six children and they picked her to put in an orphanage . . .

I had a crummy childhood. I didn't want to have a crummy life. I was going to live on Riverside Drive and look at Jersey instead of vice versa.

GARY ROSS, cowriter, *Big*; director, *Pleasantville, Seabiscuit:* He's a very intense guy. You're not gonna get involved in a working process with Jim and it's breezy or casual. It was very, very intense, a lot of it pleasant, some of unpleasant, but ultimately all of it rewarding. And you could no more separate kind of the stormy part of Jim's personality from the genius in Jim's personality. It all comes together.

Brooks attended NYU, but he dropped out, working menial labor before landing a job as a page at CBS in 1964, at the age of twenty-four.[5] He eventually got a job writing for the *Nightly News;* two years later, he was in LA, selling scripts to *The Andy Griffith Show, My Mother the Car*, and *That Girl.*[6] A friend of Brooks intimated that during his earlier, leaner years in Hollywood, in meetings with execs, he would employ a strategy so quirky that it seems like it's right out of one of his films. When Brooks entered a meeting, he would deliberately hurt himself physically—banging into a table or a chair—immediately winning sympathy and gaining what he saw as the upper hand.

In 1969, he created a dramatic comedy set in a high school, called *Room 222*, which won him an Emmy. That year he also partnered with fellow TV writer Ed Burns, creating the sitcom *The Mary Tyler Moore Show* (1970–77), which became one of the most acclaimed TV shows of all time, inspiring several Brooks-produced spin-offs, including *Rhoda* (1974–78) and *Lou Grant* (1977–82). In 1978, Brooks moved on to something slightly edgier, creating *Taxi*— a sitcom about small-time New York cabbies—starring Judd Hirsch,

Tony Danza, Danny DeVito, Christopher Lloyd, and Andy Kaufman. The idea for the show supposedly came from a 1975 article in *New York* magazine, passed along to Brooks by his best friend, Jerry Belson.

KEN ESTIN, producer, *Taxi, The Tracey Ullman Show*: We would have a room full of writers—very expensive writers and the best in the business 'cause it was *Taxi*, and *Taxi* at the time was the top show on TV. And the scene wasn't working and Jim just dictated an entire scene himself and nobody even butted in 'cause he was on a roll. I've never seen anybody else do that.

JUDD HIRSCH, actor, *Taxi* (to *Entertainment Weekly*, 2004): He would go further than anybody. He would think of the most embarrassing situation you could imagine in human life, and allow it to happen onstage. He would dare to write it.

KEN ESTIN: He seems to think in ways nobody else thinks. Most of us have to sit down and take a long time to put our thoughts together. When I was running *Taxi*, I would spend a long time coming up with story ideas for the coming episodes, and if I'd go to Jim and I'd pitch the idea, he'd think about it for a second and suddenly have the way to go with it. It's like he had a sixth sense about situation comedy. Jim used to just be able to do it—like Mozart did music, I guess.

I remember one episode we wrote. [*Taxi* writer/producer] Ed Weinberger didn't like it at all and made us rewrite the whole thing. And then Jim Brooks got a copy of the script and called up and said it was perfect the way it was, and even Ed, who had great credits and confidence, immediately reneged on his objections and said, "Go back to the original script." People just felt that way about Jim Brooks.

GARY ROSS: I think that within a comic structure he investigated the nooks and crannies of character. He is relentless in examining all the nuances of that character and being incredibly thorough. It's never glib. He inhabits and completely investigates a world. It's very much about the examination of human behavior. And to him the nuance of the subtlety of human behavior is the movie moment, so to speak.

Brooks was a brilliant writer, but he also had his mercurial side. People who work with him note that although he could be magnanimous, he was also sometimes difficult, narcissistic, and demanding, both on the set and off. Along with being brilliant, funny, and playful, he is often described as uncompromising, misanthropic, and fatalistic. "The glass was never full," one longtime friend of Brooks told me. "It was always half empty. It was always less than half empty. The world was always ending."

ANNE SPIELBERG, cowriter, *Big*: He is very generous with his time. He really listens. He has a temper that I think explodes if he feels someone isn't living up to what they should be doing. He made me feel, alternately, very talented and very stupid.

KEN ESTIN: He was crazy. Sometimes he was very depressed and sometimes he was very excited. I don't know if he was a manic-depressive, but he seemed to have his swings. Sometimes he'd get angry. One time when I was brand-new at running the show, David Lloyd wrote a script. [Lloyd had written for *The Dick Cavett Show* back in the day and was a writing colleague of Brooks's and Weinberger's from *Mary Tyler Moore* and its spin-offs, but not a staff writer on *Taxi* at the time.]

Ed Weinberger told us, because of David's years of success and his brilliance, "Don't change anything because he doesn't like the idea that you young guys are gonna fool around with his work." Well, when we brought it to the table for the table reading, it didn't work very well, and Jim Brooks, in front of the actors and the director, everybody, started screaming at me—that I should've been ashamed to bring a script like this to the table, that I shouldn't call myself a producer. He just chewed the hell out of me in front of everybody. Yelling at me, yelling, not talking. That's the kind of thing he would do, and he never waited to hear the explanation.

I have enormous respect for him as a writer. As a person, he's a little messed up, but maybe that's because he's a genius. Maybe geniuses are messed up. I don't know. Jim didn't yell a lot.

By the time *Taxi* finished in 1983, Brooks had moved on to film, taking with him nine Emmys and two Peabody Awards (and these were just the awards Brooks himself received; collectively, his sitcoms earned sixty Emmys). While there were a few failures, like 1978's *Cindy*, as well as a lawyer drama he'd concocted in 1979, called *The Associates*, they had barely blemished his résumé. His reputation in 1983 was strong enough for Paramount to let him write, direct, and produce his own feature, a film based on Larry McMurtry's novel *Terms of Endearment*, the story of a domineering mother's relationship with her free-spirited daughter.

POLLY PLATT: Jim really didn't know how to direct when he did *Terms*. He didn't understand a lot about the camera and the technicalities of it. But he knew what he wanted, and he knew what he wanted to see.

Albert Brooks has compared the risks taken in acting to jumping without a net. Working under Jim Brooks's direction allowed him to take any risk, because he was certain that his best work would end up on the screen.

In 1986, with help from 20th Century Fox, Brooks created his own production company, Gracie Films, named after the comedian Gracie Allen. Brooks established Gracie to provide real writers with a vehicle to get their movies made. As a filmmaker, Brooks was famous for undertaking a Herculean amount of research, casting, shooting, editing, and reshooting. Using the best actors, he would still do twenty, sometimes twenty-five takes for a single scene.[7] This drive for perfection and strain for independence would underpin the early years of *The Simpsons*. Much of *The Simpsons'* success can be traced to two main sources: an independence from network interference and a complete dedication to the writing, no matter how many drafts, or how expensive that process became.

In its early years, Gracie produced *Big* (written by Anne Spielberg and Gary Ross and directed by Penny Marshall), *The War of the Roses* (written by Michael Leeson and directed by Danny DeVito), and *Say Anything* (written and directed by Cameron Crowe). Later, Gracie was the company behind *Riding in Cars with Boys*, *Jerry Maguire*, and *Bottle Rocket*. Meanwhile, Brooks wrote, directed, and produced *As Good as It Gets* and the less acclaimed films *I'll Do Anything* and *Spanglish*.

ANNE SPIELBERG: Jim believed—and was the only person in town at that time, and maybe still now—that the writers were the center of the project, that it was a writer's medium, and he operated Gracie with that premise.

At one point the studio wanted us to work with a particular actor, and Gary [Ross] and I did not want to work with him, because we knew he brought his own writers in, and so we didn't have to. The studio wanted to know who the hell we thought we were. We didn't like the idea of somebody rewriting our script, and I believe it was Jim who was right behind us saying, "You don't have to do what you don't want to do."

JAMES L. BROOKS (to *American Film*, 1989): Screenwriters have real authorship of movies . . . The justification for Gracie was to try this idea out.

ANNE SPIELBERG: I started hanging out around the place sometimes. It was like a house—I remember buying them a popcorn machine. There were a lot of people working on different projects there at the time, and we'd all goof off and gather together in the kitchen. Michael Leeson was around, doing *War of the Roses*, and Cameron Crowe was doing *Say Anything*. Gary Ross and I had been friends for a long time and decided to do this thing [*Big*] on spec, and the first person we gave it to was Jim.

JAMES L. BROOKS (to *American Film*, 1989): The first two years [of Gracie] . . . was sort of an ideal period in my life.

A filmmaker who "cares desperately about everything," Brooks wants to control every aspect of whatever film he is making. And yet for all the self-involvement and ego ascribed to him, he can also be extremely generous with his collaborators. If someone throws a good idea his way, he's known for exclaiming, "Oh, my God! You saved the movie!" For Brooks, every moment is the most important one. Having his own production company meant that he needed to be just as involved and meticulous with the work of others, a challenge he rose to admirably on most occasions.

ANNE SPIELBERG: He was hard. He was difficult. He liked to just fling out ideas and go in every possible direction anyone could go with a possible scene. He liked to experiment. Although he was very quick-witted, I would wonder, Are we doing this all over again?

He was intense. But he laughed a lot.

We'd be quiet, and all of a sudden Jim would come up with a total non sequitur, as if he had the first half of the sentence in his head, and then he said the second half of it, which didn't seem to be related to anything we had been talking about. His mind was jumping around a lot—that was a typical Jim-ism.

ALBERT BROOKS: If you watch a Jim Brooks movie and you like it, the first thing you're liking is the writing and the story, and the characters.

GARY ROSS: Anne and I skirted the moment when Tom Hanks told the Liz Birkin character that he was really a child. And we kind of played that off camera. And Jim said, "You can't play that off camera. You owe it to them to at least to make an attempt at the scene." And I think that was very wise on his part.

CAMERON CROWE, Oscar-winning writer and director (to *American Film*, 1989): You get calls late at night, or early in the morning, where Jim would go, "Hey, man, I watched those dailies from two days ago and let me tell you something—that house is too clean. Don't you think that house is too clean?"

GARY ROSS: Nobody can always triumph over commercialism. And I think Jim's great strength is that he found artistic satisfaction within an environment of commercialism. Jim is commercially very successful, whether it's *Taxi* or *The Simpsons* or *Terms of Endearment* or *Broadcast News* or *Jerry Maguire* or *Big*. These are very commercially successful movies, but they're also very emotionally and artistically satisfying. Jim is at once a very successful artist and a very good businessman.

JERRY BELSON (to *American Film*, 1989): [Brooks is] a very good executive. That's probably one of the things that bothers him.

Being a "good executive" requires different attributes than being a good writer. It requires steely nerves, a mind for business, and the confidence to make decisions that will ultimately leave others in your wake. Although Jim might have had these abilities, it was not in his best interest to put them on display. After all, he was the sensitive one, the tortured genius writer, not the cold-blooded suit. He needed someone to be the bad guy, to run Gracie Films with the iron fist Brooks could not reveal was his own. He found that person in Richard Sakai.

The most complimentary adjective I have heard to describe Sakai is "devoted." Sakai is generally described as "crazy," though one interview subject called him "smart." Nearly everyone I spoke to referred to him as Jim Brooks's "henchman" or "hatchet man," and more generously as "Jim's id." He was referred to alternately as "Lurch" (from *The Addams Family*), "Darth Vader," and "a bad person." He was also described to me as "not human," a screamer, and "psychotic." One thing is certain: Sakai believed in Jim Brooks more than anyone else, and from the time he was a production assistant on *Taxi*, he devoted himself completely to his boss, suppressing his own creative ambitions and doing whatever it took to be the man behind James L. Brooks.

It is not easy to get people to speak on the record about Sakai— Jim Brooks still has long tentacles in Hollywood. But one witness ventured to remember how when Gracie was being formed, Sakai "was just desperate to become a part of Jim's inner circle in a way that meant that he was rather ruthless." Sakai spent much of his time at Gracie, dedicating himself wholly to Jim Brooks and the production of his films.

Just as you can't make an omelet without breaking a few eggs, you can't make a string of phenomenally successful films without breaking some balls. Richard Sakai was, and is to this day, Jim's chief ball breaker. Later, *Simpsons* writers would model the behavior of the sycophantic Wayland Smithers—with his undying adulation of his boss, Mr. Burns—on Sakai, one of the most important figures in *The Simpsons*' history.

KEN ESTIN: Richard Sakai was my best friend when I was on *Taxi* and we got along really well. After work we'd go to a video arcade and we'd play games together. He'd invite me over to his house; I'd have dinner with him and his wife, Patty. He was a pretty normal guy. He was just intense.

Richard started with Jim as his gofer, as an errand person. He was so good at making things happen that eventually Richard became the associate producer and was entirely in charge of postproduction. And then when I began running *Taxi*, I made him the producer with me and Sam Simon.

The thing is, Brooks had a lot of confidence in Richard. Richard, as I said, was very good and dedicated and admired Jim. They fought a bit and Jim was a little bit hard on Richard, and he endured it because he admired Jim's genius and he knew he was on to a good thing with Jim. So there's always been some confrontation between the two of them, but Richard's very loyal to Jim and he ended up becoming the president of Gracie Films, so it paid off for him.

At one point Richard wanted to be a writer and a director. He didn't intend to be the hatchet man, but it turned out that that's where his life took him, and Jim finds him indispensable. So in spite of their occasional belligerence or whatever, there's a mutual respect.

A source who knows both men confirms that Richard Sakai indeed did have creative aspirations of his own, but Jim, who "needs someone twenty-four/seven," has never let Sakai out from under his thumb. Others believe that Sakai does not have the chops to make anything worthwhile without Jim Brooks. "He'd been riding Jim Brooks's coattails for so long he had bonus miles," says an early *Simpsons* staffer. "And he developed crazy resentments."

If Sakai was the guy beneath Jim Brooks, providing the means to Jim's ends, Barry Diller was the guy above. Diller was at the helm of Fox when Brooks brought *The Tracey Ullman Show* to the network. A legendary Hollywood executive turned mogul, Diller had invented the made-for-TV movie at ABC in the seventies and knew Brooks well from Paramount, where Diller had been CEO and overseen the production of *Taxi* and *Terms of Endearment* (as well as other monster hits like *Cheers*, the Indiana Jones films, *Saturday Night Fever*, and *Grease*). In 1978, Diller took steps to create a fourth major television network, Paramount Television Service, to compete with the Big

Three, but the idea quickly crumbled (the network was to be launched on the strength of a follow-up series to *Star Trek*, called *Star Trek Phase II*—no joke). This misstep aside, Diller was a TV visionary and the natural choice to run a new network when, in 1985, Australian billionaire Rupert Murdoch purchased 20th Century Fox, the legendary studio of Darryl Zanuck, from oil wildcatter Marvin Davis.

While Diller and Brooks are old friends, their relationship was described to me as complicated and at times combative. Fitting with his personality, Jim Brooks likes to feel that he is, as another producer put it, "Joe Lunch Box," an employee with a boss whom he resents and can rebel against, a role easily provided by the domineering Diller and his control of the purse strings at Paramount and Fox. Conversely, it seems that that Jim's tendency to break new ground pushed Diller to explore unique creative opportunities.

HARRIS KATLEMAN, former CEO, 20th Century Fox Television: The relationship between Gracie and Fox was never wonderful because Barry and Jim had this hostile relationship, but I think it was a love-hate relationship. Jim would always push Barry to the brink. But that's Jim. Jim is a creative genius.

While still in his thirties, Diller had helped to save and reestablish Paramount Studios. With a reputation for ruthlessness, he fostered a competitive culture among his protégés: Jeffrey Katzenberg, Michael Eisner, Don Simpson, and Garth Ancier. Known as the "Killer Dillers," these men would all go on to be (baby) media moguls in their own right. By 1984, Diller was feuding with Paramount's new chairman and quit the company for 20th Century Fox, where he would become CEO under Marvin Davis. Here again Diller chafed under his boss, who had wooed him with 25 percent of any growth he could inspire (one insider referred to their coupling as "the Stalin-Hitler pact").[8] Fox was doing badly and Davis refused to provide Diller the funds necessary to turn the studio around. Diller threatened to quit. Lawyers were called. And then along came Rupert Murdoch.

In March 1985, Murdoch partnered with Davis to purchase the half of Fox belonging to financier Marc Rich for $250 million (Rich had fled the country after being indicted for evading $48 million in income taxes). Diller was given a new contract with $3 million a year, preferred stock in News Corp, and, it was rumored, 5 percent of the new Fox Inc.'s profits.[9] That same month, Murdoch announced the purchase of Metromedia, which owned independent television stations in major markets, like New York and Dallas (the price: $2 billion; the deal was financed, in part, by junk bond king Michael Milken[10]). He and Diller then publicly announced their intention to launch a fourth television network.*

In September, Murdoch had purchased Davis's remaining half of the company for $325 million, giving him complete control over Fox Inc. (Davis had wanted to flip a coin to see who would buy the other out—Murdoch called his bluff and Davis relented.)[11] He started a new division: Fox Television Network, later renamed Fox Broadcasting Company. Though it could reach only 80 percent of the country's television sets,[12] by the fall of 1986, FBC was ready to set sail.

HARRIS KATLEMAN: [NBC President] Brandon Tartikoff made the joke, "Fox Broadcasting is a network with a coat hanger for an antenna."

Fox Broadcasting lost $95 million in its first year, launching such forgettable shows as *Duets* and *Mr. President* (starring George C. Scott, who had not appeared on television since the 1960s). Yet Murdoch had bet the farm on this new venture and was committed to making Fox Broadcasting a success. As he'd done at Paramount, Diller pitted his young turks against each other, encouraging a competitive, combative atmosphere, which achieved phenomenal results, and for which he was unapologetic.

GARTH ANCIER, former president of entertainment, Fox Broadcasting (in Daniel M. Kimmel, *The Fourth Network*): I think part of Barry's man-

*The FCC, which previously had forbidden a single owner to possess both TV stations and newspapers in the same markets, granted Murdoch—who now owned both TV stations and newspapers in Boston and New York City—repeated waivers for his takeover, until Congress ordered them to stop. Murdoch then went to court, arguing that the bill passed by Congress had unfairly targeted him, and only him. The judge agreed, and Murdoch triumphed—although by this time he'd already sold his competing news assets, the *Boston Globe* and the *New York Post*. Murdoch repurchased the *Post* in 1993 after New York governor Mario Cuomo persuaded the FCC to grant him a permanent waiver of their cross-ownership regulations.

agement style is to have those kind of rivalries going on between executives in the hope that the best person will rise to the top. My problem, personally, is that I don't respond to that kind of sibling-rivalry situation very well.

ROB KENNEALLY, former executive VP of series, Fox Network: It was 1987 and I was twenty-six. I go to Fox to become their VP of development at 20th Century Fox Television, the studio. The network launches, and I'm at the sister company.

So I'm in my office after my very first up-front* as a studio executive, and I get a phone call that Barry Diller needs me in his office. First of all, it's like God's calling. Second, what would he want with me? So I'm walking across the lot and into his inner office and then into his office, and the first thing he says to me as I sit down is "How does it feel to sell so few shows?"

And I get fairly defensive and say, "What are you talking about?" And I go through the litany of things we've sold, and he puts his hand up like, Be quiet. And he says, "I need you more here," and he very dramatically kind of taps on the desk referring to the network, and then wipes it dismissively, "than over there." And I was pretty surprised. I remember kind of saying to him, "Wow. That's—really? Me?" And he says, "Yes, this is your seat at the table." I didn't know anything about networks. I didn't know what affiliates were. I didn't know what ratings really meant. I'd only been a studio executive for a year. And he said, I remember very distinctly, he thought that was great.

And the more I sat there, the more I realized he was serious. This was a real job and he was offering me to oversee all of programming. He got me really enthusiastic, but I also had the presence of mind to say to him, "I hope you can appreciate the fact that I'd like to mull this over." And he said, "I respect that." So I walked back to my office. It was Friday afternoon. I am thinking about a thousand things, the implications of that meeting, what this means, when I'd start, what I'd do about the studio. It's not a small move.

And I went back up to my office and I called my wife, and as I'm dialing my wife, my assistant yells out, "It's Barry Diller on line three."

*Up-fronts are essentially a series of meetings among network execs, the press, and TV advertisers, when the networks unveil their lineups for the coming fall or spring, and gauge which shows will make money and which ones will be ditched.

And I pick up the phone and he goes, "Well?" That was the beginning.

Barry's MO was he hires people way over their head and makes them kind of rise to the occasion, because it gives him license to beat you into the executive you should become, if you can live through the process.

You'd go away for the weekend and you'd come back on Monday and he was always there before everybody, so you wanted to be there—you wanted him to see your car. That was all part of the culture.

You had a Diller phone line and it had, you know, almost a Pavlovian effect, because it would ring and it wasn't like your other phone on your desk. I learned quickly to keep a running notepad next to my phone from Friday evening, because I could typically expect to get a phone call somewhere at the front end of Monday morning, you know, 8:15, 8:30, 9:00, and he would want to know where things were.

GARTH ANCIER: Honestly, Barry is probably one of the best bosses I've ever had. He's not necessarily the easiest boss to work for. I think he's the first person to own up to that, but as a creative executive, most of my best habits were forged under Barry because he's one of those people who force you to think differently than the standard creative executive in the business. I'd worked for Brandon Tartikoff for seven years before that. Barry was much more analytical, much more of an editor, and very demanding. I mean, not just demanding of the people around him, but demanding of the product. The thing that I think I learned most from Barry is that unless you make sure that every single aspect—from the idea to the writer to the execution to the casting—is right, you have a much lower shot of something working. Whereas Brandon came at it trying lots of different things. Wildly creative, but not necessarily as good an editor.

Diller saw that the major networks were getting old and tired—they were losing viewers to cable and independent networks. People wanted something new, and Diller was eager to experiment.* He and his execs quickly realized that they weren't going to beat the Big Three in the traditional sense, but they were beginning to win over

*The network's first hit, of any kind, would be *21 Jump Street* (1987–91), starring a young Johnny Depp.

young males, age eighteen to thirty-four, the demographic that is most important to advertisers.

HARRIS KATLEMAN: The risk taking was pretty good because, remember, we're the little engine that could, and we had to take chances, such as *Married . . . with Children*, which was very risqué and edgy—the network got condemned for it but that got the attention of the [other] networks at a time when the jury was still out on Fox Broadcasting.

FBC's first foray into entertainment was in October 1986, with the *Late Show Starring Joan Rivers,* intended to compete with Johnny Carson and David Letterman. Rivers was the big-name yet edgy star the network was banking on to draw a hip young audience, but she failed miserably, fought with executives, and was replaced after less than a year.* Meanwhile, in April 1987, the network launched a beachhead into prime time with *Married . . . with Children, The Tracey Ullman Show,* and three other sitcoms broadcast on Sunday nights.

GARTH ANCIER: We probably started out a bit too conventionally and then fairly quickly, in TV years, realized that the stuff that was working was the stuff you couldn't find elsewhere else.

RUPERT MURDOCH: Our first successful show, or that showed *any* ratings, was *Married . . . with Children*. And then came *America's Most Wanted*.

Jim Brooks made a loosely arranged production deal with Fox Broadcasting, which was banking on his Midas touch to make them a hit. He came up with *The Tracey Ullman Show,* a half-hour variety sketch program that showcased the talents and impeccable mimicry of its British star. Brooks assembled his cabal of Gracie producers

---

*Rivers, who had been Johnny Carson's permanent guest host since 1983, had deeply offended and alienated Carson by taking the job with Fox without informing him in advance. Not only was she not asked to replace Carson when he retired, she was never invited on the show again, and Carson refused to speak to her for the rest of his life. Subsequent hosts of Fox's *Late Show* included Arsenio Hall, Suzanne Somers, and Richard Belzer. All crashed and burned.

and writers, and together they collaborated on what would be Fox's first critical hit (the ratings for *Ullman* never did much—the show is best remembered for launching *The Simpsons*).

GARTH ANCIER: Basically, I went to Jim and said, "Look, I know you're a big movie producer now." I mean, I knew him before *Terms of Endearment* [Ancier had been an exec on *Taxi*], and he had a movie deal at 20th Century Fox. I went to him literally on bended knee, something I was very used to doing at Fox in the early days, and said, "Look, is there any way I can entice you back into television? Is there any project that you feel passionately about enough to do it for this start-up network?" And he said, "Well, there's one thing with this woman named Tracey Ullman whom I'm kind of intrigued with to do a sketch show," and that's where *Tracey Ullman* came from.

KEN ESTIN: I worked with Jim Brooks and Heide Perlman and Jerry Belson, and created a pilot. At first Jim didn't know what he wanted to do. We considered doing a sitcom with [Tracey], but because of her versatility we decided to do a variety show, which nobody had done for a long time and the networks wouldn't do. But Fox wanted to be in business with Jim Brooks and the rest of us on this project and said we could do it any way we wanted.

Jim had just finished *Terms of Endearment* and I think he had finished *Broadcast News* by then, and he said I could do a movie with him if I would come to do *The Tracey Ullman Show*.

ANNE SPIELBERG: Tracey had done a special that Jim had seen, and he wanted to talk about doing a series featuring her. She was new to the States at the time. He had a couple of people coming in to shoot ideas around and wanted to know if I wanted to be part of the group. It was Jerry Belson, Heide Perlman, Jim, and myself. And I felt, especially in the presence of Belson—they could come up with ideas so quickly—rather intimidated.

To accompany Tracey's outlandish characters, the producers needed to find a supporting cast that could keep up with the talented performer. Jim Brooks convinced his old friend and *Rhoda* cast member

Julie Kavner (whose spouse was David Davis, the cocreator of *Taxi*), to join the cast. Kavner, who would eventually provide the voice of Marge Simpson, accepted on the condition that she would have no contract and hence would be free to do other projects, including Woody Allen's movies. For Dan Castellaneta, the future Homer Simpson, producers Tracey Ullman and Heide Perlman went to Chicago, where they met a casting agent who took them to see Castellaneta perform at Second City. Castellaneta stood out, and Tracey loved him immediately. She thought he had the face of a clown.

With the producers and talent lined up, and the structure of the show in place, all that was left to do was fill in the content. Jim Brooks, Barry Diller, and Tracey Ullman were about to meet the Simpson family.

THREE

When Bart Met Tracey

In which *The Simpsons* is almost a show about a talking bean . . . *someone* shows James L. Brooks how to die in LA . . . and Matt Groening unwittingly outwits a Fox.

I breast-fed those little devils.

—*Tracey Ullman*

KEN ESTIN, producer, *Taxi, The Tracey Ullman Show*: Jim Brooks had us all go to Ojai, California, and stay at a country club there and decide what to do with the Tracey Ullman variety show. At the time, Heide Perlman and I wrote the pilot for *The Tracey Ullman Show* with Jim's supervision and Jerry Belson's help.

Since each sketch involved several scenes, we didn't know how to separate the sketches from the scenes. When the sketch was over and something else started, we wanted to make it clear that that was not a cut to another scene of the same sketch.

We sat there in a suite at the Ojai Country Club—Heide, Jim, Jerry, and Richard Sakai—and we said, "How are we gonna separate that?" We thought of different things. The one that we almost agreed on: we were gonna have talking animals. At one point we decided on a talking bear. I don't know why we were so into a bear. Nobody was in love with that idea, but we just couldn't think of how else to do it. In most variety shows it was just sketches that were so short that they didn't have to worry about going from one to the next. Nobody had ever really done this before.

Richard Sakai had given me a drawing made by Matt Groening from *Life in Hell*. He gave it to me as a gift for my birthday or for a holiday some time before we had this meeting, and for some reason it occurred to me—as long as we're thinking about animating a bear's lips or even doing an animated bear—"This cartoon that I saw from a guy named Matt Groening for something he calls *Life in Hell* was really funny."

It was very different. It was smart. It was unusual. It was drawn poorly, which I thought added to the charm, with his overbites and things. And I said, "What if we have this guy do these little cartoons in between the scenes? Is that possible? Does anybody like that idea?" They all said they liked the idea. This is how Matt ended up being our guy.

POLLY PLATT, production designer, *Terms of Endearment*: I was nominated for an Academy Award for *Terms of Endearment* and I wanted to give Jim a thank-you gift. Matt did a cartoon called "Success and Failure in Hollywood." So I called Matt and I bought the original.

[Jim] was thrilled! First of all, he loves to get presents. He really does. He just laughed and laughed and hung it on his wall in his office. It was a brilliant cartoon. Success and failure come out to exactly the same thing in the cartoon [i.e., death].

My suggestion to Jim: I thought it would be great to do a TV special on the characters that he [Matt] had already drawn. I never envisioned anything like *The Simpsons*.

DEBORAH GROENING, Matt Groening's ex-wife: We got a call from Polly Platt's assistant, so I brought over a big portfolio of Matt's original art, which I would sell for cheap (though at that time we didn't think so). She said, "I want to give it as a birthday present to James L. Brooks, who doesn't know about Matt." So I sold it to her, and I sold one to Richard Sakai. The one that she got for James Brooks was "Los Angeles Way of Death," and the point was, even if you're successful, or if you're not successful, you're still miserable.

GARY PANTER, friend of Groening's, cartoonist: I saw Matt going to *a lot* of meetings. I went to a lot of pitch meetings when I lived in LA, but he probably went to, like, hundreds of pitch meetings.

Panter's "Rozz Tox Manifesto," published in the 1980s and influenced by Groening, was a post-Marxian theory of art, which rejected the idea of the artists working against the system. Instead, it encouraged artists to effect change by working within the capitalist environment, thereby attracting larger audiences to their causes. "Popular media are bigger than fine art media. Aesthetic mediums must infiltrate popular mediums. We are building a business-based art movement. This is not new. Admitting it is," reads Item 10. "Capitalism good or ill is the river in which we sink or swim and stocks the supermarket," the essay concludes.[1]

DOUGLAS RUSHKOFF, media critic: The way you look at it from the beginning, the way Gary Panter would've explained it to Matt Groening—when they were starting out and when he was trying to sell out in this way—was an argument that I've made very often: "Fuck it." These corporations aren't alive anyway. There's nobody at home; they don't know what they're doing. Let's use that fact to push media through their tubes and they have no idea what it is. In other words, we can be subversive because they don't know what's going on.

KEN ESTIN: Now, the story that Jim's associate producer, Polly Platt, gave Jim a cartoon of Matt's years [before] is probably true, and she may have even given one to Richard, which is maybe why Richard gave it to me. But the idea of ever incorporating Matt into *The Tracey Ullman Show* was entirely my idea. It did not come from Polly. It did not come from Richard.

Both Estin's and Platt's accounts fit with Deb Groening's account of selling several drawings to Platt, one of which was intended for Sakai. Whose "idea" it was to incorporate Matt's drawings into the show is up for debate—if both accounts are true, it could be that Platt suggested his drawings for some kind of TV special, while Estin suggested incorporating them into Ullman's show.

KEN ESTIN: When we met with Matt Groening, my concern was that Matt was an artist, and kind of bohemian, and I didn't think he would do it. I said, "There's a possibility he's gonna say, 'It's too commercial and I can't do tiny sketches at less than a minute in total.' "

We figured we'd have four moments to throw his cartoon in. So we said, "Could you possibly do a one-minute segment and break it up into three or four pieces for us?" I really thought Matt would say no. Matt said, "Of course. Sure. No problem."

So Matt goes away, and meanwhile Heide Perlman finds a woman named M. K. Brown. She was also an artist who was not well known who did a character, a woman psychiatrist, and Heide liked her better. So we met with her too and she agreed to do the same thing. When we were ready to go into series, both of them submitted stuff. And then Matt disappeared and all we're doing is meeting with this woman.

I was one of the creators and runners of the show, so we're busy writing scripts and sketches and we're getting stuff from this woman, but we're not hearing anything from Matt. So I went to Richard Sakai one day and I said, "What ever happened to the Matt Groening idea? I like his stuff better." He told me Fox wanted to take over merchandising *Life in Hell* as part of the deal and Matt had passed. He'd been making a living, not a good one, but he'd been surviving by merchandising those characters through small papers and by selling items through the mail. And he didn't wanna give up his full share of the merchandising for *Life in Hell* for just a piece of it.

So I said to Richard Sakai—and this is the truth, and I don't know if they remember it or they don't wanna remember it or what—but I said, "Well, why don't you ask him if he has some characters that he's willing to allow Fox to merchandise for him?" So Richard goes away and comes back and says, "Yeah. I talked to him and he says he does have other characters and he would be willing to do it, so he'll send us a drawing of the characters and see if we like them."

GARTH ANCIER, former president of entertainment, Fox Broadcasting: Richard had sent me Matt's books 'cause he was excited about the *Work Is Hell* series that Matt had done. We talked about it and he said, "I'd love to do either Binky or some of the characters from *Life Is Hell* and *Work Is Hell*, etc." And the problem they had was that the publisher would not allow us to use those characters on a TV show without Matt getting a large percentage of the revenues. So Richard said to Matt, "Can you go home and draw new characters that we don't have to pay the publisher for?" And the story is that Matt went home and came back the next day with—drawn out on a piece of paper—the Simpsons, the family.

PHIL ROMAN, former president of Film Roman; animation executive producer, *The Simpsons*: Matt didn't want to give up [*Life in Hell*]. Valerie Kavanaugh [a Gracie Films executive] told me this story: they picked Matt up, and they were going to go talk to Fox, and they asked him, "Do you have anything yet?" And he said no. And they said, "Well, we're having the meeting." So, on the way over there, he started making some sketches. He created that show on the drive to Fox.

Groening has said that he made up the characters while in the waiting area of Brooks's office. Regardless of the exact location, the idea that the Simpson family was created moments before the meeting with Brooks is probably a myth. For some time Jay Kennedy, Groening's friend and the editor in chief of King Features Syndicate, had encouraged him to move away from his rabbits and to draw more marketable, human forms. Speaking at Kennedy's funeral in 2007, Groening credited him with helping him to develop the Simpsons. While Groening named the family after his own—a father named Homer, mother named Marge (Marjorie), sisters Lisa and Maggie— he created Homer's middle name, Jay, as an acknowledgment of Jay Kennedy's contribution.

KEN ESTIN: Well, two, maybe three days after I spoke to Richard, Matt sends us a drawing of the Simpsons exactly as—well, not exactly— almost exactly as they are. Anyhow, everybody said, "Fine. That's fine. We like them." And Matt made his deal with Fox.

We went into production, and for the first half of the season we used both cartoons. All of us except [*Ullman* producer] Heide Perlman liked Matt much better—she continually fought for the woman to be the sole drawer and to get rid of Matt. The rest of us wanted Matt, and eventually Heide gave in and we let the woman disappear.

Other early *Ullman* staff remember it differently: Heide Perlman had liked both M. K. Brown's work for the *National Lampoon* and Matt's *Life in Hell* in the *LA Weekly*. While Perlman promoted Brown's work early on, it eventually became clear that Matt's material was working better, and it was never a case of Perlman promoting Brown's work over Matt's.

The deal Matt struck with Fox would prove extremely lucrative, particularly because he retained such a large portion of revenues from merchandising, which became ubiquitous. To this day, Groening signs off on every piece of *Simpsons* merchandise that goes on the market—and gets a piece of the proceeds.

KEN ESTIN: Fox gave Matt a much bigger piece than anybody will ever get again 'cause they had no idea. At that point no sitcom other than *M*A*S*H* had ever merchandised, and the merchandising for *M*A*S*H*, although far greater than for anything else, was still insignificant. So they were just playing hardball with Matt wanting to merchandise the characters 'cause that's what they do. They screw everybody they can. What they did is give him a much bigger piece than they thought would ever matter [by giving Matt a bigger share of future merchandising, they could pay him less for his cartoons appearing on the show]. Now Matt's probably worth hundreds of millions of dollars because of that.

ART SPIEGELMAN, Pulitzer Prize–winning cartoonist, *Maus*: I pleaded with Matt and advised him strongly from my elder-statesman position to not work with Fox. "Whatever you do, don't work with those guys! They're gangsters! They're gonna take your rights away!" I told him. He's never let me forget it.

POLLY PLATT: What's funny now, because he's so rich, is that I was driving home from my office at Paramount very shortly after that, and I saw Matt sitting at the bus stop. He didn't even have a car. I had no idea he was so poor.

Turning Groening's drawings into animated cartoons, something Brooks and company were clueless about, would require an animation studio. They settled on a tiny company in Hollywood called Klasky-Csupo, run by an eccentric Hungarian immigrant, Gabor Csupo, and his wife, Arlene Klasky.

KENT BUTTERWORTH, director of first *Simpsons* episode: Klasky-Csupo's studio was located on the second floor in the Bob Clampett building on Seward Street in Hollywood. This used to be the animation studio where the *Beany & Cecil* show was produced in the sixties. It was an old Hollywood building from the twenties or thirties with old hard-wood floors and lots of character.

Gabor had escaped from the Iron Curtain with a couple of his animator friends, Steve and Tibor. He was into a lot of the Eastern European graphics of the eighties.

PHIL ROMAN: When I was directing the *Peanuts* specials, way back in the late seventies, Gabor came by. He had just come over from Hungary, and he showed me his reel that he had compiled in Hungary, and I kind of liked him and what he'd done, so I said, "Okay, I'll give you some work to do, some scenes to animate." I might have given him some of the first work that he did.

GABOR CSUPO, animation executive producer, *The Simpsons* (1987–92): My partner and I had a small animation studio doing commercials and music videos and all kinds of stuff. And we got a call one day from Gracie Films, saying, "We looking for an animation company that could animate one-minute cartoons for this new show for Fox." So we went in there, meet the producers, and found out we were one of roughly two hundred companies they were looking at, so we were thinking, We're never gonna get this gig. But apparently our reputation was good, and they were telling us, "Listen, if you guys give us a good bid, the job is yours." So we gave them a price that they thought was pretty reasonable, but they said they actually got a better price from somebody else, which we thought was impossible.

When Jim Brooks originally saw Matt Groening's drawings on his wall it was just a clipping from a magazine, just the line drawing, no color or anything, and that's how he wanted to do the show. And we said, "Well, you know, it's not going to be very, how can I say it, accessible for people to watch, especially if you want to tell little stories, with just line drawings." So we offered them color for the same price, and all of a sudden their eyes lit up and he said, "Okay, you guys are on."

The characters were so beautiful but, let's face it, primitively designed, so we thought that we could counterbalance that design with shocking colors. That's why we came up with the yellow skin and the blue hair for Marge. We colored it in and we created the whole look for the show. Even for the backgrounds we used the same kind of flat-cel paintings, which no one ever used before. And at that time we didn't have computers, so everything was done by hand.

MARGOT PIPKIN, animation producer, *The Simpsons*: Klasky-Csupo was a really tiny little place. We had three animators on it—Bill Kopp, Wes Archer, and David Silverman—three young guys. Everyone was free-lance at Klasky because it was so tiny. The only full-time people were Gabor, the receptionist, and Arlene. We hired those three guys to ani-mate *The Simpsons*' bumpers ["bumpers" or "interstitials" are the names given to the short, one-minute cartoons that Gracie used to fill space between Tracey Ullman's sketches]. So they did the layout. They did the animation. They did the in-between. They did everything. And then Gyorgyi Peluce did the color design.

Matt said in a recent interview that he found the colors used for human beings in previous cartoons "freakish," so with *The Simpsons* Gyorgyi Peluce chose yellow skin. In the same interview he noted that she has never received proper credit.[2] This could be because until the date of the quotation above, June 2007, Matt never gave her any. In all my research for this book, which spanned twenty years of interviews and feature stories where Groening was quoted, this was the only time he mentioned Ms. Peluce.

GYORGYI PELUCE, color designer, *The Simpsons*: I knew Gabor from Hungary. We worked together at the Hungarian Film Studio, and when he needed some color design, I did it for him on a freelance basis.

I love color a lot. I knew the show was going to be very quick fillers, so I wanted to do something very different, something that was really going to pop, and something that would be a lot of fun. If you look at those drawings, they have a tendency to look a little crude, or primitive, if you will. They're not cartoony. I think they're a category of their own, because it didn't look like anything that was done before. And that's why I wanted to give them a color that didn't look like *anything* else that had come before.

What is the first thing that comes to people's minds about the Simp-sons? Yellow skin and the blue hair.

MARGOT PIPKIN, animation producer, *The Simpsons*: Gyorgyi came up with the colors, and at first everyone balked at it over at Gracie Films, and then Gabor kinda talked them into it, that it was such a funky design. They really needed funky color design too.

GYORGYI PELUCE: Gabor liked it. He knew it was good. He knew it was different. He knew there was nothing like it before.

MARGOT PIPKIN: Gyorgyi brought that crazy coloring style, which Matt would not have chosen on his own. And then when he saw it, Matt had the good design sense to say, "You know what? That works."

GYORGYI PELUCE: I've seen *The Simpsons Movie*. It's very nicely done colorwise—but that's not exactly a direction I would have taken with it. It looks a little bit too normal. I like to do weird colors. I had Asian people with slightly green colors at the beginning; I had black people with purplish colors—I don't think it really lasted—but what does it matter what color you are? We are universal.

For the voices of Homer and Marge, the producers used Dan Castellaneta and Julie Kavner, actors who were already regulars on *The Tracey Ullman Show*. (Marge's rasp is Kavner's normal voice, almost uninflected.)

Bonnie Pietila, the Ullman casting director, remembered that Yeardley Smith had a funny voice and asked her to read for Bart. When that didn't work out, she tried Lisa on for size, taking her voice up a few octaves. Conversely, Nancy Cartwright was brought in to try for Lisa. When she saw a picture of Bart and a description of his character, she let out a "Whoa, man, yeah!" in a voice that was just a small variation of one she'd done on *The Snorks*. Matt Groening instantly said, "That's it! That's him. That's Bart."[3] Hank Azaria was in a play no one was coming to see at the time. When Matt and Sam called him in to try for Moe, he used "a bad Al Pacino impression." After Azaria made his voice more gravelly, *The Simpsons* had their Moe (and the hundreds of other characters that came with Azaria).

Harry Shearer came on board because Sam asked him to. Shearer initially balked, but Sam promised it would be only an hour a week. "He lied," Shearer has joked.[4]

The *Ullman* bumper episodes were amusing snippets of the dysfunctional family's daily life, focusing mostly on the kids being kids, and the grief they caused their parents: Bart and Lisa engage in a burping contest; the parents unintentionally terrify Bart, Lisa, and Maggie with bedtime stories, resulting in loss of sleep for all; Bart directs the pallbearers at a funeral as if he were the foreman on a construction site; Bart tries to catch a football from Homer and in the process runs into a wall, runs off a cliff, and catches it in his mouth—then they all go out for frosty chocolate milk shakes. Without a ton of personality (Homer was an angry, moody dad, Marge a traditionally doting TV mom; Bart and Lisa were bratty kids who fought and played pretend), the edgy, nontraditional feel of Groening's *Life in Hell* had bled into the cartoon spots, with the rampant anti-conservative statement left behind. The bumpers were indeed different, but the show's comedy was basic—the Cro-Magnon version of *The Simpsons* man who would evolve, become civilized, and build empires. Here you can see some of the DNA of the show's earliest themes: Homer as the grumbling, stumbling father, trying hopelessly to keep his kids in line while not providing much of an example; the parents' well-intended behavior toward their kids going awry; Bart's contempt for authority causing havoc but its all turning out all right, or for the better, in the end. Yet many of these themes could be found in any sitcom, going back to *Leave It to Beaver*, whereas the special characterization, smart, subversive humor, and tender emotionality that would become hallmarks of the series were at this point almost entirely absent.

WESLEY ARCHER, director, *The Simpsons* (1987–97): At the time, there wasn't really much out there, so I knew people would like it. Matt's little scripts were very funny, and his design style was attractive to look at; it commanded your attention.

MICHAEL MENDEL, postproduction supervisor, *The Tracey Ullman Show, The Simpsons* (1989–92, 1994–99): Matt would just show up with a two-page script and go, "Here it is. This is the cartoon we're doing this week." It was sort of guerrilla-style animation. We would hang out on the stage of *Tracey Ullman*, and in between block and rehearsal, we would

grab the actors and record their lines. It was me and Matt and the animators and a couple directors—a really small group of people working
on this little one-minute cartoon every week.

WALLACE WOLODARSKY writer/producer, *The Simpsons* (1989–92): We
knew Matt's work from *Life in Hell*, just as fans. So when we saw the
bumpers, we saw a lot of those ideas being reflected in an animated
forum and we really connected to it because so much of Matt's work at
that time was about childhood—the trials and travails of being a kid. So
that was something we really responded to.

GABOR CSUPO: Every week we had to do a minute and a half of animation. And Matt turned in the script on, let's say Thursday, and on Monday we started with a new show. And then we had to finish by Friday, so
it was really a lot of work. We stayed around the clock.

GARTH ANCIER: *Tracey Ullman* just didn't quite . . . as good as the show
was, and as much work as Jim and a really great team put into it, we
never quite cracked that show, even though it was a critical darling.

Julie Kavner, for her part, has said that she did the best work of her
life on *The Tracey Ullman Show*.[5]

WALLACE WOLODARSKY: *The Simpsons* was viewed as poor relations by
the writing staff of *The Tracey Ullman Show*, and we secretly always felt
that [it] was the funniest part of the show.

Groening would ask Tracey Ullman to do guest voices on the
bumpers, but the show's producers said she was "too busy."

MICHAEL MENDEL: We started putting all these one-minute episodes
together on a tape. Seeing these cartoons play, one right after the other,
in front of a live audience, that's when it dawned on me that this was
something special.

Jim Brooks later explained to Charlie Rose that because Tracey Ullman could spend up to three hours in makeup, the audience would

get incredibly restless. To quell their hostility, the crew would string together a number of *Simpsons* bumpers, which ended up getting the biggest laughs of the entire show.

Another important factor in helping Brooks imagine *The Simpsons* as its own series was the cheerleading of David Silverman, the director of many of the bumpers, as well as of the series' early episodes, and who had approached Brooks with the idea at a Christmas party. Although Silverman had been drunk at the time, and quite young, Brooks had never had anyone speak to him so passionately about what it would mean for the world of animation to get an animated series on prime time.

Meanwhile, back at Fox, some at the studio (headed by John Dolgen) were looking to kill the *Simpsons* spots, because they were costing something like $15,000 per spot and were the lowest-testing part of the show.

BARRY DILLER: We all thought the Simpsons were really cute, but their shorts weren't making any noise, nor was *The Tracey Ullman Show*, for that matter, which was unfortunate. I never saw *The Simpsons* as a series. What made the difference was Jim Brooks.

No one would argue with the above. But Brooks didn't do it alone. Far from it. Brooks and Groening make up only two-thirds of the holy trinity responsible for *The Simpsons* genesis. There was also a veteran TV writer who had worked with Jim Brooks since *Taxi*: the cigar-smoking, hard-gambling, brilliant Sam Simon.

FOUR

Sam "Sayonara" Simon

In which *The Simpsons* hosts a war . . . Matt Groening is called a "fat fuck" . . . the Emmys become a scene of rivalry and petty resentments . . . and Roland Barthes lets everyone off the hook.

The man James L. Brooks chose to partner with Groening in developing the series was Sam Simon, a veteran writer/producer who had worked with Brooks on *Taxi* and *Ullman* and had written for *Cheers*. It was Simon who assembled the original *Simpsons* writing room, which has become the stuff of legend. Credited by many as the chief architect of *The Simpsons*, he took the one-minute shorts from *Ullman* and transformed them into the hysterical half-hour episodes that America fell in love with.

Simon would depart from *The Simpsons* after its fourth season, leaving behind much acrimony with Matt Groening over creative differences and compensation. Simon's lawyers negotiated a lucrative deal for him; he left without much severance but retained a piece of the show (which earns him between $20 and $30 million annually to this day). While many of the early staff, particularly the writers, remain loyal to Simon, calling him an "unsung hero," it is clear that Simon was difficult to work with and not an ideal collaborator for Groening, whose reputation as a "nice guy" and genuinely easygoing still holds up today.

Simon told *60 Minutes* in 2007, "Any show I've ever worked on, it turns me into a monster. I go crazy; I hate myself."[1] For his part, Groening has said, "I think Sam Simon is brilliantly funny and one of the smartest writers I've ever worked with, although unpleasant and mentally unbalanced."[2]

BRIAN ROBERTS, editor, *The Simpsons* (1989–92): Sam personally assembled the writing staff: John Swartzwelder, Jon Vitti, George Meyer, Jeff Martin, Mike Reiss, Al Jean, and eventually Rob Cohen. He hand-picked Jay Kogen and Wallace Wolodarsky, whom he pulled over from *The Tracey Ullman Show*. So here you have this guy who personally assembled the equivalent of the Manhattan Project, or the 1924 Yankees [as the original *Simpsons* writers room would come to be regarded by TV writers]. The greatest testament to Sam's impact on the show is that even after his departure that writing team stayed together and continued the pattern and the template that Sam set up.

JOSH WEINSTEIN, writer/producer, *The Simpsons* (1991–97): [Weinstein was among the first outsiders to join the original room.] It was like walking into the pantheon of comedy gods.

JAY KOGEN, writer/producer, *The Simpsons* (1989–92): He was a tough critic. So if you pitched something he didn't like, he'd let you know it right away. You couldn't have a thin skin.

CONAN O'BRIEN, writer/producer, *The Simpsons* (1991–93): I remember Sam coming into the room, and pitching to him, and initially being really intimidated. He's hilarious. It was fun to try and make him laugh. If I could make Sam laugh, I was excited.

DARIA PARIS, assistant to Sam Simon, *The Simpsons* (1989–93): Sam's basically an asshole—whom I *adore*. As crazy as Sam could be—and he could be extremely crazy—he's brilliant. He's one of the funniest people I have ever known. I found that the staff, the producers, the writers—most of them were very intimidated by Sam, so I wound up being the go-between. They would come to *me* to talk to him because there are very few people I'm intimidated by, and I wasn't intimidated by Sam. I mean, he could be scary. He can have a bad temper. And he could get very passionate about things. And people were afraid to approach him.

WALLACE WOLODARSKY: writer/producer, *The Simpsons* (1989–92): Of any of the people [on *The Simpsons*], Sam was the person I was most involved with and learned the most from at that time. He was the person who sat in the room with us day after day.

Sam opened our eyes to the possibilities of what an animated show could be, which is to say we could go anywhere in the world, we could do anything, and that was incredibly liberating, coming from live action, because you were obviously limited by so much.

BRAD BIRD, executive consultant, *The Simpsons* (1989–97); director, *The Incredibles, Ratatouille*: I think the unsung hero has always been Sam. I was in the room when he took some pretty mediocre scripts and just sat there in his chair, with all the writers in the room and a cigar, and went through it, line by line. He would get people to pitch lines, but nine times out of ten he came up with the best line. And if someone came up with a genuinely better line, he'd put that in.

BRIAN ROBERTS: When you see the opening credits and all those characters go by, they're all right out of Sam Simon's imagination. I think *The Simpsons* was, in a way, the perfect storm for Sam in that he's a pretty accomplished cartoonist himself. I remember him drawing a lot of the characters out on cocktail napkins. I wished I'd kept 'em; they'd be worth a fortune now.

Sam is said to have actually defined the look of Mr. Burns, Dr. Hibbert, Chief Wiggum and the cops, and nearly all the early characters voiced by guest stars. But in a different way Simon shaped many, if not all, of the citizens of Springfield from the first four seasons by developing their characters. For example, Krusty the Clown was inspired by Rusty Nails, a pathetic clown Matt Groening as a kid had seen on TV, but Sam turned him into the chain-smoking, hacking, shamelessly self-promoting character who took advantage of kids.

DARIA PARIS: He's a very smart guy. He went to Stanford. He got his first job I think when he was twenty-three, and he started in animation.

COLIN A.B.V. LEWIS, postproduction supervisor, *The Simpsons* (1989–97); producer, *The Simpsons* (1989–97): Those first two seasons, those first two quote unquote "brilliant" seasons, that's Sam. Sam put together the models.* Sam was the head writer. If you like *The Simpsons*, you like Sam Simon's work. He was the one who was able to take a sitcom format and make an animated sitcom rather than a cartoon that's adult. That comes from Sam and Jim.

DARIA PARIS: Whenever I was the angriest at Sam (and there were many occasions), my way to get back at him was not to laugh when we were in the writers room and he'd pitch a joke to me. But he always got me. There was something he would say that just did it. He's a very funny man. And he was really very good-hearted.

The most public airing of the ill will between Simon and Groening happened in the pages of *The Washington Post*, just months after the show had debuted. "My contribution to the writing of the show should not be minimized," Matt said. "I'm involved in every creative aspect, from conception of ideas to writing scripts to directing voices to designing characters." Sam retorted, "He's doing a lot of other stuff for the show, merchandising and things like that. He's the show's ambassador." "That's a little bit condescending," Matt shot back. "There's definitely a power struggle here,"[3] he added.

BRIAN ROBERTS: I was a big fan of *Life in Hell*—I read it every week— and, sure, *The Simpsons* and *Life in Hell* emulate each other. *Life in Hell* is funny, but Sam created the biting sarcasm and the dysfunctional family. It was based on Matt's thing, but still, it's an awful long ways from taking a twenty-second interstitial cartoon on *The Tracey Ullman Show* and turning it into an actual series that's run for eighteen years. So this concept of Matt as the creative driving force behind *The Simpsons* is just plain bullshit.

JAY KOGEN: I love Matt. As a person, Matt is fantastic. He's funny. He's smart. He's witty. He's pleasant. If anybody I knew was going to become a gazillionaire, just for being a nice guy, why not Matt Groening?

---

*The model is the basic set of drawings that make up a character's physical look. The model for a given character's aesthetic is what the animators work from.

WALLACE WOLODARSKY: The thing about Matt is that he did supply the template for the show. And that's undeniable. Sam was able to take that template and make it into an even bigger world and really flesh it out with characters. He brought a broader perspective to it. He made it bigger than just the family. What's such an important part of *The Simpsons* is the world of characters it exists in.

JAY KOGEN: Matt wasn't always in the room. So it's hard to fight with everybody and have a real say if you're not there. He's also a very pleasant, easygoing guy, and the writers room can be a tough place. But, you know, ultimately Matt got what he wanted. When he pitched stuff, he got what he wanted. [Many sources from the early days disagree with this last statement.]

Creatively, Matt Groening and Sam Simon saw things very differently. The mistrust of institutions and whimsical cynicism of *Life in Hell* would persist in *The Simpsons*, but Matt was not a TV writer and didn't know how to structure his jokes and concepts into a pithy twenty-two minutes of television. Sam was a master TV writer and was openly disdainful of Matt's attempts to include himself in the writing process. Creative differences could spill over into budget crises (scripts being rewritten late in the process are costly), as well as issues of power, control, and credit. Sam and his writers were the ones making the show, but of course *The Simpsons* would always be Matt Groening's idea. The differences between the show's two chief developers would devolve into an all-out "war," especially as the show gained notoriety and the millions began rolling in.

POLLY PLATT, production designer, *Terms of Endearment*: Matt did not get along with Sam. Nobody got along with [Sam]. He's kind of an awful person. If he was at any meeting, it just seemed that everyone would turn on each other.

GAVIN POLONE, former agent for Conan O'Brien, *Simpsons* writers; executive producer, *Curb Your Enthusiasm*: I remember Sam Simon yelling at me and telling me I was an [asshole]. I don't remember anybody ever doing that before. He was angry with me because I would try to get [my clients] as much money as possible. But, you know, with Sam either you do what he wants you to do or you're an [asshole].

SAM SIMON (to Joe Morgenstern in the *Los Angeles Times*, 1990): I've never worked on a good show where there isn't a certain amount of creative friction. I've seen brother turn against brother in a rewrite room.

BRIAN ROBERTS: In the beginning it was all really happy. Everybody was ensconced in Marilyn Monroe's old bungalow—that's where Gracie Films was. And it was all very impressive: Jim had a wall full of Academy Awards and a million Emmys. And since the editorial side of the show took place six to eight months ahead of when the animation would come back [from Korea], for those six to eight months it was probably the happiest time on *The Simpsons*. I mean, Matt and Sam were getting along. You know, they were happy. We were recording really funny shows—just the sound tracks were hysterical.

And then it seemed as if the little bubble that we'd been living in for eight months burst. It didn't burst because of anything negative. It burst because all of a sudden Bart Simpson became the iconic graphic image of the early nineties and then the next thing you know the show ended up on the cover of *Newsweek*. And that's when it all really started to go sideways.

There was a party. I remember it specifically because somebody had created the world's first *Simpsons* pinball machine. I think Sam and I had had a little too much to drink. We were outside of this party and Sam was really upset. He was beside himself because Matt was glory hogging the spotlight and taking credit for everything, and Sam didn't get any of that attention.

DARIA PARIS: I didn't like Matt very much. I used to call him "Fat Fuck Groening," because he caused Sam a lot of problems and because I was a Sam supporter in the war. Matt used to go out there and grab all this attention for himself, like he did it all. Well, he didn't do it all, you know? And I suppose I felt that was very ungracious and unfair.

COLIN A.B.V. LEWIS: Sam had been around Jim since *Taxi*, and he went on and did *Cheers*, and so in the TV world he was pretty high profile to begin with. Jim Brooks is Jim Brooks; everyone knows Jim Brooks as a director, and even on screen, from the movies. Matt was the face of *The Simpsons*. He was the "creator." Matt had become a public figure, because he's the person whose name was on the show. Matt Groening. He was *The Simpsons*. Everyone thought, He's drawing all the cartoons, he's directing all the episodes, and he's writing all the shows. But Sam was this guy no one knew. He didn't have a face.

JAY KOGEN: Matt Groening got all the credit, or most of the credit. Jim Brooks got some of the credit. Was the credit awarded appropriately? No. But is credit awarded appropriately on any show? Apparently not. I keep reading books about *Star Trek* where Roddenberry was not the guy who was necessarily at the head of it, or the stuff about *The Godfather*, where it's Coppola *and* it's a bunch of other people. It turns out that what they say about TV and movies being a collaborative effort is really true. It's a large collaboration. But those are hard stories to tell for the press. They like to make stars out of people, so they pick one guy and say, "This guy's the guy who did it." And that's a pretty good story.

An example from a 1990 article in *The Boston Globe*: "Groening's skill as a writer is such that, in *The Simpsons*, as in *Life in Hell*, he can weave contrasting strands together . . . He has a sharp eye for detail and nuance; he likes little jokes within bigger jokes; his humor often carries the sting of truth. And, in his situations and character-izations, there are plenty of shocks of recognition." In the same arti-cle, it was mentioned that Groening was "working with" James L. Brooks and Sam Simon. Groening seemed comfortable taking credit for a writing process which, according to those people who were in the room, he was not significantly involved in. From a 1991 inter-view with the *San Francisco Chronicle*: "We work late into the night, rewriting scripts. By the time a show gets on the air, we've heard the same jokes hundreds of times, so we really have to like them . . . If we think that a line doesn't quite work, we'll change it."

There was a running joke at *The Simpsons*: Matt had been assigned a script in the early days of the show, which over the first seasons never materialized. As years went by, people would comment sarcastically that it was going to be turned in "any day now."

BRIAN ROBERTS: This was my ham-fisted attempt at trying to make Sam feel better. I said, "Listen, you know America loves a success story. Here's a cartoonist making cartoons out of his fucking garage. Polly Platt picks up a cartoon, gives it to Jim Brooks. The next thing you know it's a hit series. It's legendary, right?

"Listen, if I was at the news desk at *Entertainment Tonight*, I'd go, 'What would make a better story? Slick Industry Insider and Brilliant Writer Come Up with Funny Show, or, Starving Artist Hits the Lottery and Is Now King of Television.' I'd go with the other story every day of the week. It's just more interesting."

It started to become extremely dysfunctional at about that time.

CONAN O'BRIEN: You heard things, but it wasn't discussed that much.

JAY KOGEN: It was clear that there was animosity back and forth. It was a tough position for Sam to be in, because Matt was getting *all* the accolades. I would think that if you were pouring your life's blood into something and getting none of the credit, it would be irritating. If you look at the original *Simpsons* cartoons, those are closer to Matt's drawings, but Sam reshaped them and redrew them. He had experience in sitcoms. He had also worked in animation, and was also a very talented cartoonist himself. He's really smart and handled storyboards and all that stuff. He knew what he was doing all the way down the line. And then the story that broke was, "Independent Cartoonist Changes TV."

DARIA PARIS: It's a very weird thing because even though it was Matt's idea, it's basically Jim and Sam's show.

BRIAN ROBERTS: After it went sideways, the rift between Matt and Sam got greater and greater and there were lots of incidents. You know, like Matt snubbed Sam at the Emmys. Sam didn't get to sit at *The Simpsons* table. Matt somehow—as the story went that I pieced together—went behind Sam's back and started rearranging where people were sitting, so that he could sit next to Jim, and Sam ended up sitting somewhere else.

And it all started to get really petty, to the point where they weren't talking to each other.

Unfortunately, it was me who was in the middle. When we'd do a screening it was Matt, Sam, and I. And they were like two five-year-olds not speaking. We'd be watching an episode and Sam would say, "Do this." And Matt would say, "Will you tell Sam Simon I think that's the stupidest idea I've ever heard." Sam would say, "Would you tell Matt Groening that he doesn't know his ass from third grade." We were all sitting shoulder to shoulder! It was extremely uncomfortable for me.

DARIA PARIS: At the time, we all had offices on the same floor of this one building. We were at one end, there was a short hallway, and then there was Matt's office. So there was a lot of tension, I mean there was a *lot* of tension, a lot of yelling here and there. Sam can be volatile.

CONAN O'BRIEN: Matt didn't want *The Simpsons* to be a cartoon where Homer can run off a ledge like Wile E. Coyote and keep running. He wanted respect for the laws of gravity, the physical properties of the basic elements. And I would run up against that sometimes.

I remember with the monorail episode, there was a moment where, at the end of the episode, Leonard Nimoy says, "My work here is done." And Barney says, "You didn't do anything!" And he says, "Didn't I?" And then I wanted him to beam out. I remember there being a discussion with Matt, like, "I don't think we can do this, 'cause this can't happen in the physical world." I think Mike Reiss and Al Jean had to pitch it to Matt or tell Matt, but Matt was okay with it, because I think it was consistent with the *Star Trek* reality. For whatever reason, we got it, and I was happy about that.

He wanted to make sure that we didn't wreck this beautiful machine that he had built.

DARIA PARIS: There were times in the room when Matt would come up with the stupidest ideas. And he had this one: we were going to do an episode where Marge finally lets her hair down, and Matt's idea was that once she let it down the audience finds out she has rabbit ears, which was ridiculous. And Sam said no.

So things like that would come up and they definitely differed on the vision of the show. It's silly, you know, and Matt would get a little stubborn about it.

JAY KOGEN: In another episode, Bart's going to jump over Springfield canyon. Before he does it, Homer takes his skateboard away from him.

He hops on the skateboard and starts going down the ramp and then over the canyon. And he says, "I'm king of the world!" (which was before *Titanic*, by the way; we like to take credit that *Titanic* stole that from us). And then Homer falls down the canyon. He hits his head on the rocks and he gets bloody and falls down to the bottom and then is hauled up by emergency people. He's put into an ambulance. The ambulance takes off, hits a tree, the gurney he's in falls out of the ambulance and goes right back down the canyon.

Matt didn't want that to happen. We explained, "No. He's getting really hurt. He goes to the hospital. He smashes his head. He gets bloody. It's not like a Warner Bros. cartoon."

He was against it. And at one point we found out that he had canceled the animation for it, without telling anybody, because he didn't like it. Sam Simon had to reorder the animation at the last minute to get it done. Eventually I think Matt came around and said it was one of his favorite pieces. But at the time he just felt really strongly that it was not appropriate—it was too cartoony for his cartoon.

While only Sam and Matt will ever know what was ultimately at the root of their split, the lion's share of the credit going to Matt is a likely culprit. And though their enmity produced the Cain and Abel story of the *Simpsons* genesis, their rivalry did produce something valuable. For effective art, even in television, you need tension, and it was the creative forces of Sam Simon, Matt Groening, and Jim Brooks, pushing and pulling the show in three different directions, that produced a half-hour comedy that can stand up to anything on television.

BARRY DILLER, former chairman and CEO, Fox: I was totally aware of [Matt and Sam's] problems and often mediated them on behalf of everyone. For a while it was not a happy place. But I think it ultimately made the show better.

MICHAEL MENDEL, postproduction supervisor, *The Tracey Ullman Show*, *The Simpsons* (1989–92, 1994–99): A lot of the foundation for the show and the reason why I think it's successful was laid down during those tumultuous times.

The question of authorship and *The Simpsons* comes up again and again in this book, and there's no easy answer. The shorts were Matt's and Gabor Csupo's and Gyorgyi Peluce's and David Silverman's. The series built on these, with authorship going to Sam and Jim in the writing room, but also to Jay Kogen, Wallace Wolodarsky, Al Jean, Mike Reiss, and the others. Matt Groening too. When it comes to a work as collaborative and postmodern as *The Simpsons*, it may not be possible to distribute credit to one, a few, or many individuals. The literary critic Roland Barthes argued that this conception of authorship is practically irrelevant, that words are already so loaded with meaning and cultural context that he who puts them on the page barely matters. In the essay "Death of the Author," he says that "writing is the destruction of every voice, over every point of origin . . . It is language that speaks, not the author . . . A text is made of multiple writings, drawn from many cultures."[4] *The Simpsons'* "author" is all the works that contributed to the language, signs, and symbols that make up the show, including the infrastructure in which it was created. Seen this way, Rupert Murdoch, Barry Diller, *MAD* magazine, *Saturday Night Live*, Fox, and Bill Cosby all had a hand in making *The Simpsons*, as did all the crappy sitcoms it was responding to, as well as the conservative culture that produced them.

The overarching point is that Sam Simon deserves more credit than he gets, but authorship is more involved than who had what idea, who wrote what joke, and who drew which character. As a wise magazine editor once explained to me, "Idea is spelled with a small 'i.' "

Sam Simon, who we will meet again in later chapters, is inextricable from *The Simpsons'* success, and its history. But before the war, before he was even brought on to run the show, the idea to give the Simpsons their own half-hour show had to pass muster at Fox. This was the Simpsons' first battle, which placed them against the suits and the suits against each other.

FIVE

Welcome to Springfield

In which Matt Groening nearly becomes Mickey's bitch . . . Barry Diller threatens torture . . . a nineteenth-century governor of Wisconsin inspires Bart's creation . . . and everyone at Fox supports *The Simpsons* unequivocally.

MATT GROENING (to the *New York Daily News*, April 8, 1999): The executives like to think they have something to do with the success of their shows, and with *The Simpsons* . . . they can't say that; the shows are done with complete independence. And I think that grates on their nerves.

Though critics liked *The Tracey Ullman Show*, the series wasn't a big hit. But, then again, neither was much else on the network. While the execs might not agree on how the idea for *The Simpsons* as its own series came to Diller, or how enthusiastic he was about it, one thing is certain: *The Simpsons*, as a series, was far from a sure thing.

BARRY DILLER, former chairman and CEO, Fox: I know it was originally Matt's drawings, and I'm sure Sam Simon made his contribution, but the show never would have happened, or have been successful, without Jim Brooks.

At the time, Matt was taking many meetings with studio execs who were interested in having him to do a cartoon show. But until he was approached by Jim Brooks and Fox in the mid-eighties, these meetings never went anywhere. "Just saying 'Rocky and Bullwinkle' was enough to get them nervous . . ." he told *The New York Times*.

HARRIS KATLEMAN, former CEO, 20th Century Fox Television: One day, sitting talking to Jim Brooks and Matt Groening, we decided we'd take seven one-minute episodes of *The Simpsons* and put them together and see how it looked [there would be forty-eight bumpers in total]. I purposely didn't share this with any of my colleagues in the company because of a comment that Barry Diller had made to me about *The Flintstones* being the last successful animation show and how prime time would never buy another one.

So we developed the seven minutes, and we tested it, and it tested through the roof. The testing was incredible.

Yet Barry Diller was highly skeptical of those results.

ROB KENNEALLY, former vice president of series, Fox Broadcasting: So myself, Garth Ancier, and a guy named Kevin Wendell actually put a bunch of these shorts together and screened them for Diller, and he didn't particularly care for them and he ultimately sort of pushed us back, 'cause in animation, there's a lot of lead time, and it's awfully expensive, and Jim Brooks wasn't going to do anything like a pilot.

HARRIS KATLEMAN: I was running Fox Television [which financed, produced, and sold TV shows to all the networks], and we had more shows on the air than any other studio. We had *L.A. Law, In Living Color, M*A*S*H,* and *Trapper John.* My division was highly successful, and I had to walk a very careful line because Fox Broadcasting wanted me to give them all our shows. And I told them, "I have a fiduciary relationship with Steven Bochco and David Kelley and all these people to explore all the studios. I just can't do an exclusive deal with Fox Broadcasting 'cause that wouldn't be ethical."

Still, they were struggling and I did everything I could to help them. I gave them *In Living Color*, even though HBO wanted it. And with *The Simpsons*, I said to Barry, "This show's a home run." And then Barry went to Rupert 'cause they had to commit to me for $13 million 'cause each episode cost $1 million.

RUPERT MURDOCH, CEO, News Corp: I was at a program meeting with Barry Diller and the people at Fox Network and afterward Barry said, "Come into my office, I want to show you something." He had a tape there about twenty minutes in length of all the little thirty-second bits that had been used on *The Tracey Ullman Show*. And he played it, and I thought it was just hilarious. I said, "You've gotta buy this tonight."

Of course, nothing in the TV business is ever that simple.

Harris Katleman: I showed it at the time to Bob Iger, who's now the CEO of Disney but at the time was president of ABC Television and a good friend of mine. And Bob looked at the seven minutes and said, "I'll buy it." I told him that first I had to show it to Fox Broadcasting because it was technically part of *The Tracey Ullman Show* and I had a responsibility to them.

So I showed it to my colleagues at Fox Broadcasting and they poohpoohed me. They were not all gung-ho. None of them really wanted to do anything. And I let them know I had thirteen episodes ordered from ABC, at which point Barry Diller got into it and said, "Do you want me to commit for thirteen episodes?" I said, "You're gonna have to 'cause if you don't ABC's gonna buy it."

Although Diller would eventually green-light the project, other execs remember having to push the CEO to give *The Simpsons* a shot. Murdoch, for his part, takes no credit in *The Simpsons'* creative development. "It was all them," he told me, referring to Jim, Matt, Sam, and the writers. But in terms of executive decisions with regard to *The Simpsons,* and the development of other shows, Murdoch is more assertive about his involvement, as for example, when Diller left in 1992, and Murdoch named himself chairman of Fox. "Let's put it this way," he told *Variety* at the time. "Seven years ago I bet News Corp on buying FOX for $2 billion. It's not as if I've been asleep for seven years."[*][1]

---

*Among execs, Diller is seen as somewhat of a snob. For him, it was a much classier proposition to do something like *The Tracey Ullman Show* than *Married . . . with Children* and the other schlock that Fox became known for producing and distributing (called "tabloid TV" and "guerrilla TV" in the press). In the same interview cited above, Murdoch tried to call out Diller on his elitism, adding, "Without intending any criticism, go look at the taste of every movie Barry ever made or anybody else in Hollywood. I read today that Barry was the last gasp of morality here. That's liberal bullshit."

A former Fox exec who spoke to Daniel Kimmel for his book, *The Fourth Network*, said, "The reality is that there were not many ideas that came out of Barry Diller's head . . . There wasn't one show on our air that Barry Diller dreamt up . . . He's been dramatically overpaid. But that's the way Hollywood is with people like Barry Diller."

And yet such criticisms are few and far between. When Diller abruptly left Fox in 1992—he had approached Murdoch about becoming a partner; Murdoch's reply, "There's only one principal at this company"[2]—it caused an uproar, and the press speculated that it could spell big trouble for Murdoch, Fox, and News Corp. "The very thought of Barry leaving Fox is mind-boggling," *Beverly Hills 90210* producer Aaron Spelling told *USA Today*. "This changes everything."[3] And yet Diller left 20th Century Fox in immeasurably better condition than he'd found it. Hits like *Home Alone* and *Edward Scissorhands* had helped Fox studio regain its footing, and Fox Broadcasting had finally made money in 1990, enjoying a 40 percent uptick in revenues the following year. Diller was confident about the position of the network he was leaving behind. "Fox has landed," he said. "It's a reality. Nobody can take it away."[4]

The question of how much Diller actually had to do with developing *The Simpsons* remains open—but at the end of the day, it was under his supervision that the show was given the go-ahead. As far as which execs were responsible for convincing him to do so, that answer changes, depending on whom you ask.

CHARLIE GOLDSTEIN, former executive vice president in charge of production, Fox Television: There were a lot of people who were not as hopeful, who doubted whether the show could make it as a series. It was all brand-new. Nobody knew. John Dolgen was a big supporter of the show for the studio, for Brooks. He was a visionary. He was president of Fox Studios, and he answered to Diller. A very smart businessman. He wanted it to work. I was really close to the show from a production standpoint, and if it wasn't for a guy like Dolgen, the show never would have been made. It would have been *dumped*.

HARRIS KATLEMAN: Oh, I don't believe that. I think John Dolgen supported it equally with me. John was very supportive. You know, it wasn't easy going against Barry and Rupert in those days 'cause nobody really knew if Fox Broadcasting was gonna work. So whenever you're spending big money like we were, you needed a solid front, and John Dolgen and I presented a solid front to management.

Other top Fox execs remember it differently, that Dolgen and Fox Studio wanted to kill *The Simpsons* spots when they were on Ullman, and that the real champion behind the series was Fox Broadcasting president of television, Garth Ancier, who, while laughing, called other execs' accounts "revisionist."

ROB KENNEALLY, former executive vice president of series, Fox Broadcasting: Garth was totally into it, but he wasn't willing to go to the mat. I mean, he couldn't, and Barry was fairly intimidating. And when I came in, Garth was already reported as having had his anxiety attacks. Barry had pressed him pretty hard.

CHARLIE GOLDSTEIN: Can you imagine saying, "I think we could do a series based on a show called *The Simpsons*. You know those interstitials? We'll do a whole series." People would go, "Are you out of your fucking mind?" Even I thought, on that one, You guys are nuts. But what do I know? I wish I'd got a piece of it.

Katleman may have been wise to approach Diller with some backup—the man ran his network "with fear" as a prime motivator. Once, during a company retreat in the mountains of Colorado, Fox executives were stunned at how friendly and cordial Diller was being. "I think Barry has altitude sickness," John Dolgen exclaimed. His staff used to half joke that Diller's phone number at the office was 203-P-A-I-N. Harris Katleman, whom Diller would accuse of having a "bunker mentality" for being one of the few people who disagreed with him, would stand up to the Fox president. "I'm gonna do what I want to do," Katleman would say. "If you don't like it, fire me." Diller used to joke in return, "I'll keep you and torture you."

While surely Katleman, Dolgen, Ancier, and others played their part in getting *The Simpsons* series on the air at Fox Broadcasting,

Jim Brooks was the true driving force behind the network's acceptance of it.

ROB KENNEALLY: The way we got Barry to finally say yes was, "Well, let's do a Halloween special. Let's do a Christmas special." And ultimately when we pitched that to Jim Brooks and his group, their response back was, "We don't make pilots."

MICHAEL MENDEL, postproduction supervisor, *The Tracey Ullman Show*, *The Simpsons* (1989–92, 1994–99): Barry Diller just wanted to make specials and Jim Brooks put his foot down and said, "It's a series or nothing." The network wanted to play it safe, and they weren't sure if this was going to work. I don't think that happens today. I don't think anyone gets on the phone with Barry Diller and says, "Take it or leave it. It's a series."

RON KENNEALLY: So—it's over. We tried every which way. We couldn't get Jim Brooks to do a Christmas special. We tried to convince him to do a series of specials. Couldn't get that. Couldn't get Diller to move. It dies. It literally sits on the development room floor. The way *The Simpsons* ultimately got made was in the renegotiation of Jim Brooks's overall deal at the studio. It was put in the deal that they *had* to do *The Simpsons* as part of it. The studio was desperate to hang on to Jim Brooks for films, and the lawyers at the time pressed the studio—thank God for all of us in the TV department—to make *The Simpsons* as part of his renewal.

GARTH ANCIER, former president, Fox Broadcasting: You know, once we got to the homestretch of the thing, Barry was actually quite encouraging of *The Simpsons*. He saw the potential of it, there's no question that's true.

BARRY DILLER: I wanted to do anything that did not involve making a commitment of thirteen episodes. But Jim said, with six months of lead time, it wouldn't work any other way.

GARTH ANCIER: It was a tense atmosphere, because there was so much at stake and there was so little that any of us really knew. We would spend probably several hours a day together, talking through with

Barry in particular, what we were trying to accomplish and how we got there.

The Simpsons certainly fit the criterion we were following at that point, which was, How do we do something different from the other networks? The question was, Could you tell a half-hour story that would maintain the pace of what they were doing on the vignettes? I totally give credit to Jim, because he was the one who visualized how you could do that.

MATT GROENING (in George Mair, *The Barry Diller Story*): I designed *The Simpsons* to be a TV series. That was always my secret plan. The idea of putting animated characters on at prime time was considered very controversial. I was worried that just having one shot at getting people's attention would not do it.

BRAD BIRD, executive consultant, *The Simpsons* (1989–97); director, *The Incredibles, Ratatouille*: First of all, nobody had really done a show like that—to some extent *Rocky & Bullwinkle* and *The Flintstones*. The idea of doing an animated show for adults in prime time was considered really off-the-wall at the time. And because Fox was a new network, they were willing to try that. They sensed that they could do a different kind of comedy than the kind that was traditionally done for sitcoms, meaning they could afford to jump around the world and go somewhere elaborate for the sake of a single-shot joke. So they were beginning to see that they could accelerate the comedy and go a lot more different directions at once. But they also knew they had to give it substance. So Jim Brooks, being the genius that he is, wanted to make sure it was more than an expanded version of the one-minutes that were on *The Tracey Ullman Show*. And that it had a plot and a subplot, and that underneath all the goofiness there was some emotional realism.

GEORGE MEYER, writer/producer, *The Simpsons* (1989–2004) (to *The Believer*, September 2004): Launching a new TV show is probably one of the most difficult things that a writer can do. In the early days, it's like a baby crawling across a freeway. It's such a miracle if it gets across.

While most execs saw that *The Simpsons* had potential as its own series, any and all doubts about the show ultimately came down to

cost. Unlike dopey Saturday morning cartoons, which cost in the low thousands of dollars per episode to create, *The Simpsons* would cost hundreds of thousands per episode. Early on, these costs were frustrated by the producers' lack of experience in animation.

RUPERT MURDOCH: You look at it in today's figures, and the risks of making *The Simpsons* its own series weren't that great. But at the time, we were very conscious of how much money we were spending on production.

BRIAN ROBERTS, writer, *The Simpsons* (1989–92): For the first six to eight months, nobody knew who we were. There was the writing staff in the building across from the Gracie compound. In the editing room we were operating out of this little trailer. During those sessions, it was me, Matt Groening, and Sam Simon, and sometimes Jim. And for eight months [before the show first aired] it was a joke. We couldn't even charge food from the commissary because nobody knew who we were.

The Simpsons moved onto the Fox lot in 1988, with the writers settling in the Gracie bungalow, and the postproduction folks setting up shop a few yards away. The other appendage of *The Simpsons'* operation, the animators at Klasky-Csupo, got to work in their offices on Seward Street in Hollywood.

MARGOT PIPKIN: As soon as *Simpsons* became the series, it was about managing a huge studio of people. I mean, we went from this tiny little studio at Klasky-Csupo to a studio that could do a big prime-time series.

SHERRY GUNTHER, animation producer, *The Simpsons* (1990–92): We quickly found that, as talented as some of the veteran [animators at Klasky-Csupo] were, they weren't capable of rethinking and doing the pose-to-pose animation that we were establishing as a look for *The Simpsons* and that worked really well with the timing of the comedy. So we really had to get very creative, not only in the way that we structured the show and the production itself, but also in whom we hired and where we found all these people. And we ended up getting really, really talented young people whom we didn't have to unteach. We had a lot of first- and second-year CalArts students coming to work for us.

The young animators hired by Klasky-Csupo would ultimately define *The Simpsons'* **signature look.**

BRIAN ROBERTS: David Silverman [who had animated some of the shorts at *Ullman*] had a style going all the way back to film school, and some of his early cartoons had very specific shapes and a smooth style that he applied to *The Simpsons*. If David Silverman hadn't been there, I honestly don't think that the characters would have developed in the way they finally did.

DON BARROZO, animation editor, *The Simpsons* (1987–present): I had to use this white clapboard garage that was just outside of the main building [at Klasky-Csupo]. That's where my editing was. But it wasn't wired for that kind of stuff. So I was constantly blowing fuses—I had a whole big box of fuses that I would change just about every other day.

But it was nice. There were only about thirty people on the show at that time. That was August of '89. A very, very small crew.

The artists were all in a central room. The windows were always wide open. And the pigeons were literally walking around on the floor. And everybody was really young, mostly just CalArts graduates all in their early twenties.

WESLEY ARCHER, director, *The Simpsons* (1987–97): [When the show became its own series] we just moved upstairs in the same building—the windows didn't have screens and the pigeons would hang out in there. Sometimes if I didn't like a drawing I would just toss it out the window, because there was a Dumpster below.

DON BARROZO: Back then, each director, each one of their crew was in a separate room. Gabor's office was right there in the middle of everything, so he was never apart from anybody. And those were fun times. Frank Zappa and his kids were big *Simpsons* fans. So Moon and Dweezil Zappa were both taking live drawing classes at night a couple of times a week.

MARGOT PIPKIN, animation producer, *The Simpsons*: It was a lot of work, and what I remember at that point was just really trying to bring the animation up to the level of the writing, because I was noticing that these scripts were very good and we didn't have a lot of artists or a lot of time.

Unlike *Looney Tunes* or *Tom and Jerry,* where the humor was mostly slapstick, the writing in *The Simpsons* scripts required a whole new level of attention from the animators. Comedy on *The Simpsons* often came from the reaction of the characters in exchanges of dialogue, or in layered, subtle jokes—the humor was no longer as simple to animate as a coyote falling off a cliff.

WESLEY ARCHER: A lot of animation artists were used to working on shows where the writer was at the bottom of the [totem pole]. They were either Hanna-Barbera artists or Disney artists. Wherever they came from, we had to tell them, "Look, you gotta see how funny these scripts are and trust the humor of these scripts." And not everyone really understood the humor.

MARGOT PIPKIN: Well, when it went on to become a series, we as animators had to relearn how to do a television series. Richard Sakai brought over a bunch of *Taxi* episodes and showed us how to pull back so we didn't do the big, exaggerated cartoon take; we had to do a much more contained sitcom take. And that really works on *The Simpsons.* We didn't realize that's what Jim Brooks wanted.

KENT BUTTERWORTH, director of first *Simpsons* episode: It was decided I would direct the first episode, since I had the most experience with series television. Matt and Sam Simon were working out of a trailer on the Fox lot, near Gracie Films's bungalows. We had meetings several times a week at the trailer. It was at this stage that a lot of the basic setup of the show was established: What car did they drive? Where was the dent on the car? The kitchen. How important is it to have a realistic layout for the house? What exactly is it that Homer does at the power plant? All these things were being discussed.

MATT GROENING (to the *San Francisco Chronicle*, 1990): I love it because it has the feel of an early sixties sitcom. And that's as it should be. What is *The Simpsons* but a hallucination of the sitcom? And that has to be the ultimate American nightmare.

The show was ultimately successful in threading a line between what could be considered the American nightmare and what others could see as a much more realistic impression of the American dream. What impressed early audiences and critics about the new series was how "real" it was: the characters, their emotions, and their reactions to the fairly normal challenges that confronted them were believable. At the other end of the spectrum, more conservative viewers saw Bart's sassiness, Homer's beer swilling, and the family's constant state of uproar as a challenge to the myth of family values that had been propagated for generations by TV families. The tension was rooted in the fact that this was a nuclear family: a dad who worked nine to five; a mom who took care of the baby, shopped, and did chores all day; a bratty preadolescent son; a brainy eight-year-old daughter; and a dog. And yet the writing was so knowing, and the actors so talented, audiences who so desired were able to feel that these cartoons were closer to their real lives than anything else on TV. And with few exceptions, *The Simpsons* explored fairly realistic situations: Homer lived in fear of losing his job; the Simpsons were short on money; Marge was a dissatisfied housewife; Lisa's intellect and sensitivity were underappreciated by her family. These were problems experienced by families everywhere.

KENT BUTTERWORTH: Matt and Sam had different opinions about everything, and there was a lot of debate about every detail. I remember there was an extensive discussion about what kind of underwear Homer wore—this went on for weeks! Matt would come by the studio every week or so to talk with the artists. Gabor would walk around the artists telling them to "make it funn-key."

BRIAN ROBERTS: I was there when they recorded the theme song, which was amazing. They took one of the last great remaining orchestra recording stages, which happens to be located at Fox, and an eighty-piece orchestra came in and the choir was there, and Danny Elfman was conducting, and I'll fucking never forget it. It was our first look at the opening title of the show. We'd never seen it before and of course we'd never heard Danny's score. He conducted this orchestra right through that really complex opening theme song, which is sort of a mix of *The Jetsons* and *The Flintstones*, and Danny Elfman blended it all together.

To me, that was part of TV history.

For the series, they would require more voice actors to fill out the remaining roles of Springfield's citizens. Brooks's casting agent and producer, Bonnie Pietila, decided on Hank Azaria (Moe, Chief Wiggum, Apu), Pamela Hayden (Milhouse, Jimbo), Tress MacNeille (Agnes Skinner, Dolph), Maggie Roswell (Maude Flanders, Miss Hoover), Harry Shearer (Principal Skinner, Kent Brockman, Mr. Burns), Russi Taylor (Martin Prince, Terri), and Marcia Wallace (Mrs. Krabappel). Employing top improvisational actors as voice talent was just one of the innovations that enabled *The Simpsons* to assert itself as something that was progressive as well as wholly original.

JAMES L. BROOKS (to *The Washington Post*, October 11, 1990): On the shows where we're doing the job right, you forget it's animation. The characters are real to us.

GEORGE MEYER (to *The New Yorker*, March 13, 2000): When you and I were kids, the average TV comedy was about a witch, or a Martian, or a goofy frontier fort, or a comical Nazi prisoner-of-war camp. That was the mainstream. Now the average comedy is about a bunch of people who hang around in some generic urban setting having conversations and sniping at each other. I remember watching, in the sixties, an episode of *Get Smart* in which some angry Indians were aiming a sixty-foot arrow at Washington, and Max said something like "That's the second-biggest arrow I've ever seen," and I thought, Oh, great, shows are just going to keep getting nuttier and nuttier. I never dreamed that television comedy would turn in such a dreary direction, so that all you would see is people in living rooms putting each other down . . . One of the main reasons is the tyranny of live studio audiences, which I think have ruined television comedy. *Leave It to Beaver*, unlike most sitcoms today, was not taped in front of a live audience. If that show were in production now and Beaver made some kind of gentle, sweet remark about his collection of rocks, or whatever, that line wouldn't get a laugh from the audience during rehearsal, and it would be cut. With a live audience, you always end up with hard-edged lines that the audience knows are jokes. Audiences hate it when they have to figure out whether something is funny or not—I think because people have an anxiety about laughing in the wrong place, almost like a fear of speaking in public. That's why the biggest comedy stars tend to be people like Robin Williams and Jim Carrey, because audiences never have to guess when they're trying to be funny.

MATT GROENING (to Charlie Rose, July 30, 2007): When we went to turn it into a TV series, Jim said, "We have to go for real emotion. We have to know what makes these people tick and we have to feel for them. I want people to forget they're watching a cartoon." And we did.

GEORGE MEYER (to *The New Yorker*, March 13, 2000): I think we can get away with a little more on *The Simpsons* because the setup is so traditional. The Simpsons are an intact family unit . . . I think it was a smart choice not to go in any really interesting direction with the core of the show—just to be very traditional, and then make the execution odd and quirky. Because people can take only so much before their heads explode.

CONAN O'BRIEN, writer/producer, *The Simpsons* (1991–93): There is a strong lack of sentimentality on *The Simpsons*, but there's also something that's important, which I know Sam Simon and Jim Brooks and Matt Groening stressed: this is a family. That kind of talk can start to sound pretty treacley, but it is a family and you can't have an episode where Homer sells Bart or harvests his organs. You can't do *that*. So I think one of the things that maybe *works* is that respect for that unit was always kept intact.

JAY KOGEN, writer/producer, *The Simpsons* (1989–92): The Simpsons are more than just cartoon characters; they're relatable characters. I think the show, when it first began, certainly had a heart. Lisa was smart and stuck in a family that she was better than. Also Marge. The women in the family had more brains, and also more heart. But Homer's heart was in the right place too. And as far as dysfunctional families go, it was a pretty good, smart dysfunctional family. And pretty funny.

A classic trope of traditional sitcom is that the family at its center is firmly rooted in a town or city that—with the exception of the occasional birth or boy down a well—never really changes. For *The Simpsons* this was Springfield, a traditional town with traditional values, turned completely on its head. Springfield is both landlocked and near an ocean, rich and in terrible economic decline, open-minded yet completely subject to mob rule. It is, in short, whatever the writers need it to be.

MATT GROENING (to *The Washington Post*, May 13, 1993): The reason why the town is called Springfield is because when I was a kid I watched *Father Knows Best*, which took place in a town called Springfield. And I always assumed it was the next town over . . . We get letters from people all over the place telling me they know it's their Springfield because their Springfield has a toxic waste dump and a nuclear power plant. It's very sad, the number of letters we get like that.

There are forty-nine Springfields in the United States (there are more Lincolns, but Groening has said he thinks Springfield is a funnier name). In a move to promote *The Simpsons Movie,* a contest was held, in conjunction with *USA Today,* where competitors, who lived in real Springfields, made videos demonstrating their enthusiasm for *The Simpsons,* in order to determine which Springfield could call itself the "real" one. Although Springfield, Vermont, was named the winner and got to host *The Simpsons Movie* premiere, Matt Groening has said repeatedly that the real Springfield exists only "in your heart." Early on, viewers' hearts were captivated by one resident of Springfield above all others: a prepubescent hellion named Bart.

Bart Simpson started out as Dennis the Menace updated for the nineties: Dennis in the age of Ritalin, without a Ritalin prescription. He was a prankster, a daredevil, a smart-ass, and a wit. In the early years, he lived to subvert the authority abounding in his life: his principal, his teacher and, of course, his bumbling, caustic father, Homer. Bart was subversive, but he had heart—some of the show's most touching early moments had the little hellion coming to terms with his bad behavior and reconciling with his family or friends.

Later, as Homer became simpler, and the show moved its focus more toward him, Bart became, more often than not, his dad's partner in crime.

WALLACE WOLODARSKY, writer/producer, *The Simpsons* (1989–92): We used to joke that Bart was the original *Peck's Bad Boy,** which was ancient reference. Bart was an amalgam of our childhoods smashed into one character. At the time there were no women on the staff, so it was very heavily skewed toward what boys thought was funny. When you're a kid, you like to see adults getting away with stuff, because you hope to join them one day in anarchy and mayhem.

JENNIFER TILLY, actress, poker champion, ex-wife of Sam Simon: We were really young, and I didn't want kids, and Sam didn't want kids, but to make up for it, we had—as couples often do—this imaginary kid running around that was always getting into trouble. Our imaginary kid was always taking the Porsche out for a spin. Or we'd leave a store, and Sam would say to him, "What do you have? What are you holding?" He was this incorrigible kid who was always getting into trouble. And a lot of the character of that kid that we had in our relationship as a running joke ended up being Bart.

GEORGE MEYER (to *The New Yorker*, March 13, 2000): The thing I like about Bart is that even though he will put on his grandfather's dentures and bite the ceiling fan and spin around, he is not cruel or nasty.

Aside from being the star of the show (after Season 2), Homer Simpson has become one of the great characters in the history of entertainment. While he started out as a gruff parent and foil to Bart's pranks, he has evolved into perhaps the most complete and complicated simpleton the Western canon has to offer. While work-

---

*Peck was a character from the newspaper funnies of the late nineteenth century. In the cartoons, served to illustrate short stories, Peck is constantly pranking his elders, like the deacon, his father, and the grocer (although at one point he does set a girl on fire, albeit just a little, with fireworks). The series was created by George W. Peck, a humor writer who went on to be governor of Wisconsin. Peck's stories were later made into a film with Jackie Cooper. You can see them at: www.guten berg.org/files/25488/25488-h/25488-h.htm.

ing a dead-end job as the safety inspector at the local nuclear power plant—a job he is completely unqualified for—Homer manages to drunkenly stumble his way through each day, numbing the drudgery of life—with Duff beer and thoughtless, often dangerous antics—until he can crawl into bed with his beloved wife, Marge.

WALLACE WOLODARSKY: Homer always felt to me like a bigger, dumber version of Ralph Kramden. Ralph Kramden was always one of my favorite characters in television, because he's trying so hard and always getting in his own way, so that kind of character is really fun to write. And because it's telelvision, they needn't ever get ahead, because every week you can start at the beginning again.

GEORGE MEYER (to *The Believer*): As in the real world, the most oblivious people are often the happiest. Someone like Chief Wiggum, for instance, who is pretty satisfied with his life despite being an absolutely catastrophic police chief. I also think Homer is pretty happy, if only because deep in his bones he realizes that he's indestructible. There's not much that can hurt him.

MATT GROENING (to *Playboy*, June 1, 2007): One of the great things about the character Homer . . . is that he is ruled by impulse. He wants whatever he wants at the moment, with all his heart.

GEORGE MEYER (to *The Believer*): I don't think [Homer and Marge] have the greatest marriage. I'm always surprised at how that never comes across to some viewers. There'll be an episode where Homer passes out drunk on Christmas, or sells his family to Gypsies, and people will say, "It was funny and you did your jokes, but that's a family that really works. That's a good marriage." It blows my mind. They have to see that, even if it's not there.

Marge Simpson is at once a clever and cynical twist on the classic housewife archetype. She is June Cleaver, Harriet Nelson, Alice, Clair Huxtable, and Annie Camden all rolled into one (with an occasional hint of Lucille Ball and Gloria Steinem thrown in for good measure). Marge does the impossible: deals with Homer's unpredictability, Bart's troublemaking, Lisa's perspicacity, and Maggie's diapers. She revels in her role as supermom and yet feels the need to rebel sometimes. While *The Simpsons*' writers admit that Marge is the hardest, and their least favorite, character to write for, what started out merely as the nagging voice of reason at 742 Evergreen Terrace has progressed—with the help of Julie Kavner's enormous talents—to a more challenging, fleshed-out, adult female character.

GEORGE MEYER (to *The Believer*): Marge needs to have a loose-cannon guy in the house. She likes being the authority figure, and Homer gives her something to wag her finger at. And obviously Homer needs Marge to keep him alive.

JONATHAN GRAY, author, media critic: Marge is your sort of traditional sitcom mom who is surrounded by a real family. She can't just tell the son, "Do this," and the son does it. She actually has to deal with these real people. And so you get these moments where Marge is being asked to do everything and to hold everything together and she can't. There are eight or nine episodes where Marge has one or another kind of meltdown—she gets addicted to steroids or she starts losing her hair or she freaks out in other ways. It's showing that asking the moms to be these sort of superwomen was just too much.

And then there is Lisa. Poor, smart, underappreciated Lisa. Originally a little precocious for her age, Lisa's IQ has expanded exponentially over the years, as has her role as the family's moral center: its voice of reason, its critic, the single opposition to the consumerist, irrational behavior that defines the residents of 742 Evergeen Terrace and really all of Springfield. Hence, she is the perpetual outcast, often even within her own household. In later years, she's a vegetarian, environmentalist, and all-around cause-head, but in the earlier days, while she certainly had that sensitive, questioning voice of right and wrong (it was fear of losing his daughter's love that caused Homer to give up the free cable he stole in the first season), she also had the voice of an eight-year-old girl: unjaded, inquisitive, hungry for love, attention, and acceptance.

JEFF MARTIN (Season 3 DVD Commentary): I always liked Lisa episodes. I always find them the most effortlessly emotional and touching.

MATT GROENING (Season 3 DVD Commentary): I think Lisa's a great character . . . She's the one character not completely ruled by her impulses.

JEFF MARTIN (Season 3 DVD Commentary): And as a result, she's in pain, all the time. Or it's never far from the surface.

JONATHAN GRAY: I'd maintain that Lisa is probably the best and certainly longest-running feminist character that television has had. She's the heart of the show and she quite often questions the gender politics.

But *The Simpsons* didn't jump from the sketchy archetypes we saw on *Ullman* to the fully fleshed-out characters described above. To breathe life into this family, Sam Simon would assemble a writing team of television comedy's best and brightest, complete with Harvard diplomas.

SIX

The Room

In which the West Side Pavilion Mall is the first *Simpsons* writing room . . . Conan O'Brien invents a sport . . . *The Simpsons* hires a black guy (not really) . . . and Jim Brooks wants blood.

He's probably some geek Simpsons *writer's kid.*

—*Michael Bluth,* Arrested Development

The Simpsons writers room, where scripts are devised, written, and edited, has come to be considered one of the great temples of comedy. Although many of the original writers had substantial television credits, Sam Simon plucked spectacular talent from nontraditional places, beginning a trend that would continue long after his departure (subsequent showrunners hired mathematicians and lawyers). Perhaps his key find was George Meyer, editor of the humor magazine *Army Man*—distributed sparingly in Hollywood in the late eighties and somewhat of a shibboleth in the comedy-writing community. In 1991, Conan O'Brien, one of many *Harvard Lampoon* veterans on the staff, Bill Oakley, and Josh Weinstein would be the first writers to be added to the original room.

Writing is important to any sitcom, but on an animated series there would be beautiful actors or topical humor to keep the viewers enthralled, so the writing room carried special significance at *The Simpsons*. It is important to remember that this was before the likes of David Chase (*The Sopranos*), Ricky Gervais (*The Office*), Alan Ball (*Six Feet Under*), Mitchell Hurwitz (*Arrested Development*), and Aaron Sorkin (*The West Wing*) made television something closer to a respectable medium for writers. This was the era of *Full House* and *Family Matters*, where smart, incisive, funny writing was hardly prevalent. *Late Night with David Letterman*, *Roseanne*, and *Cheers* were anomalies in an otherwise dismal comedy landscape.

For the first four or five seasons Sam Simon's writers room not only created the best episodes of *The Simpsons* but also established the show's inimitable voice. Over the years, many of the show's critics and commentators have tried to define that voice—a combination of rebellious, ironic, highbrow, silly, crude, intertextually hyperactive, iconoclastic, sly, witty, and retarded. The men in that room—Nell Scovell is the only woman with a writing credit from the initial seasons—built a family sitcom that was not only funny but also resonant, first with kids, then critics, and then everybody else, for the next twenty years. If *The Simpsons* has reshaped what we find funny and how we communicate, the writing room and its workings are worth examining, because it is the touchstone of *The Simpsons'* universe.

The original room included Sam Simon, Al Jean, Mike Reiss, Jace Richdale, Jon Vitti, George Meyer, John Swartzwelder, Jay Kogen, Wallace Wolodarsky, Jeff Martin, and Matt Groening (sort of).

CONAN O'BRIEN, writer/producer, *The Simpsons* (1991–93) (when he was asked to join the room after Season 2): It was as if that first Olympic Dream Team, with Larry Bird and Magic Johnson, called and said, "Do you want to come shoot baskets with us?"

BILL OAKLEY, writer/producer, *The Simpsons* (1991–97): It was like being hired at *Saturday Night Live* in 1977. It was like going to work at *Your Show of Shows* in 1955, when you had Mel Brooks and Neil Simon and all those guys there on the writing staff. The show was at its absolute height and it was all the original guys and Conan.

JAY KOGEN, writer/producer, *The Simpsons* (1989–92): We were on board even before there was a writers room. Wallace Wolodarsky and I would walk around the West Side Pavilion Mall with Matt Groening and Sam Simon and pitch out a show. Sometimes we'd go to lunch; it would just be the four of us.

DARIA PARIS, Sam Simon's assistant, *The Simpsons* (1989–93): There'd be usually four or five writers in Sam's office, and we'd go through the script and they would change things, pitch ideas, that kind of thing. And basically out of that they'd fashion a script. At the time, Jim Brooks was in Ireland, I think, and he would call in and we would take notes from him and then incorporate them. Jim was more of a consultant—he'd get a script, he'd call, he'd send notes or whatever. He was not usually in the room.

BRIAN ROBERTS, editor, *The Simpsons* (1989–92): Jim was never around a lot. Matt was around, but he was isolated and not really a part of the inside gang. Jim would come, though. And the thing that I really credit Jim with, and I don't think there's anybody who would argue with this, is that he would give the family some heart.

Jim's thing was that deep down they really loved each other. Deep down, I think Jim understood that if they didn't truly love each other, at the end of the day, nobody's gonna watch.

And so he'd come in and he'd sprinkle his fairy dust in little places here and there, to the great improvement of the show. And that's where I think Jim's contribution begins and ends on *The Simpsons*. And that's no small contribution.

HANK AZARIA, voice actor, *The Simpsons* (1989–present): Fox had two hits: they had *The Simpsons* and they had *Married . . . with Children*, and *The Simpsons* was very believable and *Married . . . with Children* was more like a cartoon. And there are episodes, I think particularly the Lisa episodes, where they really involve the journey of a little girl and what would realistically happen; those are beautiful, realistic little stories.

I think of Matt's *Life in Hell* cartoon. It's very cynical, but it's got a lot of emotion at the same time. It's usually very negative. Like those Jeff and Akbar cartoons: they'll have very realistic arguments with each other about pretty deep, interesting issues, and they're both kind of unattractive and yet we relate to them so much that we feel a lot for them. I think that's what really what Matt brought. You know, the family of *The Simpsons*—they're so flawed and kind of ugly that we all relate because we all have a dysfunctional family of our own.

SAM SIMON, creative consultant, *The Simpsons* (1989–93) (to Joe Morgenstern in the *Los Angeles Times*, 1990): If you bring up any subject in a story conference, if it's a field trip, or what it's like to go to the nurse's office, or what it's like to be called in by the principal, [Matt's] recall is near total and astonishing. I think that's a real rare talent.

WALLACE WOLODARKSY, writer/producer, *The Simpsons* (1989–92): Matt had an incredible ability to recount events from his childhood and also events and feelings that were resonant with us from childhood. It made him an endless source of amusement. In the early days, we didn't really care that much about stories, and Jim insisted that we tell real human stories, and so did Sam. What I cared about was telling jokes.

COLIN A.B.V. LEWIS, postproduction supervisor, *The Simpsons* (1989–97): George Meyer was this long-haired guy. Swartzwelder was this big tall Sasquatch sloppy guy. Vitti always was in cords and a nice shirt, almost looking like a substitute teacher. Al Jean wore high school basketball shorts like Cousy used to wear, and inappropriately tight clothes. You'd see all these guys and you had no idea; you would talk to them and have really intelligent conversations about politics and art. You'd go to parties with them and they were regular guys. If you talk to a writer on any show, somehow he'll guide you toward, "What do you do? What show are you on?" And with *The Simpsons*' writers, it was the opposite. They were guys who were having fun, doing what they were doing and making a good show, but they were the geekiest, most unassuming guys.

DARIA PARIS: It was usually the same people in the room. At the time it was a fairly small writing staff, and they were just great and very different. Jon Vitti, very quiet. John Swartzwelder wasn't very quiet. And then everybody pitched in, including me. And the great thing about Sam as a showrunner was that no matter where it came from, if it was funny, he took it.

BRIAN ROBERTS: Jeff Martin was the go-to guy for all the jingles and he was brilliant at them. Mike Reiss is probably the nicest human being on planet Earth and absolutely hysterically funny. And then Al Jean, whose style is a little more reserved, is also just fucking funny.

These guys would throw lightning fastballs and it was after that experience that I got addicted to writers rooms because they're just brilliant, fun places to be.

ROBERT COHEN, production assistant, *The Tracey Ullman Show*, *The Simpsons* (1989–92): It was very friendly. These guys seemed excited that they were creating this show and everybody was bringing something different to the table. I don't think anybody was sitting there thinking, We are going to create groundbreaking television. I think they just wanted to do really funny shows. I've been in a lot of rooms since that did not have the same enjoyable mellow vibe.

BRIAN ROBERTS: The legend is that Cohen was the model for Milhouse, or the way he looked, anyway. And there's all kinds of inside stuff like that in the show. I used to answer the telephone in the editing base like, "Bay of Pigs, Fidel here," or "Joe's Crematorium. You kill 'em, we grill 'em." And the writers put that into one episode because they were probably bored with Bart's prank phone calls for that day, so they used one of my lines. I remember feeling honored that somebody found that funny.

GEORGE MEYER (to *The Believer*): We'll slip in references to "golden showers" or "glory holes," stupid things that are only there to make us laugh. We had a "chloroform" run for a while. We just thought chloroform was funny, so we tried to include it in as many episodes as possible. Somebody was always pulling out a rag soaked in chloroform and using it to render somebody unconscious for no good reason. We get these crazes every now and then. There was a period when we were obsessed with hoboes. Specifically, hoboes and their bindles. In the boxing episode, Homer was fighting a hobo who kept turning to check on his bindle. [Laughs] Stuff like that is basically about wasting the audience's time for our own amusement . . . My personal favorite internal gag that nobody outside of the show will ever see . . . [is a] hobo spinning a yarn, and Lisa interrupts with a story of her own. The hobo snaps, "Hey, who's the hobo here?" And in the script, his dialogue note is "[ALL BUSINESS]." [Laughs] I love the idea that a hobo would be "all business."

Rob Cohen was a PA in the original room. One of his jobs was to set up regular poker games, led by Sam Simon (Sam placed forty-first in 2008's World Series of Poker, winning over $10,000.[1] His ex-wife,

Jennifer Tilly, won the tournament in 2005, and in 2008 placed thirtieth[2]).

ROB COHEN: The poker game started at *The Tracey Ullman Show*. My job was to basically arrange the poker game and get the food and secure the room. But then when I was at the game, I was one of the guys, one of the players. And it would be weird. Garth Ancier, who was running Fox at the time, he would play, and Jim Brooks would play, and these other guys. They had a lot more money than I did, but it was really cool; it was just playing cards with the guys. There was no pecking order during the game.

Sam's leadership dictated the room's atmosphere and ensured its variety.

JAY KOGEN: Sam Simon really led that process: the hiring process and also what the show should be. Sam can be tough, but he's really, really funny. George can be bitter, but he's also really funny. Al can be too logical, but he's really, really funny. Jon Vitti can be too quiet, but he's hysterically funny.

BILL OAKLEY: Jon Vitti, whom I believe to be the best first-draft writer in the history of *The Simpsons*, would often sit silently in the room for forty straight minutes, but then he would come up with a gem, whereas Conan would be talking all the time.

CONAN O'BRIEN: I actually have a picture of me, Jeff Martin, Jon Vitti, Matt Groening, George Meyer, Al Jean, John Swartzwelder, David Stern, Mike Reiss sitting around that room, and it really is an accurate portrayal. People would be shocked. If this was a common room at a university, I think the students would sue. It was pretty small, and it didn't really have a good air conditioner.

WALLACE WOLODARSKY: The room was like a dilapidated dorm study room. The garbage cans were always overflowing with Styrofoam containers of take-out food. Swartzwelder and Sam used to smoke, so there'd be overflowing ashtrays. There were empty cans of soda everywhere. Hygiene was not at a premium.

BILL OAKLEY: There was a crummy old shag carpet. There was some sort of haunted house pinball machine in the room. There was an old pink couch that people gradually tore apart.

JOSH WEINSTEIN, writer/producer, *The Simpsons* (1991–97): It's actually in a building that used to be the set of an old motel, and ironically it was called the New Writer's Building, but it was really crummy, and the furniture looked like it had been there for a long time.

Even with all that talent, and fodder for scripts all around them, the writers could go a little stir-crazy. It is impossible to be funny all day long—you need a break or ten. Fittingly, the writers found uniquely hilarious ways to waste their time.

BILL OAKLEY: It's not like Dick Van Dyke crazy gag after gag every second. There would be periods where an entire room of people were sitting silently for close to an hour trying to think of one funny gag.

CONAN O'BRIEN: So you're there, and you're trying to be creative, but over these long stretches of time. There were periods of time where you felt like, Gee, I think I lost my mind a little bit during certain stretches.

I used to walk around the Fox lot, and once I found two pieces of a broken pool cue in an alley. There were two pieces that screwed together, with a brass fitting, and then unscrewed. Jeff Martin and I developed a whole game around unscrewing it, flipping both pieces in opposite hands, and screwing it back together, and seeing how many times you can do that in one minute. And then we developed all these complicated rules involving how far your wrists had to be apart, and we took it really seriously.

It got to the point where Jeff had the record for forty-five flips in one minute, but then there was the time I broke it and got to forty-six; we were elated. And other people in the room would watch sometimes. I remember times where Jeff and I were doing it, and there was a circle of people around us watching, and it got very intense.

If you're trapped on a deserted island, you can build an entire religion around a seashell. It was that feeling. That's an illustration of how we were driven to the edge of something, I don't know what.

Another time we took my Ford Taurus for a spin around the Fox lot.

Imagine a Ford Taurus creeping around a completely empty Fox lot and Jon Vitti and I looking for scenes where they had shot episodes of *Batman*. That is about as low as it gets.

TIM LONG, writer/co–executive producer, *The Simpsons* (1999–present): I remember George Meyer—whom I consider the king of this business—saying he was going to try and figure out what the optimal ratio of goofing off to hard work is, and he concluded it's about two-thirds goofing off. Even when you're really under the deadline gun, there seems to be just this natural tendency to start betting on football. Remember when everyone got excited about dumping Mentos into Diet Coke? We saw that, and we got *so* excited. We sent the PAs out and we bought several hundred dollars' worth of Mentos and Diet Coke, all of which came, I would hope, straight out of Rupert Murdoch's pocket, and set them off. And that was a day we were facing some pretty significant deadlines, but there's a really gratifying consensus that that stuff is important.

Speaking for myself, I can probably focus, at most, four minutes at a time, at which point I start thinking about food or my car, or just wanna take a nap.

No matter how much time they wasted, the fact that the room was composed of intelligent, articulate, educated people could not help but filter down into the scripts.

GARY PANTER, friend of Matt Groening's; cartoonist: When you get a whole bunch of comedy writers together, it can get pretty mean. Because they're really smart and they're trying to entertain each other, and they're trying to outdo each other. So I'm often surprised *The Simpsons* can back away from being as scary or outrageous as it could be.

BRAD BIRD, executive consultant, *The Simpsons* (1989–97); director, *The Incredibles, Ratatouille*. No matter how bizarre the situation is, there are recognizable emotions, and there's a structure to the emotions. On the best episodes that I worked on, there was about forty-five minutes' worth of material packed into twenty-two minutes. They were very sophisticated scripts and they moved along very quickly and they frequently took you by surprise. And as screwed up as Homer was, he did intend to do the right thing. I think that comedy works best when people connect with characters and understand the emotions.

GEORGE MEYER (to *The Believer*): [Fans] seem to believe that we have unlimited time and resources for each episode, and that we're able to examine everything from every possible angle. And really, the show is more like a hurricane swirling around us. Every joke can't be dazzling.

Although Sam would not add anyone to the original room until the third season, he did accept freelance scripts. Michael Carrington, who wrote "Homer's Triple Bypass" with partner Gary Apple, was also asked to do voices on the show.

MICHAEL CARRINGTON, episode writer, *The Simpsons*; producer, *That's So Raven*, *Cory in the House*: They liked my voice—they put me into a lot of episodes, which was great. I consider myself the minor black character. If you see a black character with fewer than five lines it's usually me. I played Jimi Hendrix in an episode, Sideshow Raheem, I played a black stand-up comic. I'm the guy who says, "You know white people drive like *this*. Black people drive like *this*."

It was a color-blind show. You know, they're really cool. I've been the only black guy in the room on a lot of shows. Luckily, with the Simpsons, they're yellow, so it really didn't matter. But on a lot of shows they always ask me, "What would the black guy say?" Sometimes we just say hello. We don't always have jive, you know.

The degree to which *The Simpsons* is color-blind may be up for debate. Carrington was never a staff writer. The few nonwhite staffers over *The Simpsons'* twenty years include a single African-American man (Marc Wilmore), a single Asian-American man (Danny Chun), and a single Hispanic woman (Rachel Pulido).

There have been approximately ten female writers on staff at *The Simpsons*. One veteran writer attempted to explain it by saying that, generally, women are better at writing about human relationships, while men are more prone to being joke machines. At *The Simpsons*,

the ability to come up with a fast, clever joke obviously was considered paramount, beginning with Sam Simon, who staffed his writers
room with zero women.

BRENT FORRESTER, writer/producer, *The Simpsons* (1993–97); writer/
producer, *King of the Hill, The Office*: It was all boys, yeah. I mean, there
were no women hired. When I was there, there had only ever been one
woman there. I forget her name now.

Bob Kushell found a novel way to get the producers' attention: theft.
Kushell eventually became a staff writer in Season 5, under David
Mirkin, but he'd been trying to get on the show since before the first
episode had even aired.

BOB KUSHELL, writer/producer, *The Simpsons* (1994–95): I was working
at Fox on these non-Guild shows called *Malibu Beach Party* and *Fox
Across America* [in the late eighties]. I was getting paid a few hundred
dollars a week to write on these things and I knew that they were doing
The Simpsons. I was such a huge fan of the interstitials on *Tracey Ullman*
I had to become a part of it. I would sneak up into the executive offices
in the middle of the day, while nobody was looking, and steal scripts. So I
ended up having all of the original *Simpsons* scripts, from Wallace Wolodarsky and Jon Vitti. And I wrote a spec *Simpsons* based on those scripts.
You know, literally four to five months prior to the show ever airing.

Rob Cohen was a PA at *The Simpsons*, and I don't know why he did
it, but out of the goodness of his heart, he got my spec script to Jon Vitti.
And Jon Vitti read it, and called to tell me how much he enjoyed the
script. He was such a mensch, such a great guy, and I'll never forget him
for it.

Years later, when I ended up on *The Simpsons*, Jon Vitti came in to
write an episode, and I mentioned my spec script to him. And he not only
remembered it, he quoted a joke from it. Working with your heroes of
comedy was unbelievable, but for Jon to have remembered that one joke
in that one script I had written years earlier just meant the world to me.

Cohen's karma came full circle. The writers encouraged the young
talent, who had been a PA since the Ullman days, to get a script
produced.

ROB COHEN: I started writing weird stuff on the side. When the music video for "Do the Bartman" came out, they needed somebody to write the intros: So I was getting all these weird side jobs, like they paid me $300 for that. And I guess they liked the job I did, so then I submitted a list with a bunch of crank calls that Bart would make and I got paid a little cash on the side for that. Then I decided to take a whack at writing a *Simpsons* episode. I think *Die Hard* had just come out, so I wrote a script that was kind of a *Die Hard* thing at Mr. Burns's power plant. They really liked it, but because I was an employee of Gracie, and they had a policy there against buying from within, they didn't want to buy the script from me.

I got so pissed off that I quit.

As I was walking across the parking lot to go turn in my notice—somebody had heard that I'd quit—Sam met me in the parking lot and basically said, "Now that you've quit, we'd like to give you a shot at an episode." Obviously I said yes. I needed the money, too. Because I'd been around and knew the process, my one request was that I be involved in every step of the process. He agreed. They were all very cool about it. Jay [Kogen] was really helpful and gave me a lot of guidance on how the writers wanted things done.

So I worked with them all the way through it, and then the best part was, because I was still wrapping up my PA duties, my last responsibility as a PA was to distribute the script, as I normally did with other scripts. So my last run was distributing my own episode, which was great.

I was psyched! I couldn't believe the episode had my name on it. And also it had Aerosmith, whom I had really fought to have involved. It blew my mind.

One producer remembers the writers coming back to Cohen with changes for his script, and Cohen being resistant, which seems a little far-fetched (especially considering that, according to another former producer, Jay Kogen had actually rewritten the majority of the script's first draft).

ROB COHEN: I definitely did not sit there and go, "No no no no no. Forget it." That'd be crazy. I know there was one thing I disagreed with, and they yielded.

Cohen's situation was unique. Most of the early writers found their way to *The Simpsons* after working at the *Harvard Lampoon* and from other comedy shows like *Saturday Night Live*, *The Late Show with David Letterman*, and *The Tonight Show*. Regardless of a writer's TV pedigree, some of *The Simpsons*' best material came from their real lives.

WALLACE WOLODARSKY: It was lots of people telling their personal stories and figuring out how to put those into the show. And then lots of what you call "room jokes," people being really funny, making everybody laugh even though it would never go into the script.

JAY KOGEN: Mike Reiss's father had made him a clown bed. The headboard was a clown face and the footboard was big clown shoes. It was supposed to be adorable for his kid, but it turned out to be horrific and scary. We put that in the show.

In "Blood Feud," Season 2's final episode, Mr. Burns discovers he has a rare medical condition and needs to hit up his employees for a blood transfusion (Bart is a match). It apparently came right out of a situation with Gracie Films's own gazillionaire boss.

BRIAN ROBERTS: Sam's way to get back at everybody was to write them into the show. Jim and Richard Sakai didn't start out as the models for Burns and Smithers, but as the animosity grew around the office, things that came out of Burns's and Smithers's mouths were based on Sakai and Jim's relationship. The most famous of all the stories was that Jim had some sort of anemia, a temporary blood condition. And he sent out a memo to all the staff at Gracie, asking for blood.

In the memo, Brooks phrased his request for blood in a manner that made it seem like it should be a privilege for staff members to give him their blood. "That's how we read it," remembers one early staffer. "Like, 'You could really be helping a very important person out!'" While in *The Simpsons* Smithers had made an emotional appeal over a loudspeaker at the plant, Brooks's memo was anything but emotional or pleading in its tone, causing Sam Simon to edit the episode's script to reflect Burns's high-handedness.

Sam's refusal to buckle under to Brooks and Sakai would ultimately lead to his undoing at Gracie, but his assemblage of the first *Simpsons* writers room would be the most important creative decision made on *The Simpsons*. Yet as Brooks, Simon, and Groening were about to discover, with a cartoon, there was only so much the writers could do.

SEVEN

The First Episodes

In which the world holds its breath with an eye on Korea . . . a bear drinks the blood of a Happy Little Elf . . . the critics give nine thumbs-up . . . and dysfunction beats the hell out of the Huxtables.

Once the episodes were written, and rewritten, they had to be drawn up by the animators at Klasky-Csupo, shown to the producers, and redrawn. The process of interpreting the first scripts, of giving *The Simpsons* its signature look and feel, was arduous, fraught with complications. Should there be a consistent floor plan to the house? Who are Bart's friends? The answers to these, and a million similar questions, had to be drawn and redrawn until everyone was satisfied.

MATT GROENING (from *The Simpsons Season 1* DVD, director's commentary): The deal with animation is you basically are creating your own universe and your own rules. Disney has its own rules. Warner Bros. had its own rules . . . And we were establishing our rules on *The Simpsons*. And I think part of the problem . . . with [the] early episodes is that we hadn't really nailed down what our rules were.

Groening wanted to move away from Disney's world of animation where characters' appendages seem to be on "cushiony springs" (when Disney characters move, it often looks as if they're dancing). He also wanted to differentiate his world from that of Chuck Jones, where characters' bodies move in a much more extreme way—Bugs Bunny and Wile E. Coyote often move like elastic bands, extending beyond themselves and then snapping back.

WESLEY ARCHER, director, *The Simpsons* (1987–97): The first season was really spent trying to figure out the production and how to organize it and how to get people to draw in that Matt Groening style. A lot of animation artists were unable to draw that way.

The energy devoted to the specificity of the characters' design would be instrumental in creating a visual world that was both original and fit with the sharp, cynical scripts that were coming out of Sam Simon's writing room. Groening has noted that his characters are not the only ones on television with large, round eyeballs (googly eyes), and yet he argues that his are the only ones that look inherently alienated. He points to the cuteness of characters from *Garfield* and *Sesame Street*, contrasting them those with *The Simpsons*. He cites the small size of the pupils on his characters as the source of their alienation, as well as his dictum that the eyes on *The Simpsons* must look in the same direction (they can't go cross-eyed), giving them a vaguely human, realistic feel.[1]

MARGOT PIPKIN, animation producer, *Simpsons*: We had to redesign the characters from the bumpers and make them look much more rounded and much more easy to animate and turn and move, 'cause you look back at those original shorts—they look a lot more like Matt's style, with what he calls the potato-chip lip.

KENT BUTTERWORTH, director of first *Simpsons* episode: In those days, we had to shoot it all on film with an animation camera, and this was a big deal—very expensive. Gabor had never done that volume of work and had not worked with overseas studios, and he was concerned about his ability to deliver. There was a lot of discussion of how "cartoony" the show should be—how much "stretch and squash." A lot of it was "Let's try this" and "Let's try that."

DOMINIC POLCINO, animator/director, *The Simpsons* (1990–2001): The artists who worked on the show from first through fifth seasons, we felt like we were pioneers. We would get a script that had, like, "Homer drunk" or "Bart dances a jig" or "Itchy sucks Scratchy's intestines out through a straw," and we would go to town, because we were doing it for the first time.

Everything that came along in the first seasons was a brand-new toy to play with. And we felt like we were making television history in a way—like Chuck Jones when he first did Bugs Bunny.

GARY PANTER, friend of Matt Groening's; cartoonist: The challenge with any show is trying to get your vision through other animators. When you hire a production company, they already have their own style and people want to make their own statement, and then you're in the position of having to be tough or insistent or persuasive or whatever it takes to get people to make it look the way you want it to look.

Once the animators had finished drawing an episode, it was still in skeletal form, an expanded storyboard. This outline, once approved by the producers at Gracie—along with extensive stage directions, camera instructions, and the voice record accompany—still had to be sent to South Korea, where hundreds of artists would fill in the animation (by hand, at slave wages) over a period of several months. For the first episodes, sent to Korea in the summer of 1989, this was an extremely stressful period at Gracie, Fox, and Klasky-Csupo; once the first episode came back, it would be the first time anyone would see a *Simpsons* episode in its completed form. What arrived back in the fall of 1989 was far from what anyone—Jim Brooks, the writers, the animators, Barry Diller—expected.

BRIAN ROBERTS, editor, *The Simpsons* (1989–92): I think the network was really apprehensive because of the gigantic lead time between when the shows were recorded and when you actually got to see anything. Imagine taking some great pictures and then not getting them back for six months. They made this gigantic investment and I think they were obviously very nervous.

When the first episode came back, fifty people jammed into the screening room to watch the show. It was packed. Everybody was really excited—Jim, Sam, Matt, Mandel. It was literally as if Lindbergh had just landed and everyone was running to the airport.

It truly was an amazing moment. Everybody, even the people who didn't have anything to do with the show, ended up in this conference room, and we played the first episode. It was fucking awful. It was unwatchable; the animation was terrible. It was the Bart and the babysitter episode, with Penny Marshall playing the babysitter.

MICHAEL MENDEL, postproduction supervisor, *The Tracey Ullman Show*, *The Simpsons* (1989–92, 1994–99): The first show came back from Korea and it was a complete disaster. It was unairable. We had to recast some voices. The director just went off and did a bunch of stuff on his own.

At one point in the episode, the Simpson kids are watching a cartoon called "The Happy Little Elves Meet the Curious Bear Cubs." To the horror of everyone watching, Butterworth and his animators had decided to have one of the bear cubs tear the head off one of the elves and begin drinking its blood.

BRIAN ROBERTS: So the episode ends and there's dead silence in the room and Jim stands up and says, "Do you think we can we can thin out the ranks a little bit?" And fifty people—you've never seen a stampede for the door as quick as that—the room emptied out so quick it created a vacuum. And unfortunately, I was one of the people who had to stay since I was the editor. So it was me, Matt, Sam, Jim, maybe a couple of the writers and there was this sense of, What the fuck are we going to do? This is fucked. We are fucked. It's all fucked up. And now what? So we tried to keep it quiet and everybody figured, We'll just bury it later in the season.

GABOR CSUPO, animation executive producer, *The Simpsons* (1987–92): It was a very, very raw first assembly of the scenes, and some of the scenes were still missing, or had the wrong colors, or the wrong angles. So it was a disaster. Jim sort of got into it, started to laugh for the first five minutes, and then all of a sudden his face started to turn green and yellow, almost matching the *Simpsons* characters. He got really disappointed because none of the jokes worked, and then all of a sudden he started to scream and yell, saying, "What is this?" He just went off and he even started to demand extra camera angles, which was the funniest thing ever—he never did animation in his life. He asked for coverage like when you're shooting a live-action movie. "So where are the other camera angles?" My producer and I were just looking at each other.

I was just so angry and embarrassed at the same time that they forced us to show this raw footage before we could even correct it. Jim was screaming and yelling that "this is not funny!" And I said, "Well, it may be not funny because you didn't write it funny." And then everybody looks at me, obviously thinking, Oh, my God! You dared to say that to Jim! But I felt I had nothing to lose.

Matt Groening, on the Season 1 DVD commentary, remembers Jim Brooks's pronouncement, sitting there in the screening room, having seen the first episode, "This is shit."[2] Brooks, on the same commentary, recalled Gabor Csupo's response being "Maybe this shit isn't funny," a line Brooks pointedly repeated to Csupo while they posed together for a photograph after the show had received its first Emmy. Brooks admitted that the comment was "small of me" but laughed it off, saying that he and Csupo now "hang out all the time together."[3]

This last bit is actually not true, or what those of us outside of Hollywood might call a "lie." By the time the first season DVD came out, in 2001, *The Simpsons* had long ago fired Gabor Csupo and taken much of the staff to their new animators, Film Roman. Jim and Gabor did not "hang out all the time together."

WESLEY ARCHER: I was working late that night and Gabor Csupo came back and he was really upset at Gracie Films.

KENT BUTTERWORTH: Brooks decided to shelve this episode and get back to it later. Meanwhile, he would let Fox know that the delivery of the series would be delayed in order to get the quality they needed. Needless to say, my employment on *The Simpsons* was over.

DON BARROZO, *Simpsons* animation editor (1987–present): [Gabor] didn't really have a fully formed idea of what this was supposed to look like, either. Nobody did.

HARRIS KATLEMAN, former CEO, 20th Century Fox Television: It was out of sync. The color was off. Everything was awful. And I remember we were sitting in my office and Barry was there and John Dolgen and Jim Brooks. And Diller looked and me, and he said, "What have you done?" I said, "Look, we'll get it fixed." Then he looked at me and he said, "What do you mean? How you gonna fix that?" I said, "Out of sync you can fix."

BRIAN ROBERTS: I think we were all put under twenty-four-hour guard so that no word of this would be leaked, and it's ironic because *everybody* was there.

Jim Brooks recalled thinking the show was in serious jeopardy because "you couldn't call the emperor anything but naked at that moment."[4] For his part, Groening could not sleep that week, thinking that the first episode had spelled the end for him and animation.[5] The next episodes, directed by David Silverman and Wesley Archer, would be the deal breakers.

DON BARROZO: The word was they were either just gonna pull the plug right now or just wait until the David Silverman show came back, which was show two. And so everybody just sat tight for a few weeks. And then that show came back and the screening for that one went much better. We could see it was gonna work.

HARRIS KATLEMAN: You had to have brass balls to tough this out because management was really after me, and after Jim and Matt, because everybody felt that this thing was a train wreck.

BRIAN ROBERTS: Fortunately, "Simpsons Roasting on an Open Fire" came in next. If you take those two shows and actually run them side by side, you just see a tremendous improvement in the animation, a tremendous improvement in the quality of the characters, and I personally credit Silverman with really refining and making it palatable.

The show was pushed back from its original debut date, and instead *The Simpsons* would premiere with "Simpsons Roasting on an Open Fire" as a Christmas special.

BARRY DILLER, former chairman and CEO, Fox: I remember when we screened the first finished episode for a number of Fox executives. We all went down to their bungalows over at *The Simpsons*, and not a single person in the room was laughing, except for me and Jim Brooks. No one had done an animated sitcom since *The Flintstones*, and it was just like, What is this? But we put it on, and it became more and more successful every week.

HARRIS KATLEMAN: When *The Simpsons* went on the air, the attitude was, We got a home run here. The first broadcast numbers—we were all shocked, including myself. We couldn't believe the numbers we got.

The numbers were good indeed. The Christmas episode scored 6.2 Nielsen rating points[6] (each point represented a percentage of America's 92.1 million TV-watching homes), the second highest in Fox's history. The numbers improved as the show caught on; the first regular episode was second, nationally, in its Sunday, 8:30 time slot. By May 1, *The Simpsons* was number one in its time slot and a Top 20 television show.[7] This was when Fox Broadcasting could reach only four-fifths of the country. If you added the other 20 percent, *The Simpsons* was coming close to being one of top-rated sitcoms on TV, period.

BRIAN ROBERTS: I'm telling ya, man, it was like we went from zero to a thousand almost overnight.

With its bright colors and sight gags, not to mention a view of the world (where teachers, bosses, and parents tend to be the obstacles in life) that corresponded with young people's, the show was an instant hit with kids. But as Groening and others would repeat constantly, this was a sitcom that happened to be animated—a cartoon for adults—and it drew in teens, college kids, and ultimately their parents, as well.

RICKY GERVAIS, guest voice, *The Simpsons*; creator, *The Office, Extras*: Like all my favorite things, I didn't like it immediately. I was put off by it. I think I saw that video "Do the Bartman" and I thought it was an awful, brattish, American thing for whiny kids. Then when I saw [an episode], I thought, Well, how is this a kid's show? It's one of the most intelligent things on television. It's fantastic.

I think it's one of the most remarkable TV shows of all time. It's a beautiful setup, the characterization's amazing, it takes that dysfunctional family and looks at every single aspect of life. It's wickedly satirical. It's audacious. The subject matter is on two levels, so brilliantly, for kids and adults.

BARRY DILLER: In terms of ratings and financial terms, it really built the network, but also in terms of giving Fox its attitude. Some of that was already there with *Married . . . with Children*, but *The Simpsons* is by far the network's most successful show.

JAY KOGEN: A lot of care and love went into the show, to make something really special and interesting. Same thing is true for *Cheers*—a lot of people cared for it and loved it—but I don't think it had quite as wide an audience adoring it. And it wasn't that fresh because it wasn't *that* new. Having a cartoon like this seemed very new.

After the first regular episode aired, on January 14, 1990, there was already buzz. *The Simpsons* "scored second in its time slot nationally . . . With a wave of merchandise almost ready to go, there is every indication of fadish success," wrote John Stanley in the *San Francisco Chronicle* a week later.

WALLACE WOLODARSKY, writer/producer, *The Simpsons* (1989–92): To be honest, we thought the show was going to be successful. Months and months before the show premiered, we were seeing the raw episodes and we all thought they were really, really funny. So we felt other people were going to respond to it. Its success was not a surprise, but nobody anticipated just how successful it was going to be.

Initially reviewers were cautious, comparing the show to its live-action Fox neighbor, the raunchy, over-the-top *Married . . . with Children*. This was a comparison at which Matt Groening bristled. "I suppose there's some similarity," he said in an interview with the *Chicago Tribune*. "I guess the big difference is that *Married . . . with Children* is more cartoony."[8]

Groening might have been right; the writing on *The Simpsons* was slick, smart, and poignant, while the Bundys went for gross-out or sniping jokes whenever there was an opportunity. Where the comparison was apt was in its grouping of a new brand of very successful sitcoms that displayed a darker, more caustic, and less idealized interpretation of the blue-collar American family. The very idea of what it meant to be a family was at question in these new series—something that *Will and Grace* would also invoke, though much more safely, many years later.

JONATHAN GRAY, author, *Watching with* The Simpsons: *Television, Parody, and Intertextuality*: In terms of its cultural importance, it was part of that triumvirate along with shows like *Roseanne* and *Married . . . with Children*. It really came in and blasted domestic sitcoms out of the point that they were in.

Reagan was the ultimate optimist, right? And it's one of the things that a lot of people liked about him—and still like about him even if they didn't agree with his politics. But you can only have so much optimism before you need to start making fun of it.

TOM WERNER, creator, *The Cosby Show, Roseanne*: I think America was ready for a more dysfunctional and weird take on family. The whole history of television was creating families that were safe and comfortable, so I think that both [*Roseanne* and *The Simpsons*] were trying to create some more dissonance over what the family could be.

It may have been that America was ready for that five or ten years earlier and the networks weren't. I always feel the audience is more comfortable with something fresh and something honest. There were millions of women who were balancing their role as mother and their role in the workplace, something like 50 million women who were not being represented on TV.

Roseanne was a mother whose mantra was "If the kids are alive at the end of the day, I've done my job." To say the least, this was a different mother than on *Father Knows Best* and *Leave It to Beaver*. She was living in an economic position very different from that of the Huxtables. We had one episode where the [Conners] were kiting checks to put food on the table. We were trying to capture what the real challenges of a two-income family were: kids who wanted expensive sneakers, but their parents weren't going to pay for them. There was a whole swath of the working class not really being represented on television, and they were portrayed in a very blunt way.

The Simpsons were lowbrow in their form (cartoons after all are traditionally part of "low" culture), lowbrow in their family dynamic and the problems they faced, and definitely lowbrow in terms of their own tastes and the culture they embraced.

D. G. ARNOLD (from his essay " 'Use a Pen, Sideshow Bob': The Simpsons and the Threat of High Culture"): For Homer . . . and the rest of the family (except perhaps the precious Lisa), culture functions at a very low level [Arnold cites, as an example, Homer watching a finance drive for public access, hosted by a Garrison Keillor type, and responding by smacking the TV and yelling, "Stupid TV. Be more funny!"]. They have acquired this minimally functioning culture, the show suggests, as a result of a slipshod educational system, an all-encompassing environment of consumerism and commodification, careless and misguided parenting, and, of course, television.

AL JEAN, writer/producer, *The Simpsons* (1989–   ) (to media analyst David Rushkoff, 1992): Some of the most creative stuff we write comes from just having the Simpsons watch TV.

Roseanne, which premiered in 1988, was the number one show by 1990.[9] While *The Simpsons* wasn't quite there in the ratings, the critics were seeing something worthwhile. The first review appeared in *Newsweek*, on Christmas 1989: "Wild, acerbic, and sometimes deeply cynical, *The Simpsons* is hardly the stuff of Saturday-morning children's programming." *USA Today* asked, "Why would anyone want to go back to *Growing Pains*? Crammed with sly visual and verbal gags . . . [*The Simpsons* is] adult entertainment that's just as hip for kids." And the Associated Press called it "Well animated . . . cutting humor . . . clever writing."

Much of the early press about *The Simpsons* focused less on reviewing the program than on profiling Groening and his remarkable ascendance from cartoonist for alternative newspapers to TV big shot. They quoted the cartoonist widely, on everything from the inspiration for the show's insouciantly cynical humor to his ambition to make audiences forget they were watching a cartoon.

The New York Times got around to writing about the series midway through February with a mixed but positive review by John O'Connor: "The record so far: impressively on target." O'Connor was, by turns, astute in his criticisms: "The show can fall flat . . . There is, admittedly, a fine line between being hilariously perceptive and just plain, even objectionably, silly. While habitually teetering on that line, *The Simpsons* has shown a remarkable ability to come down on the right side most of the time," and wildly reductive: "Bart's spike haircut suggests he has been profoundly influenced by Jughead in the old *Archie* comic books" (which is like saying that Homer's hefty carriage meant that he is heavily influenced by Mr. Weatherbee or The Penguin). A little late to the game, like its older, more sophisticated readership, the *Times* was ready to accept *The Simpsons*.

As the larger population was swept up in the show's first season, the media began to see its sophistication and potential. Tom Shales described what he considered the emergence of new family television institution, signified by *The Simpsons'* dominance of the prime-time Sunday ratings, which, over the decades, had bowed to the likes of *The Ed Sullivan Show, Lassie,* and *Candid Camera.* "Sunday night is what we watch. Sunday night is who we are." Shales called the cartoon "sparkling" and the animated family "crazed, wonderful and bitterly funny . . . "They're the flip, dark side of the Nelsons, the Andersons, the Bradys and all other sitcom families from the dawn of television . . . The show inhabits a rarefied realm that enables it to be both fiercely funny and absurdly poignant."[10]

Of course, there was the occasional exception to the praise: "*The Simpsons* . . . is strangely off-putting much of the time," wrote *Time* magazine. "The drawings are grotesque without redeeming style or charm (characters have big beady eyes, beaklike noses and spiky hair), and the animation is crude even by TV's low-grade standards."[11] One couldn't have expected much more from a magazine that still dedicated a number of its covers, every year, to questions like "Is the Bible True?" As Rupert Murdoch would later point out to me, *The Simpsons* was first popular on the two coasts—it took a little longer for Middle America to catch on.

By the end of the first season, though, the expansive appeal was clear-cut: "Young viewers love the show's exuberant humor, its aggressively crude drawings, its false-to-life colors," wrote Joe Morgenstern. "Grown-ups relish its broad gags, just as the kids do, but also respond to its emotional complexity and its wickedly deadpan social comments—*The Simpsons* has some of the most incisive writing on TV."[12]

JAY KOGEN: Sam kept saying to write things that were funny to us. We took him at his word and came up with things that *we* thought were funny.

BRAD BIRD, executive consultant, *The Simpsons* (1989–97); director, *The Incredibles, Ratatouille*: When we first started that show, the studios in Asia that were doing the episodes didn't know us from *Teenage Mutant Ninja Turtles*. So they gave us the same attention, or lack thereof, that they'd give any other show. And they'd ignore a lot of our instructions, because it slowed them down. When we got a little more successful, we were better at either figuring out ways to trick them into doing what we wanted, or saying, "Come on, you gotta do it right if you want our business. We're gonna be on the air for a while now." That's another reason the quality improved; we had more clout to make them follow instructions.

Critically, comedically, monetarily, in every way possible—from ratings to fans to marketing—by the end of their thirteen-episode run, *The Simpsons* was an unbridled success. An April 23 *Newsweek* cover story perhaps summed it up best: "*The Simpsons* has emerged as a breakaway ratings hit, an industry trendsetter, a merchandising phenomenon, a cultural template and, among its most fanatical followers, a viewing experience verging on the religious."

Ratings were so good, in fact, that the network was at a loss for what to do when the thirteen episodes had finished playing. Murdoch and Diller wanted to keep rerunning them all summer, while Sam Simon, Matt Groening, and Jim Brooks were worried that the momentum they'd created would be exhausted by the repetition before the new episodes were ready to go the next fall. "It's not a happy situation," Matt Groening told *The New York Times*.[13] This was an instance where the executives were proved right. They reran the episodes, fans kept tuning in, and word of mouth brought new viewers with them.

For the fall of 1990, while expanding Fox's programming schedule from three nights a week to five (the baby network was still not quite ready for seven days of programming), Murdoch and Diller hatched a bold plan: beginning with *The Simpsons'* second season, it would be moved to Thursday nights, where it would take on the reigning television champion, NBC's *The Cosby Show.*

BARRY DILLER: We were at a scheduling meeting, and there were about fifteen people there, and we were figuring out what to put up against *Cosby* on Thursday nights at eight o'clock. *Cosby* had been the biggest thing on TV for God knows how many years. Rupert leaned over and whispered to me, "What about *The Simpsons*?" And I stood up and went over to the board and moved the little magnet that said "Simpsons" to Thursday night at eight. And it took a solid minute before someone said, "You know what? That could work." And it was a big deal, little Bart Simpson going up against big Bill Cosby. So it was a dragon-slayer story.

RUPERT MURDOCH, chairman, News Corp: We were sitting down with Barry, reviewing the schedule. We looked at it and I said, "We gotta be more aggressive . . . let's put it up against *Cosby*. Cosby must be coming to the end of his run—he's been there forever." And everybody in the room was horrified and sort of laughed at me. Except Barry Diller, who said, "No, let's think about this."

The media, already smitten with *The Simpsons,* was intrigued by the possibility of Bart toppling Cos:

"Bart Vs. Bill"—Los Angeles Times
"Simpsons to Compete with Cosby"—The New York Times
"The Simpsons: They're Scrapping Again—But This Time It's a Ratings Fight" —The Washington Post

Tom Shales, in his *Washington Post* column, elaborated, "Much has been written about this supposedly monumental face-off. *The Cosby Show,* it's been said, embodies the optimism and materialism of the '80s, whereas the Simpsons personify the sadder but wiser pragmatism of the '90s. Thus, Their Time Has Come."[14] Johnny Carson even alluded to the coming battle in a monologue, seemingly siding with *The Simpsons* when he commented that the cartoon family was closer to the real thing than the perfect Huxtables. Cosby took all the attention in stride—during an episode of *The Cosby Show* that season, one of his kids surprised him by wearing a Bart mask. Some twenty years later, however, Cosby commented, somewhat ruefully, that Bart Simpson was "sent to destroy *The Cosby Show*."[15]

WALLACE WOLODARSKY: None of the writers cared about the scheduling move. It was just an opportunity to make fun of *Cosby* and be impudent about it. The writers never had a stake in the ratings; you never cared about that. That was always viewed as a business decision.

The same could not be said for the producers, who saw all their success slipping away with schedule changes, which never did positive things for a show's ratings.

JAMES L. BROOKS (to Tom Shales, *Los Angeles Times*, October 11, 1990): Suddenly a show that was a hit is fighting for its survival . . . There have been two weeks in my life when a show I was associated with was number one in the ratings, and on Sunday night, we had a chance to be the number one show in the country.

The Fox execs knew what they wanted, though. This was about more than *The Simpsons* to them—this was about taking on the Big Three, moving up to five nights of programming, and becoming a real player in the network game. Peter Chernin, who had taken over as Fox Entertainment president, told the *Los Angeles Times*, "There's no one in this company who looks at this as 'Let's take on *The Cosby Show*.' We think that if we're really lucky and very fortunate we'll come in second place to them because the other two guys [CBS and ABC] aren't as strong. We're hoping to establish a little bit of a foothold there."

BRIAN ROBERTS: In Fox's great wisdom, they decided they were going to go against Bill Cosby, take him out. And a lot of people on *The Simpsons* weren't very happy about it, least of all Sam. Sam thought it was the stu-pidest move ever. So in typical Sam Simon fashion, he created a charac-ter by the name of Dr. Hibbert, who is always wearing a Cosby sweater, who's always going "heh heh heh," and is an idiot doctor. This was *The Simpsons* sort of like fastball over the plate at Bill Cosby.

And we had a lot of fun with Dr. Hibbert that year.

RUPERT MURDOCH: So we did it. And at the end of the first year, Cosby announced his retirement. We started behind him, but I think we'd caught up by the end of the year; certainly the writing was on the wall.

From late August 1990 until October, *The Cosby Show* was running first-run episodes of their new season against reruns of *The Simpsons* and was inevitably beating Fox in the ratings (as was CBS, with the short-lived *The Flash*, based on the DC Comics hero). When the big night of *The Simpsons* premiere arrived, Bart did his parents proud (this would be daddies Barry and Rupert, and maybe Jim too), finish-ing with an 18.4 rating share behind *Cosby*'s 18.5,[16] and even taking first place on the West Coast. "Simpsons Edge Cosby in Overnight Ratings," trumpeted the *Los Angeles Times* the next morning. Cosby was still number one on Thursday nights, but it was clear who the real winner was. Fox Broadcasting still reached only four-fifths of the country—add that 20 percent to their numbers and it was once more a *Simpsons* victory. Even if *The Simpsons* failed to achieve the 27 per-cent audience share that sponsors had reportedly been guaranteed,[17] by capturing *Cosby*'s younger viewers Fox could declare Mission Accomplished (in the classic sense of the term). *The Simpsons* offi-cially beat *Cosby* at Thanksgiving (by three-tenths of a ratings point, tying it for thirty-seventh place[18]), but by then the competition was over. It was official: *The Simpsons* could compete with anyone—Fox and their skateboarding scamp of a mascot had come to play, and come to stay.

DONICK CARY, writer/producer, *The Simpsons* (1996–99); creator, *Lil' Bush*: They invented a network. In a lot of ways, the Fox Network wouldn't exist without the longevity and the amount of viewers that *The Simpsons* has consistently brought.

HARRIS KATLEMAN: They didn't save Fox. Rupert's got deep pockets and he was determined to make Fox Broadcasting work. Did *The Simpsons* get us noticed? Absolutely. *The Simpsons* made the other networks say, "Wow. Look out. This is a network waiting to happen."

WESLEY ARCHER: We didn't know if there was going to be a Season 2 while we were doing Season 1. And while we were doing Season 2, we thought there would probably be a Season 3. Then when we were doing Season 3, we were pretty sure there was going to be Season 4. And the merchandise was kicking in and we thought, Well, this could go on for seven or eight years.

EIGHT

Bigger Than Jesus

In which no one really wants to relive the Depression with George Bush Sr. . . . a stranger tries to starve James L. Brooks's children . . . and Matt Groening finds great pleasure in the ass of a ten-year-old boy.

Do the Bartman. It was as ridiculous as it sounds. In a fervor moment worthy of parody (which would come later—the metahappy *Simpsons* never had issue satirizing itself), Bart Simpson had his own dance, and real people everywhere were doing it. "Do the Bartman" as well as "Deep Deep Trouble" played on MTV to a point far past overkill. He had music videos, a gold album, coffee cups, air fresheners, talking dolls, and T-shirts, all of them plastered with his image. One (awesome) trend that emerged involved middle-class kids horrifying their parents with the letters BART shaved into their hair. There were magazine covers and controversies. The media called him a "fad," "cult hero," and "America's sweetheart." If Bart had been a real preadolescent, this is when the paparazzi would start popping photos and champagne bottles.

The show was Fox's biggest ratings hit, reaching a high at the end of its first season when it cracked the Top 10 (the only Fox show to do so that year). Fox struck a deal with Mattel and fifty other product licensees, beginning a merchandising boom the likes of which television had not seen before or since. Bart was more than just a beloved cartoon character; he was a cultural phenomenon. Things became so crazy that Barry Diller, worried about overexposure, began discouraging the show's staff from cooperating with print and TV journalists.

Bart was brazen and obnoxious, but he said all the things we wished we could say to the authority figures in our own lives—our father, our boss, or the Man in whatever form he took. In an early example, when Bart is told to say grace at dinner, he offers, "Dear God, we pay for all this stuff ourselves, so thanks for nothing." With that wise-ass remark, Bart touched on our resentment of religious piety, the debate over deist involvement in our lives, and the religious inculcation of children by parents everywhere. That single joke also alludes to the family's unity and its observance of some of the traditional family values promulgated by sitcoms: this is a family that sits, eats, and prays together regularly. It was also pretty funny. And all of this in just one line—no wonder he and the show were catching on like wildfire.

Bart's catchphrases such as "Underachiever and proud of it" and "Don't have a cow, man" became hallmarks of the early nineties lexicon and his popularity courted disapproval from teachers, parents, and "values" spokespeople of the religious right, including the Bushes (whose battles with cartons were not limited to *The Simpsons*—Garry Trudeau's *Doonesbury* characters also felt the wrath of George H. W. Bush). Naturally, the negative attention only sparked greater fervor for the sassy little troublemaker. When *TV Guide* put *The Simpsons* on its cover, it sold more copies than any other issue that year.[1] *Newsweek* ran *The Simpsons* on their cover in April; "Why America Loves the Simpsons—TV's Twisted New Take on the Family" (on the same cover: "Gorbachev's Ultimatum; A Blockade of Lithuania"), and *Time* followed suit, making Bart its "Best of '90" cover boy. Fox purchased twenty-four episodes for Season 2, and then 3, then 4.

By 1991, six animated sitcoms, all inspired by the success of *The Simpsons*, were being developed by the networks, with major production muscle behind them. Steven Spielberg and Tim Burton produced *Family Dog* for CBS, about a caustic suburban family seen through the eyes of its pooch, while Steven Bochco (producer of *L.A. Law* and perhaps the biggest name in television at the time) came up with *Capital Critters* for ABC, a show about a mouse who moves to the basement of the White House, after seeing his Midwestern family exterminated—ugh. Both CBS and ABC made thirteen-episode commitments, at approximately $600,000 per episode[2]—for shows that turned out to be complete failures. Facing a similar fate was *Fish Police*, a Hanna-Barbera-animated mystery comedy that took place under the sea. "Call it fish noir," Hanna-

Barbera's CEO told *The Wall Street Journal*. You could also call it canceled—the show lasted three episodes. (*Family Dog* lasted only two, but the entire series was later available for purchase—on laser disc). And these were the good ones: *The Jackie Bison Show*—a cartoon series featuring a buffalo, based on Jackie Gleason, with a talk show—was thankfully never picked up by NBC.

Like a real celebrity who had reached his zenith, Bart did have a fall, but it was far from the Feldman/Haim, Spears/Lohan variety. As Bartmania tapered off, and Bart dolls found their way to the discount stores and the prize racks of carnival booths, the writers were discovering that there was more comedy gold in Homer than could ever be written for Bart. (With a ten-year-old, there are only so many situations you can exploit: a kid covets an item, he gets in trouble at school, he develops a crush, etc.)

WALLACE WOLODARSKY, writer/producer, *The Simpsons* (1989–92): The Homer stories were always the easiest to write, and then the second easiest were Bart stories, and then Lisa stories. Marge stories were always the toughest, because we were a bunch of boys, really, and nobody had any understanding of what it meant to be a mother or a woman, so those stories Jim invariably insisted on us doing and I thought they turned out really well.

But in the first years of the 1990s, it was all about Bart, the foul-mouthed (for his time), disobedient voice of a new generation. The numbers for *The Simpsons* were a godsend to Fox, and they milked it for everything they could. Licensing deals came through Fox Broadcasting by the bushel.

TIM LONG, writer/co–executive producer, *The Simpsons* (1999–present): When the show started, I was a sophomore in university. I remember thinking, This is the fastest, funniest show ever. I cannot believe this show is on the air. It just felt like a miracle.

BILL OAKLEY, writer/producer, *The Simpsons* (1991–97): The idea that there would be a cartoon in prime time, other than *The Grinch Who Stole Christmas*, was astonishing to people. The fact that a boy would be sassy to his principal and say, "Eat my shorts," was amazing.

ROBERT COHEN, production assistant, *The Tracey Ullman Show*, *The Simpsons* (1989–92): It was just amazing, because you could see the show going crazy. And you could see something that was worked on quietly with these guys, who were busting their ass on it. It was starting to just really become hip and take off. And for me in particular, the first "holy crap" moment was during the Hollywood Christmas parade, which is this dopey parade that goes down Hollywood Boulevard, and stars of yesteryear wave from convertibles; it's this very weird parade. It was the second season, and they'd asked the Simpsons to be in the parade, so they hired some dancers to put on costumes and Jay Kogen and I wore our Simpsons crew jackets. We piled into this car called the Graciemobile, which was this big old El Dorado convertible painted with the Gracie logo. The plan was that we would drive the Simpsons down the street in the parade. When we pulled out on to the street and it was parade time—I was at the wheel—the people mobbed us to the point that the car could go only about twenty yards. The sheriff's department had to veer us outta there because it was like a riot. And they weren't interested in us. They were interested in these actors in Simpsons costumes. Obviously they weren't even the real Simpsons. That's when I realized, Holy crap. This thing's outta control. Because it was just hundreds of people mobbing stinky felt costumes that represented the show. I knew the show was popular, but I didn't realize how popular until that moment.

WALLACE WOLODARSKY: When you're twenty-six, and you're a part of something that is *that* successful, it's good if you're single. In the end, we were just a bunch of nerdy guys and it gave me a kind of cachet that I never could have gotten any other way.

JAY KOGEN, writer/producer, *The Simpsons* (1989–92): We were working really hard on the show. We didn't have a lot of time to do a lot of other things. It was hard.

Simpsons mania—and Bart's appeal in particular—transcended race and class lines. "From Harlem to Watts, black variations of the popular cartoon grade-schooler . . . have been the most enduring T-shirt images of the year," reported the *Chicago Tribune*. "Wearing gold chains . . . or sporting the colors of the African National Congress, Bart has appeared in the personae of Malcom X, Michael Jordan ('Air Bart'), Bob Marley ('Rasta Bart') . . . No other nonblack figure, born or drawn, has been so freely appropriated by young blacks." The black Bart spouted either Bart Simpson's familiar lines or slogans of racial pride; a rasta Bart's caption read, "Watch it, mon!" Russell Adams, the chairman of Afro-American Studies at Howard University, explained to *The New York Times* that Bart's popularity in the black community rested in his role as an outsider that spoke to black youths in a society that alienates them: "There is a suppressed rage in the cartoon that black people are picking up on."[3] The *Times* reported the sale of T-shirts featuring black Bart standing next to Nelson Mandela, against an African backdrop immediately after the South African leader had finished speaking at Yankee Stadium during the summer of 1990.[4] The juxtaposition of cultural icons and the appropriation of cultural symbolism was interesting in itself, but there was also something inexplicably cool about the pairing. None of the black Bart merchandise was licensed by Groening, who said in a statement, "You have mixed feelings when you're getting ripped off."

Of course, not everyone was thrilled with Bart as the new favorite thing of kids everywhere. Schools banned Bart T-shirts, hoping to discourage his "Underachiever, and proud of it" message—which J. C. Penney soon removed from the specialized *Simpsons* shopping sections they'd created for their stores. "Bart Simpson Is Chic, but Educators Dislike His Cheek" ran an Associated Press headline. "We feel like the Bart Simpson show does a lot of things that do not help student self-esteem, such as saying it's OK to be stupid," one principal told the news agency. Another principal who banned the shirts claimed that such a shirt was "a poor reflection on [students], their parents and their school."[5] Matt Groening issued the following statement: "I have no comment. My folks taught me to respect elementary school principals, even the ones who have nothing better to do than tell kids what to wear."[6]

If these prohibitions weren't attracting enough free publicity for the show, the president of the United States and his family decided to take umbrage with the cartoon, adding even more fuel to *The Simpsons'* fire. In an interview with *People* magazine in September 1990,

Barbara Bush called *The Simpsons* "The dumbest thing I had ever seen." Marge responded with a letter to the first lady, chastising her with the following: "I always believed in my heart that we had a great deal in common. Each of us living our lives to serve an exceptional man." The first lady wrote back, apologizing for her "loose tongue.")[7]

Later that year, visiting a rehab center Bush drug czar William Bennett noticed a Bart Simpson poster and commented, "You guys aren't watching *The Simpsons*, are you? That's not going to help you any." He later had to recant, admitting he'd never seen the show, and adding, "I'll sit down with the little spike head, we'll straighten this thing out . . . There's nothing that a Catholic school, a paper route and a couple soap sandwiches wouldn't straighten out."[8] *The Simpsons'* writers responded, "If our Drug Czar thinks he can sit down and talk this over with a cartoon character, he must be on something."[9] And then there was George Bush's own shot, taken at a campaign stop at the National Religious Broadcasters in May 1992, when he promised to make families "a lot more like the Waltons and a lot less like the Simpsons."

BRAD BIRD, executive consultant, *The Simpsons* (1989–97); director, *The Incredibles*, *Ratatouille*: We were delighted. But we also collectively thought it was idiotic. He [Bush] is talking about a cartoon family. And he sounds like someone who has never actually seen an episode because as much as it looks chaotic and insane and a somewhat gratuitous on the surface, it actually has a lot of sharp things to say about contemporary living and I think comes down on a morally sound, thoughtful side. Underneath the wackiness on the surface, if you dig into it, there's plenty there.

Bush repeated the jibe some months later at the 1992 Republican Convention in Houston (where keynote speaker Pat Buchanan gave his famous "culture war" speech, arguing that there was a battle of values raging across the United States). Three nights later, as the weekly episode was about to air (a repeat), *The Simpsons* retaliated. Seated in front of the television, the family watched Bush take a swipe at them. "Huh?" asked a surprised Homer. Lying on the floor at his feet, Bart offered the following reply: "We're just like the Waltons. We're praying for an end to the Depression too." The response, both playful and slick, was a virtuous shot back at the Bushes. It was a repudiation of all the fantasy values Bush was pushing and a reminder that there was an ongoing battle with poverty that no prayer or culture war would help win.

BRAD BIRD: They wanted to have it on TV within a week or two of him saying it. So they just took some existing animation and moved his mouth back and forth so that the dialogue roughly synced up. But they recorded the response and got it on the air really quickly. That was vintage *Simpsons*, because it was the perfect response. They embraced it rather than getting offended by it. They embraced it and then came up with the smartest response anyone could come up with.

The animators had their own fun with the Bush dustup. Bush's Waltons speech set off a contest of satirical drawings placed on the walls of the studio. Somehow the subject matter devolved from satirizing Bush to completely obscene animations of *The Simpsons*, ending with an animated scene where Grandpa Simpson was having sex with Maggie, with Lisa trying to break it up and Grandpa savagely beating her.

JONATHAN GRAY, author, *Watching with* The Simpsons: *Television, Parody, and Intertextuality*: I think the kiss of death, if you were a conservative who wanted to like *The Simpsons*, or the wonderful stamp of approval if you weren't and you wanted to like it, was when Bush intoned that we need more families like the Waltons and fewer like The Simpsons because at that point it all of a sudden dragged *The Simpsons* into the culture wars and positioned it on the opposite side of all the sort of very neoconservative sitcoms that had reigned in the eighties like *Family Ties* and *The Cosby Show* and so forth.

RUPERT MURDOCH: In the first few years, some old-fashioned people thought it was undermining family values, and it was terrible, and such. I think that's nonsense.

Before the first episode had even appeared, there were already forty-five licenses sold to merchandisers,[10] and by the end of the first season there were fifty-two.[11] "We're getting over 100 requests a day to use *The Simpsons*," 20th Century Fox's vice president of licensing and marketing, Al Ovadia, told *Adweek*. Sellers were hungry for anything allowing them to latch onto the spending power of the show's twelve- to seventeen-year-old fans, a lucrative demographic where *The Simpsons* was number one. The kids loved Bart; they idolized him—Fox had themselves a brand. "Our only problem is getting enough merchandise in," a J. C. Penney executive told *The New York Times*'s N. R. Kleinfeld. "As soon as it comes in, it sells off the shelves." There was Bart bubble gum, snow boots, notebooks, underwear, and posters, a Bart air freshener, Simpsons pasta. Burger King sold Simpson figurines with their burgers; Butterfinger had the Simpsons as their spokespeople; Bart eventually even did a commercial for Japan Air Lines. At one point, Bart T-shirts were selling at the rate of a million per day in North America.[12]

AL OVADIA, former vice president of licensing and marketing, 20th Century Fox (to the *Los Angeles Times*, September 25, 1997): The Monday after *The Simpsons* special debuted, Jon Dolgen, then chairman of Fox TV . . . called me into his office. He said, "The show will debut on January 14—go to work." Basically, go out there and secure as many deals as you can.

The revenues from the first year of merchandising were estimated at $750 million[13] (the only products that took in more money that year were *Teenage Mutant Ninja Turtles* and New Kids on the Block[14]), with Fox nabbing around 8 percent of that number. In 1991, Groening made *Forbes's* "Top 40 Richest Entertainers," with an estimated $18 million.[15]

GAVIN POLONE, former agent for Conan O'Brien, *Simpsons* writers; executive producer, *Curb Your Enthusiasm*: Everybody was making millions of dollars. Matt, Sam, and Jim (having seen profit take and things like that) collected well over $600 million . . . My recollection was that of the total pie, they had 50 percent.

Matt Groening, no stranger to the windfall merchandising could bring, was delighted by the marketing opportunities. Both he and Gracie had final approval over any *Simpsons* products, which resulted in meetings where Matt, Gracie people, and the Fox execs would essentially get to test out all the new toys. Matt was only somewhat discerning about what he put his name on. The sheer volume of *Simpsons* merchandise indicates an eagerness to make whatever he could from the brand. Both he and Jim Brooks dismissed only the occasional product they considered "too cheesy."[16]

MATT GROENING (to *Playboy*, June 1, 2007): We have turned a few things down, believe it or not. I know it's hard to tell.

Groening continues to make the hocking of *Simpsons* merchandise a priority. When he appeared on *Charlie Rose* to promote *The Simpsons Movie* in 2007, Rose brought out Simpsons posable figurines as examples of the ubiquitous merchandise. "Now you're talking my language," Groening joked. He then proceeded to insist, three times, in fact, that the toy that Rose was displaying was a "good one."[17]

MATT GROENING (to *The New York Times*, October 7, 1990): I apologize to America. But a Bart Simpson air freshener that is smell-o-rific? That's one of those things which when they ask you, how can you not?

ALBERT BROOKS, guest voice, *The Simpsons*, Oscar-nominated actor, *Broadcast News*: I'll tell you one thing that's funny: there're people who wait outside restaurants. I don't know, these people must have very big trunks, because they seem to have pictures of everybody. And I'm not a person who's out on the town a lot, but I'll go have a bite to eat with my wife and I'll come out and there'll be three people there with a picture from *Taxi Driver* or *Defending Your Life*, and they just carry around the stuff. And I've noticed, over the years, that they have some of these *Simpsons* toys, wanting me to sign Hank Scorpio. Someone last week shoved a Brad Goodman at me. I forgot about Brad Goodman. I thought, Oh, how do you like that? I said, "Where'd you get this?" "It's in my car," he said. "How *big* is your car? What else you got in there? If I was Telly Savalas, were you gonna come out with a Kelly's Heroes doll?"

In 1991, David Geffen had the idea to do a *Simpsons* music album, released in time for Christmas, which became *The Simpsons Sing the Blues.* The writers wrote humorous lyrics for the actors to perform over blues and hip-hop tracks, produced by DJ Jazzy Jeff (yes, Bart rapped) and featuring the likes of B. B. King and Dr. John. "Do the Bartman," its second single, was cowritten and coproduced (anonymously) by the King of Pop himself, who provided a guest voice during the second season (for a huge white insane cell mate of Homer's at a mental institution). "I don't think Bart would say, 'I want to be bad like Michael Jackson' [a line from the song] unless Michael Jackson actually wrote that line," Groening later told Conan O'Brien. The album went triple platinum within weeks, reaching number three on the *Billboard* charts. Jim Brooks wanted to follow up with a second, *The Yellow Album,* but apparently Matt was against it, and the album was not released until 1998, to poor reception.

JAY KOGEN, writer/producer, *The Simpsons* (1989–92): I had never been a part of anything that was that huge, ever. People were selling T-shirts of the show on freeway off-ramps. Instead of selling oranges on the freeway, they were selling *Simpsons* T-shirts. All people were talking about was *The Simpsons.* It was gigantic.

MATT GROENING (to *Playboy,* June 1, 2007): Strange things happened. Someone returned a Bart Simpson doll to my family. They thought it was lost because my name was printed very large on Bart's ass.

WALLACE WOLODARSKY, writer/producer, *The Simpsons* (1989–92): We got to do amazing things. We got to go see Foreman v. Holyfield in Atlantic city, because we were in New York recording Jackie Mason for an episode in the second season. I was a huge sports fan, so to connect to that kind of stuff was really exciting. When we did the baseball episode (Mr. Burns loads up the company softball team with ringers, including Ken Griffey, Jr., Jose Canseco, and Roger Clemens), I got to meet a bunch of baseball players and that just seemed *beyond* anything I could ever hope for.

DARIA PARIS, assistant to Sam Simon, *The Simpsons* (1989–93): Even before *The Simpsons* went on the air, I was already wearing a *Simpsons* jacket. And people would stop me because they knew who *The Simpsons* were, because of *The Tracey Ullman Show*. So they already had this recognition that was a very strange thing. And once it started it was an avalanche. I mean, it was nonstop, and I'll never be involved in anything like that again, ever.

HARRIS KATLEMAN, former CEO, 20th Century Fox Television: In May we have the selling season, when we take all our shows in and the networks buy them. The licensing division was doing merchandising rights right and left [this would be the spring of 1990, after the show had had its banner first year]. So I was in New York. That year we sold about nine shows, and I'm sitting with my whole staff 'cause you bring all your executives with you. We were sitting in my suite at the Ritz-Carlton, and they said, "What should we do tonight?" And all my people said, "We want to go to Il Molino," which was the toughest reservation in town at the time.

I called Il Molino. I said, "I'd like a reservation for eleven people." And this guy, it's the owner, Frankie, I think his name is, said, "I'd liked to go on the next moon shot." I said, "No, no. I really would." He said, "Are you crazy? We're booked up for a month." So I asked him if he has children. He said, "Of course I have children." I asked how old they were and whether they watched *The Simpsons*. He said, "Are you kidding? It's their favorite show." I said, "How would you like *Simpsons* T-shirts?" He said, "They're not out." I say, "How would you like *Simpsons* T-shirts, baseball hats—" I had the whole set in my suite. And he says, "If you got that, you've got a table. If you don't, when you come in here and you're kidding me, you won't know what hit you."

We went down there. I walked in and Frankie said, "Oh, so you're the wise guy." I said, "Here's the stuff." I had some T-shirts, I had baseball caps, I had everything we had in sample. And I said, "This is for the table." And he took us to a table—there were ten, eleven of us. God knows what the people who had reservations did. They were probably at the bar until midnight.

MATT GROENING (to the *Orange County Register*, December 23, 1990): Look, I don't own *The Simpsons*; Twentieth Century Fox does . . . So with the merchandise, it's like standing in the middle of traffic trying to stop a locomotive. I couldn't do it if I wanted to. Luckily, I like the loco-motive, so it's fun to go along for the ride.

DONICK CARY, writer/producer, *The Simpsons* (1996–99). I think the show also opened the door for a lot of marketing ideas. There were *Simpsons* burgers and cups and stuff before there were Ariel Under the Sea mugs.

GEORGE MEYER, writer/producer, *The Simpsons* (1989–2004) (to *The Believer*): I don't like that the Simpsons are spokespeople for Burger King and MasterCard and Butterfinger. In the first Gulf War, I was really upset that *The Simpsons'* characters were being drawn on tanks and bombs. But those are things that I don't control.

AL OVADIA, former vice president of licensing (to the *Los Angeles Times*, September 25, 1997): By June 1990, there was almost nothing else you could license that was in good taste.

Bootleg merchandise was soon nearly as ubiquitous as the real thing—unlicensed merchandise was popping up all over the world. For the most part, Groening found endless amusement in these imitations.

CONAN O'BRIEN, writer/producer, *The Simpsons* (1991–93): Friends of Matt's would be traveling and they would find bootlegged *Simpsons* merchandise. Sometimes they were funny and sometimes they were disturbing. Like a Marge made out of a lizard's skull, or T-shirts that were from some country—recently liberated from the Iron Curtain—that had Bart saying weird phrases that were mildly threatening or racist. I remember Matt cracking up once. "Did you see what they just found? Ceauşescu had *this* in his basement."

Fox took action wherever it could, including against an Australian beer company that began producing Homer's favorite brand of beer, Duff. When a skinhead group, the White Aryan Resistance, began selling T-shirts featuring a *sieg-heiling* Bart saying, "Total Nazi, Dude," Fox was informed by the Anti-Defamation League and had an injunction imposed.[18]

Also not amused by the knockoffs was one James L. Brooks. One story, which circulated throughout the Gracie Films building, involved Jim in New York City soon after the show had hit it big. Brooks spotted an African-American street vendor hocking counterfeit Bart Simpson T-shirts. Jim accosted him: "You're taking food out of the mouths of my children!"

The wave of *Simpsons* merch would eventually break. Mattel canceled their license in early 1991 (following Burger King, which, in June 1990, had sent thousands of Bart dolls back to their distributor[19]), sensing that America had had just about enough of Bart Simpson and had begun to run the other way. While it may have been true that we were tired of Bart, or that he was overexposed, the decline in sales of his toothbrushes signified only the end of a fad, not of the show's popularity.

CHRIS TURNER (from his book, *Planet Simpson*): The truly rare cultural force that *The Simpsons* tapped . . . was *resonance*. Pop-cultural resonance is what distinguishes the millions of records sold by the Beatles from the millions sold by Pat Boone . . . When a pop hit has resonance, it isn't merely consumed. The audience connects with the resonant cultural object, identifies itself with it, *absorbs* it.

While it may not have lasted, the merchandising explosion signified a massive success. Of the principals, Matt Groening's life changed the most dramatically.

KEN ESTIN, writer/producer, *Taxi, The Tracey Ullman Show*: Whatever Matt got, [Fox] stopped giving [to others] instantly, because in the first season of *The Simpsons* they already were making phenomenal money—money that nobody ever dreamed of. When I first met Matt, I don't even think he had a house. Once he started working [on *Ullman*], he got a house in Venice that I think he was renting. Then he bought it. Then when *The Simpsons* came out, he bought the house next door and turned it into a game house where he just had *Simpsons* things in it. He put in pinball machines and toys and toothbrushes and light fixtures, just everything you could possibly imagine—I was amazed. You'd be in one house and then you'd walk next door to the other house and there it was. It was *The Simpsons* house—his game house—but he made money so fast that then he sold both those properties and bought a huge house somewhere else.

The merchandising made the show's success highly visible, to the benefit of Groening, Gracie, and Fox, and to the chagrin of a few others, who would not be asked to share in the wealth.

NINE

Fallout Boys

In which Tracey takes on *The Simpsons* . . . Homer turns his back on his Hungarian heritage . . . and to no one's surprise, media consolidation has negative effects on creativity.

It's not show-friends, it's show-business.

—Bob Sugar, Jerry Maguire *(executive-produced by James L. Brooks)*

By the spring of 1990, articles were appearing in the trades about the phenomenal pay dirt Fox, Groening, and Brooks had hit with *The Simpsons*. Of course, with this very public windfall, the relatives came calling—and they brought their lawyers. When they were developing *The Tracey Ullman Show,* the executive producers (Heide Perlman, Jerry Belson, Ken Estin, and Tracey Ullman) had each signed a standard contract with Gracie Films, which gave them a percentage, or "points," of any earnings from *The Tracey Ullman Show* and any spin-offs. "Spin-off" being the key word here, which *The Simpsons* definitely was. As the cash came rolling in, the *Ullman* producers began to realize that Fox and Gracie weren't passing any of it along.

When questioned by the *Ullman* producers, who were also his longtime friends, Jim Brooks deferred to Fox. Fox deferred to Gracie. Lawyers were called and the fur began to fly. Jim Brooks was a mogul by this point—taking him on could be disastrous for a producer's future in the business. Heide Perlman, for instance, let the whole matter drop, because she wanted to do a series with Brooks. *The Tracey Ullman Show*'s three other producers stood up to Brooks and Fox, and lost in a big way.

The most public of these battles involved Tracey Ullman, who was very vocal with her complaints, saying of *The Simpsons*, "I breast-fed those little devils."[1] Ullman, who, like the other producers of her show, had a couple of points in *The Simpsons,* was suing for a greater stake, 5–10 percent of the adjusted gross, as well as 7.5 percent of their merchandising.[2] Fox and Gracie argued that those percentages were only for characters she created, not spin-off characters created by others, in this case, Matt Groening.

KEN ESTIN, writer/producer, *Taxi, The Tracey Ullman Show*: In her contract it said she owned any characters created on *The Tracey Ullman Show*. However, the [jury] interpreted that obviously it didn't mean characters created by other people.

After a year and a half, and probably $1 million in legal fees, Tracey Ullman had to be content with the points she had (she was the only producer from *Ullman* who would get to keep any stake in *The Simpsons*). It was presumed at the time in the industry that Ullman did not name Jim Brooks or Gracie Films when she filed the lawsuit so as not to jeopardize her relationship with Brooks. At the time of the lawsuit, Ullman was starring with Nick Nolte in the ill-fated *I'll Do Anything*, which James L. Brooks was directing. Awkward.

It's important to note that in the legal battles over *The Simpsons*, it was Fox that was being sued, not Gracie Films. *Simpsons'* pie was being divvied up by Fox, but if the producers were going to get their points, they would be coming out of the piece being given to Gracie. Gracie was directly between the two, and Jim Brooks was far from supportive of the *Ullman* producers. This was, after all, money that would be his if not theirs. He and other *Simpson* producers—though noticeably not Sam Simon—testified against Ullman in court.

KEN ESTIN: What happened is Jim Brooks and Fox decided to give none of the merchandising money to *The Tracey Ullman Show* and keep it all for *The Simpsons*. Meanwhile, Jerry Belson and Heide Perlman and I were saying, "How come we don't get a penny from *The Simpsons*? It doesn't seem right. It was a spin-off of our show."

I've seen dozens of spin-offs, and the creators of the original show always get something for the spin-offs, and we went to Jim Brooks and we went to Fox, and they wouldn't talk to us. They said, "Jim Brooks is Jim Brooks and he doesn't negotiate with people." And Fox was not gonna negotiate with us and wouldn't show us the books and wouldn't talk to us at all about it. They said, "It's over for you guys."

Another reason Fox gave for denying the *Ullman* producers their cut of *The Simpsons* was that *Ullman* had never made any money. Because *The Simpsons* was spun off from *The Tracey Ullman Show*, Fox argued that their points were worthless until the costs incurred by *Ullman* had been covered. "For the first two years of *The Simpsons* they were saying, '*Ullman*'s still in the red, so you get nothing,'" a friend of the producers remembers. "The history of Hollywood is, 'Yeah, you have points, try to get 'em.'"

KEN ESTIN: Now, nobody knew *The Simpsons* was gonna make $3 billion for Fox; we had no idea what we were losing on the merchandising. So [after the first season of *The Simpsons*] I hired my cousin just to do my negotiations—no lawyer, no real agent.

Fox comes to me and says, "We're all angry at each other right now and it's bad for everybody. We wanna be in business with you, so as a good-faith gesture"—they used these words or I never would've fallen for the ruse. They said, "As a gesture of good faith, we're willing to pay you all your piece of *The Simpsons* will ever be worth. We're willing to pay it to you now so you'll have the money now. You won't have to wait for it. Is that something that would make you feel better?" And my cousin says, "Why not, Ken? You'll take it. You'll invest it in real estate or something."

My cousin said to me, "They've told us that *The Simpsons* will never do well in syndication because it was on Fox instead of one of the regular networks."

I made the stupid mistake. I said, "Okay. As a goodwill gesture so we'll all work together again and let bygones will be bygones." Because Jim Brooks was furious at me, I said, "We'll bury the hatchet." Richard Sakai was my best friend and I said to Richard, "We'll bury the hatchet. I'll take the $400,000 less the $125,000 for my piece of *The Tracey Ullman Show* and *The Simpsons* together, and we'll all just forget this thing."

I sold my share for a net gain after my attorney fees of about

$250,000. I calculated that my share would've been worth about $10 million now, and I sold it for $250,000. I made the decision; nobody twisted my arm. But the bottom line was that when they said it was a good-faith gesture so we'd all work together, in my stupid, naïve way—and I was pretty young then—I really believed it. I later on discovered that they will say anything to anybody to make a deal.

Heide Perlman's the only one who said she wanted to stay in business with Jim Brooks. So she decided just to forget the whole thing. She did two television series with Jim and they both failed. Jerry Belson had been Jim Brooks's best friend for as long as I had known them, and they stopped talking.

Brooks and Belson's relationship went all the way back to Hollywood in the mid-sixties, when Belson, one of the youngest members of the guild, had been tapped by Carl Reiner to partner with Garry Marshall to write episodes of *The Dick Van Dyke Show*. They were part of a cabal of great comedy-writing friends that included Brooks's cocreator of *The Mary Tyler Moore Show*, Allan Burns. Jerry and Jim collaborated on projects, went on vacations with their families together, spoke nearly every day, and even celebrated holidays together.

A witness who was close to these events, and to both Brooks and Belson, related how, during *The Simpsons'* second season, Jerry Belson heard that Brooks had received a check for $6 million, while he himself had yet to receive anything. "Heard you got a big check," Belson joked with his friend over the telephone. "I'm looking forward to mine." Jim's response was reassuring, even cavalier: "Don't worry, babe, I'm taking care of you."

After more than year of waiting, with the deadline to pursue legal action fast approaching, Belson had still not seen any of the money his role as a producer of *Ullman* entitled him to. He asked his friend, "Jim, what am I supposed to do?" The answer was the same: "Don't worry, babe. I'm taking care of you. You're going to get more than you're even entitled to." Three weeks before the deadline approached, Belson complained to Brooks that he was putting him in an awkward position, forcing him to call a lawyer.

According to this witness, Brooks went "ballistic."

Belson had been diagnosed with cancer, and he and his wife, Joann, were raising a child who was severely handicapped. The last thing he wanted was to be entangled in a lawsuit. His lawyers advised him to settle. Fox was refusing to reveal how much money they were making from *The Simpsons*. Belson was looking at the daunting prospect of taking the Fox corporation to court and forcing the company to open up its books, a process that Fox could afford to drag on forever and was nearly impossible without Jim Brooks's help. Brooks held much of the leverage here. *The Simpsons* was Brooks's show; Fox wanted to keep him happy but had fewer reasons to care about Belson. "Do I want to face a team of lawyers who are going to hide everything anyway?" Belson asked. "If you don't have the support of Gracie Films, if Jim isn't going to stand behind his producers—you can't find someone who's going to jeopardize his job to go on the stand."

Belson, who has been described as unfailingly honest ("beloved" was the word most often employed), was devastated that his best friend and partner would betray him this way, all the while claiming that it was not his doing; it was Fox's. Other sources say that it was very much Jim and Gracie who were challenging the Ullman producers' claims. "Because that's who Jim is," the witness says. "He'll tell you whatever you want to hear, but it's not the truth. He's a businessman. There's never enough for Jim. It's a sickness." When all was said and done, Belson settled, taking approximately $100,000 for his percentage of *The Simpsons* that would be worth millions. A source from the Gracie side of things would not comment on whether Jim's behavior qualified as betrayal or not, saying only that Belson's claim was baseless.

Beslon and Brooks never spoke again. When a mutual friend tried to reunite them years later, Belson declined, asking how he could possibly be friends with someone who would stab his best friend in the back "for a few lousy bucks." Belson died of cancer in 2006. Brooks was deeply affected by Belson's death. Even though they had not spoken in nearly fifteen years, Brooks began to work the phone, speaking to many of their old friends, helping to organize a memorial for Jerry that would take place at Garry Marshall's theater. Although some of the friends they'd shared were surprised at

Brooks's participation, it was a sensitive time, and after all Jim Brooks was Jim Brooks, one of Hollywood's biggest machers; it was hard to say no. In addition, Brooks's involvement was seen as an expression of regret for what he'd done to his friend, especially when Brooks announced that at the memorial he would be speaking last. When his turn came, the expectation was that Brooks would finally own up to what he'd done, and as one attendee put it, "Be a mensch, take responsibility for what he did." To the shock of many, Brooks talked only about his and Belson's amazing relationship, painting a "convoluted" and "crazy" portrait of their crumbled friendship.*

To the even greater dismay of their friends, after the funeral Brooks came to the Belson house, where Joann was having a party for Jerry's "real" friends. One well-known actor who had known both men was overheard asking, "Doesn't he [Brooks] realize everyone here hates him?"

Belson and Brooks's former producing partners would not be the only casualties of the show's success. There was also Klasky-Csupo, the studio that had given the show its signature look. In January 1992, it was announced that *The Simpsons* had dropped Klasky-Csupo for Fim Roman.

SHERRY GUNTHER, animation producer, *The Simpsons* (1990–92): Part of the frustrations on the Gracie Films side was that they were used to working in live action and they were used to rewriting their show the night before air and reshooting those scenes. And with animation, there's six months' lead time between writing and air, so trying to allow them the ability to affect it and to make it funnier at any given point and to redo it is quite challenging.

BRIAN ROBERTS, editor, *The Simpsons* (1989–92): Whenever we'd get the animation back, the sitcom part of the writers would come out. They'd wanna rewrite all the dialogue.

---

*The memorial ceremony was described as part tribute, part roast. Another attendee remembers Carl Reiner's remarks as particularly hilarious. "It's a wonderful day to see you people together in the same room. I'm glad he died," Reiner said. "Then, after a long pause, he added, 'More of us should die. Gets you out of the house.'"

CHARLIE GOLDSTEIN, former executive vice president in charge of production, Fox Television: We were dealing with people like Brooks and Sakai, and everyone else who was used to having actors on stage and changing dialogue. Brooks was a multicamera guy, a comedy guy, of course. We produced *The Simpsons* shows like live shows. We actually used the animation process as rehearsals. We spent a lot of money on the first episode, because we actually did those kind of changes—but of course we were redrawing it each time and we were reanimating it, so it cost a fortune. We did that for the first episode and it cost double what we thought it was going to cost. More than double.

SHERRY GUNTHER: From day one they wanted a much bigger product than they were willing to pay for, and yet they didn't understand the process. They didn't understand the medium and the time involved. And, you know, they're the big guys. They're not used to being told no. But I kept thinking, Oh, my God, I can't animate this show overnight.

It was very challenging to try to keep everybody happy, 'cause you had a lot of young artists with no work ethic and who were feeling overworked and overwhelmed. And, on the other side you had Gracie Films going, "What do you mean, you can't do it? I want it redone frickin' tomorrow." And then you have Fox going, "What do you mean, it's gonna cost more?" The only reason I think Klasky got the job was that they were a complete unknown, because they bid at a small fraction of the price everyone else did.

In 1990, I came in and restructured and we had this big meeting at Fox, and they said, "This is the budget," and it was still minute. Minute. It was a fraction of what it is today. Salaries, quite frankly, haven't changed that much, and Fox said, "What?"

CHARLIE GOLDSTEIN: I can't remember exactly what the first episode was gonna cost. We probably spent three or four hundred thousand, which was humongous.

To address the network's financial concerns, a meeting was held at Fox, attended by Jim Brooks, Richard Sakai, John Dolgen, Harris Katleman, and several other Fox executives. The meeting, described by one of the execs as "difficult," turned into a screaming match and devolved into a he said/she said argument over the spiraling costs. Fox blamed Gracie Films, which in turn blamed Klasky-Csupo.

SHERRY GUNTHER: What happened was, in the very first season, we just ate it big-time and, you know, screamed for mercy. The second season we worked a lot of the problems into the schedule and the budget. And that's really when I was able to walk Fox through it and do a budget that was realistic.

But even with that, there were still tons of times when Gracie would say, "We wanna rewrite this whole script, or 80 percent of this script, after layouts." And so it was constantly a struggle. In the second season, I asked if we could just have revisions built in. We knew they were a fact of life. We'd been doing them. They are what make the show great. Why can't we just accept that they are part of the show? But Fox said, "No, no, no, no. That's ridiculous. Every time you get a change, you call us."

From Gracie's side, the problems had less to do with the overages than the personalities at Klasky-Csupo. "They were all nuts. They were all crazy," a former Gracie employee says. "They were great. They were young, hip, you know, wonderful artists. But, honestly, it was a madhouse."

SHERRY GUNTHER: We'd have these wonderful creative meetings with Gracie where they'd tell us what they wanted to do. Then I'd sit down with my director and he'd tell me what was involved. And then I'd have to call Fox and tell them how much it would cost. They'd call and scream at Gracie, and then Gracie would call and scream at me. It was really just not a great setup.

The situation was no single entity's fault. Fox's lack of experience in animation led to budgets that were unrealistic in the first place, while Brooks's staff's insistence on rewrites—after animation had already been completed—led to unforeseen overages, further exasperating those budgets. Klasky-Csupo, for its part, was described as "romper room," and the company seemed to be poorly managed, when you consider the fact that they never had a contract with Gracie. There was also, needless to say, an ego factor. Jim Brooks, Barry Diller, and the other Fox execs are not used to hearing the word "no" or not getting what they want. Add the strong-willed and "crazy" Gabor Csupo to the mix, and there were bound to be clashes down the line.

GABOR CSUPO, animation executive producer (1989–92): After [the first episode debacle], I think the whole relationship just kind of went downhill. Jim never really made any efforts to be friendly to us and treated us like second-class citizens. After three years of suffering, it came to a point where they made so many changes to the show that we as the animation company obviously couldn't swallow all the overages. My producers kept sending invoices back to 20th Century Fox saying that all these overages came from the fact that Gracie Films was rewriting the script last minute and then forcing us to reanimate. When they found this out they told me, "You have to fire your producers or we take the show away from you." And I said, "I cannot fire my producer because she's doing her job." So they told me they were taking the show away, and I said, "Be my guest." Because by that time, we'd been working around the clock for years without ever hearing a nice word from those guys. We felt completely abused.

SHERRY GUNTHER: The ironic thing in my eyes has always been that by the third season we had it down to a science and an art. That was honestly and objectively the best season of *The Simpsons*. They were the prettiest-looking shows. At the beginning of the third season, I was able to convince Fox to let us work at least the bulk of the changes into the budget. We were able to accommodate and do what was necessary, and it really was pretty friction-free. But by then, Gracie was intent on taking the show away. It became a vengeance thing.

CHARLIE GOLDSTEIN: I didn't want to leave Klasky-Csupo—they were doing great. I don't think they did a bad job; I think we did a bad job of managing the show. We. Me. Fox. The producers. Everybody. We let the show get out of hand. But it gets to a point where a show is doing so well on the air, way beyond expectations, and they just saw how much money they were gonna make in syndication and in merchandising that it didn't matter what it cost anymore.

SHERRY GUNTHER: It was not pretty. We had all put our lives into this thing, and it was definitely hard to take. It was our baby as much as anybody's in that sense, and it was particularly insulting because they ended up taking most of the crew with them.

Goldstein had hired an animation producer of his own, named Richard Raynis, whose job it was to make things run smoothly and keep the costs down. As far as the animation firm was concerned, his main job was in fact to analyze exactly what was being done at Klasky-Csupo, so they could easily move the show over.

 Gracie's side of the situation was that Klasky-Csupo's real problem was Gunther. Gracie saw her as "dishonest" and "utterly unreliable." The impression was that she was taking advantage of both Fox and Gracie, double-talking both parties and "gaming" them for money. Not only that, but her manner was regarded as high-handed, despite the fact that Klasky-Csupo was ultimately working for Gracie. Gunther, who was surprised to hear this was how Gracie saw things, noted that Fox never had any problems with the way she did her job, or with her personally, nor did Fox ever accuse her of "gaming" them [and she's right—they didn't]. She was a twenty-three-year-old kid, doing her best, but ultimately was just communicating Gabor Csupo's directives to Gracie, who were being uncooperative and demanding. Gracie demanded that Gunther be removed from managing *The Simpsons'* animation, but Gabor Csupo blatantly refused—despite the fact that keeping *The Simpsons* contract would have made him millions. (Gabor could easily have reassigned Gunther.) Gracie dumped them and took their business and most of Klasky-Csupo's staff to Film Roman, run by the genial and reasonable Phil Roman.

PHIL ROMAN, former owner of Film Roman: They explained to me that they were having problems with Klasky-Csupo, that they had some gal working on the project with whom they had communication problems. They told Gabor that he should replace her. He said, "You're not going to tell me how to run my studio."

So I went back to the studio and I called Gabor. And I asked, "Is this true?" And he said, "Yep. They've already told me they're going to be taking the show away from me." And I said, "Well, they offered it to me. I don't want it to appear like I'm working behind your back." And he said, "If they're going to give it to anyone I'm glad it's going to be you."

The great thing about that project was that all the crew from Gabor Csupo came along with them; the directors, I believe, were all under contract to Fox directly. So I didn't have to start from scratch, because the people that were already on the project came along with it.

SHERRY GUNTHER: It was kinda nasty. A few months before they told us they were gonna move, they said, "Let's get the directors under contract, but we want the contract to be with Fox."

And we said, "Okay. We think it's a great idea. We wanna keep these guys on the show 'cause they're key to doing it."

They put them on a contract with Fox so when they went to move, they had every right to take them. It was not really aboveboard—they basically took the entire crew and sat them down in a different studio. People would call me and say, you know, "The new producer over there is just literally walking around, going, 'What do you do? Okay, keep doing it. What do you do? All right, keep doing it.'"

GABOR CSUPO: Sam [Simon] was actually gracious. And Matt Groening, too. I can't say that they never praised any of the animators or anything. But what was coming from the top was what's important to us, from Jim Brooks and Richard Sakai. They were just truly ungrateful about all our hard work. We really felt that they never saw our hard work and they never really appreciated what we went through.

They just took two hundred of my people. The whole crew. It was a big, big crew, and basically they just walked over to Film Roman, because they knew the characters and all that. So that was a big loss, but at same time a blessing for us, because that's when Nickelodeon came by and we created six big shows for them.

DON BARROZO: It was kind of like being sent to a foster home. It was like you were uprooted from where you had grown up and sent somewhere else. And you had to get used to it. So it always felt like you were the adopted kid. Film Roman already had all these properties that were theirs, and *The Simpsons*, as successful as we were, was kind of treated like the stepchild. It was weird. But we were lucky to have a place to go.

SHERRY GUNTHER: It was disappointing and personal. It was embarrassing. It was everything that you'd assume it would be. But luckily, Klasky-Csupo still had the *Rugrats*, which was going strong, and we were in the process of selling *Duckman* at the time, and that went forward and became a successful show. And so we recovered from it, and it was certainly a relief to get rid of the negativity that went around, but it was definitely disappointing. We didn't wanna lose it.

DON BARROZO, animation editor, *The Simpsons* (1987–present): The whole vibe of the place was different. It felt very corporate. Klasky-Csupo was a small, almost family-run place. It had a real looseness to it. The intercom was going constantly with jokes. Film Roman was basically this single floor with cubicles, gray everything, and nothing on the walls. It was as if everybody had just been put in prison. It felt like, Oh, my God. Are we supposed to try and keep doing the show in a place like this?

Either because the production process was now so clearly defined, or because Roman's outfit was simply so much easier to deal with, the problems seemed to disappear. When Valerie Cavanaugh, one of the people at Gracie doing the search for a new animation house, called to interview Roman as a potential replacement, Roman was out of town, vacationing in his hometown, Fresno. A source says this strongly inclined Cavanaugh to go with Roman: apparently, after all the craziness and ego clashes with Klasky-Csupo, Kavanaugh liked the idea of someone who took vacations in Fresno. Roman, who could not be a nicer, more easygoing fellow, seemed to her to be the perfect antidote to Klasky-Csupo.

PHIL ROMAN: Gabor had told me they were so difficult to get along with, that they were demanding, and this and that—and I didn't find them like that at all. Anything they wanted was reasonable and those things that were unreasonable they paid for, so there was no real problem. It was a very pleasant situation. And then they did another series, *King of the Hill*, and we got that one too. We had a tremendous relationship with Fox: we met all their requirements, we didn't miss any deadlines, even when they had the North Ridge earthquake in the middle of production. We turned around and moved to another place and set up different units in different places and we didn't miss any deadlines.

Despite these successes (*Family Guy* would be another), Roman was eventually ousted from his own company. In 1996, Film Roman went public, with the goal of producing their own series. When the stock began to tank, the board decided they needed an MBA to run the company. They hired David Pritchard, an industry veteran with little experience in animation, leaving Roman in charge of creative. Pritchard, who almost immediately removed Phil Roman's name from *The Simpsons'* credits, replacing it with his own, complained that Roman's presence could undermine him. In early 1999, Roman was forced to resign from the company he built. Months later, when Film Roman's stock refused to recover, Pritchard was let go, and John Hyde was hired to replace him. Hyde asked Phil Roman—now running his own shop, Phil Roman Animation—to reclaim his old office at Film Roman. He was also given a place on the board. "I said, 'This is foolish. Move your office. Come back where you belong,' " Hyde told the *Los Angeles Daily News*. "He laughed, we shook hands, and that was it."

In 2003, Film Roman was acquired by Starz Media, a division of media conglomerate Liberty Media, Inc. Like the move to Film Roman from Klasky-Csupo more than ten years before, the complaints from the animators as the smaller outfit was absorbed by a much larger, more corporate studio had a familiar ring to them.

"We were no longer this little mom-and-pop operation that Phil Roman created with so much love for the artist," says an animator. "In the old building, you could write on the walls, you could run around naked, anything went. Now we were going into these stark white offices where you're not allowed to put stuff on the walls. There were so many rules, which for artists who were used to so much freedom, makes it a tough transition."

———

By 1993, Bart's animators had a new, stress-free home, and the *Ullman* producers were out of the picture, but there was one last exile to be imposed. Sam Simon remained a thorn in the side of Gracie Films. Their eventual victory over Sam Simon would not only be pyrrhic, financially speaking; it would also rob the show of perhaps its most creative voice.

TEN

Buddies, Sibs, Dweebs, and an Odd Man Out

In which free Butterfingers do not equal compensation . . . someone finally gives Harvard graduates a fair shake . . . and no one has very much sex.

While creative differences caused a divide in Matt Groening and Sam Simon's relationship, the division of *The Simpsons'* spoils created a chasm. After the first season, when the show was blowing up and the money started rolling in, Sam felt that he was not being appropriately compensated. Today, Simon has made more than $200 million from the show, but at the time, issues over money only added fodder to his war with Groening. "Once, Sam got an envelope from Fox, and opened it up, and looked at it, and angrily threw it down on the ground," says one witness from the early *Simpsons* days. "We knew it was a check, but we didn't know what it was for. Later, Sam stormed out of the room. We crept over to see what it was, and it was a check for $34,000, which Sam had felt was not enough for whatever his part of this payment was—it was merchandise—and that check sat there for a couple days on the floor. We all just looked at it longingly, 'cause to us it was still a lot of money."

DARIA PARIS, assistant to Sam Simon, *The Simpsons* (1989–94): I think a big issue came up when the merchandising started rolling in. And Sam was seeing a smaller portion of it than others, which wasn't really fair.

JAY KOGEN, writer/producer, *The Simpsons* (1989–92): I think Sam did okay. [Laughs] Part of it may have been money, but I think it was a combination of stuff.

GAVIN POLONE, former agent for Conan O'Brien, *Simpsons* writers; executive producer, *Curb Your Enthusiasm*: Back then, you used to make different deals than today. People got what was known as "adjusted gross." I think Sam may still be getting $50,000, $60,000, whatever, per episode.

BRIAN ROBERTS, editor, *The Simpsons* (1989–92): Matt used to be the king of merchandising. He would just sit in his office and sign posters and create more ways of doing merchandising. And meanwhile, Sam and the writing staff were churning out brilliant episodes. (And just as a side note, Fox is so cheap we never got any animation cels or anything. I couldn't even get one cel from the episode that I wrote. But there was no shortage of Butterfingers. You could always go up to Matt's office and grab yourself a big handful of Butterfingers, because those were free, because Matt signed that Butterfinger deal. No shortage of those. To this day, I can't eat a Butterfinger.)

The hatred between the two of them just became deeper and deeper for I don't know what reason. I think Jim sided with Matt. I don't understand it. I think Jim fell in love with the myth and the legend and said, "Hey, let's ride this deal." That was the beginning of the end, I think, for Sam.

Simon's demise at Gracie Films was gradual, and not surprisingly, Richard Sakai was involved in his being pushed out. Groening, who was being treated with contempt and disdain by Simon, often brought his complaints to Gracie. The Machiavellian Sakai, who was no fan of Sam's, and would eventually be at daggers drawn with Matt as well, leveraged these complaints to Matt's further indignation. One witness to Sakai's behavior recalls Sakai pressing Matt's buttons with incitements like, "Yeah, you know, [Sam's] really being ugly to you. He's like a toxic presence, isn't he? It's like he's poisoning the show."

Jim initially sympathized with Sam (who, it seems, really was being mean), because of their history and the fact that, in their hearts, they were both writers. As someone who knows both men put it, "If you woke Jim Brooks up at three in the morning and asked, 'What are you?' his answer would be 'a writer.' " Sam Simon was the same way. This put Sam in Sakai's sights (imagine Wayland Smithers watching someone getting close to Mr. Burns), and, according to one witness, he began ranting to Jim, "Sam didn't go to the color proof today. Sam was late at the rewrite room." He was relentless. It got to the point where Jim had to take meetings with Sam about his "transgressions."

A strand that recurs throughout *The Simpsons*' history, from Matt's *Life in Hell* to Gabor Csupo to Bart Simpson, is a distrust of authority. If there is one theme that connects the show's content with its formulation, it is this rebellious streak. And Sam Simon was no exception. Being called to task by Jim only provoked what was increasingly seen as Sam's "bad attitude." All of Sakai's whispering in Jim's ear, which earned him the nickname "Iago at Spago" around Gracie Films, was about to pay off.

After the first year of boffo *Simpsons* success, Gracie moved their offices to the Sony lot and made an exorbitant deal with ABC and its soon-to-be president, Bob Iger, to produce three series for that network. The first of these, *Sibs*, was a ratings catastrophe and a complete embarrassment when compared with the former successes from Jim Brooks advertised on its poster: "From the Creator of *Mary Tyler Moore*, *The Simpsons*, and *Taxi*. Three sisters who can't stay apart and one husband who can't relate—*Sibs*." ABC, who had paid for a *Simpsons* and received a *Fish Police*, was understandably upset.

Adding to the tension at Gracie was Sam Simon's clamoring for his share of *The Simpsons* loot. Sam felt that he was not being awarded the share of the *Simpsons* merchandising revenues to which he was contractually entitled, his contract being a complicated issue in itself. Before *The Simpsons* had ever aired, but after Simon had supervised the writing and production of the entire first season, his contract was still being negotiated (negotiations with Jim/Gracie were described to me as unusually complex and contentious by a number of sources). Early talks stalled, which caused Sam to walk away frustrated, and leave the contract negotiation to be finished after the show had aired. This would have been no problem if the show had tanked, but when it became a massive success, Gracie was in the unenviable position of making a contract with an executive producer for a show that was worth hundreds of millions, as opposed to the risky venture it had seemed when they'd first tried to nail down a deal in 1989. At some point during the second season, Sam finalized an agreement with Gracie, which gave him a chunk of the show, episode fees, and a portion of the merchandising revenues.

The continuing eruptions over Sam's share of the *Simpsons* merchandising was probably the beginning of the disintegration of Sam and Jim's relationship. Despite Sam's problems with Gracie Films and Jim, he was still contractually bound to show up for work every day and produce Gracie's shows. If he had quit, he would have had to walk away from any material interest in any of Gracie's productions, including *The Simpsons*. Gracie execs had motivation to make life difficult for Sam—for example, they threatened to put a report "in his file" about drinking on the set of *Sibs*, although many others were imbibing, including other Gracie execs—because if Sam was found to be in breach of his contract, he would lose his fees and back end points.

In 1992, Sam was made president of Gracie Television, a purely ceremonial title. The second series for ABC, *Phenom*, got decent ratings, but was quickly canceled by the network (one witness attributes this to ABC's being too furious with people at Gracie to continue working with them—countered by another who says the real issue was the poor ratings of the show, that ABC wouldn't cancel a real hit even if it were produced by Dr. Mengele). Sam held on, though. Finally, in 1993, after much posturing on both sides, Gracie and Sam cut a deal where he would agree to leave, but would retain his continuing back end and executive producer fees, and onscreen credit for the life of *The Simpsons*. Sam is still an executive producer of the show; he just doesn't have to do anything for his piece of *The Simpsons*, which provides him with $20 to $30 million a year to this day.

In terms of content, Sam is responsible for the episodes written in the first four seasons of *The Simpsons*, and even the first couple of episodes of Season 5.

The Simpsons is and always has been viewed as a "writers' show," which seems appropriate for a sitcom established under the umbrella of James L. Brooks. The writers/producers wield an enormous amount of influence, disproportionate to any other sitcom in the industry then or now. Under his supervision Simon placed two of the original writers in charge as official showrunners for Seasons 3 and 4: Al Jean and Mike Reiss. They were young and brilliant, and had both the savvy and the energy to continue on in Sam's tradition. While people will argue forever (mostly on the Internet) when the golden age of *The Simpsons* came and went, I believe it began during this period, with the show's finest episodes appearing between the second and sixth seasons. This was a time when the team Simon put together, building on the model he created, wrote amazing show after amazing show, making *The Simpsons'* voice distinctive and fully exploring the possibilities afforded to them.

Al Jean and Mike Reiss, mainstays of the original room, had previously written for the *National Lampoon*, *The Tonight Show*, *Alf*, and *It's Garry Shandling's Show*, but their friendship extended back to the *Harvard Lampoon* in the late seventies. There are a few tried-and-true paths to becoming a *Simpsons* writer, and one of them begins in Cambridge.

BILL OAKLEY, writer/producer, *The Simpsons* (1991–97): From Season 2 to Season 8, there was never a time that there were less than 80 percent *Harvard Lampoon* graduates on the staff.

TOM MARTIN, writer/producer, *The Simpsons* (1999–2001): I was maybe the first pure stand-up comedian to come to the show. I had been doing stand-up for about eight or nine years. Prior to Season 9, it had been pretty much an Ivy League institution, except for Mike Scully—he jokes about having gone to college for about a week, and then I think he actually did a little stand-up too. I'm sure I'm the dumbest guy to ever be on *The Simpsons* as far as SAT scores.

I never fit in for a lot of reasons. One reason is that, as Larry Doyle put it one day, "You remind me of the guys who used to beat me up in high school." And I thought, Well, that's strange. What do you mean? I think I was perceived by many of the group as too normal. In fact, after I left, they made a calendar of me, a "Hunky Tom Martin" calendar that they had in the room [fellow writer Ian Maxtone-Graham and sound

engineer Brian Koffman had trained with Martin for a triathlon relay—
hence the presence of "hunky" photos]. But the funny thing is, realistically it's like, No, no, guys, I'm handsome only compared to you. Not in
the real world. I'm strong and athletic only compared to you guys. But
that was what was funny about it. I'm writer handsome, writer strong,
but not really handsome or really strong.

DONICK CARY, writer/producer, *The Simpsons* (1996–99): A lot of these
guys had written on the *Lampoon* together in college, so they were sort
of falling back into their college routine, which was, basically, to hang
out all day and entertain themselves.

MICHAEL CARRINGTON, episode writer, *The Simpsons*; producer, *That's
So Raven, Cory in the House*: That's what my writing partner, Gary
Apple, always complained about. I'm from Syracuse University and he
was from Rockport. He said, "Why are the Harvard guys writing comedy? Us state school guys should be writing all the comedy and the Harvard boys should be running the country."

TOM WOLFE, author, *The Electric Kool-Aid Acid Test, The Right Stuff,
Bonfire of the Vanities*; guest voice, *The Simpsons*: I believe the sophistication of the show obviously comes from creative people who
have that same kind of education that writers either have or think
they have. I mean, most writers these days are well educated. It's true
that Hemingway, Steinbeck, Faulkner, Dreiser, if you put them all
together, you'd reach just about spring break of freshman year, but
most writers are well educated. There is so much sophistication and,
at the same time, it's done in a way so that it never loses the young
audience.

And of course, these days there are plenty of college writers, very
good ones, who don't want to write novels and they don't want to write
nonfiction. They want to write for television. And the prize is to write for
The Simpsons.

And it wasn't just *The Simpsons*. Beginning with Jim Downey (the
SNL godfather, beneath Lorne Michaels) in the late seventies, and
early *Letterman* in the eighties, television shows began to draw on

Ivy League talent for much of their writing. Graduates from Harvard and the Ivys came to dominate the staffs of shows like *Seinfeld*, *King of the Hill*, *Newsradio*, and *The Larry Sanders Show*.

TOM WOLFE: A fellow from Harvard, he was on the *Lampoon*—and they usually get very talented young people working on their magazine—was telling me how he wanted to write for television, and I said, "Write for television? You'll be anonymous. You'll never make a name for yourself. Name one television writer." Well, he named about three because they were all at Harvard when he was there, but he couldn't name a famous one.

Whether you were from Harvard or not, the writers room could be an intimidating place. Brent Forrester, who was a writer on HBO's widely respected *Mr. Show*, joined the room in the fifth season.

BRENT FORRESTER, writer/producer *The Simpsons* (1993–97); writer/producer, *King of the Hill*, *The Office*: Essentially, the way the show would go is: the scripts would come in, and they would be printed out, and everyone would have them in a kind of living room. And the head writer would say, "Okay. On page 3, we need a better joke for Homer." The room would go into silence . . . and then someone would dare pitch the first line for Homer. And there would be, hopefully, at least an appreciative chuckle. And then someone else would dare to do a line, and you would just go around.

It was so intimidating. There was one writer there who, for the first three months that I was on the *The Simpsons*, never said a word. Now, to be hired on a show to write jokes and never say a word is a true path to being fired. He knew he would be fired. But he just felt it would be better to be fired never having said something embarrassing in front of those guys. And after three months he got canned, never having pitched a joke.

My own method was to go off at lunch and try to anticipate what the next jokes would be that would need to be rewritten, and write jokes, and then come back to the room and pretend that I was coming up with them off the top of my head, which always gives them a little extra chance of getting in 'cause they seemed kind of spontaneous. That was the only way I felt comfortable competing with these legendary writers who had created and worked on *The Simpsons* for some time.

RICHARD APPEL, writer/producer, *The Simpsons* (1995–99): I don't think I opened my mouth for the first six weeks in that room. Part of it was my son had just been born. My son was, like most babies, not sleeping through the night, and there were some days where I didn't say anything not because I was intimidated but because I could barely focus. And I remember at one point actually falling asleep in the room, using that trick where you put your hand over eyes and make it look like you're deep in thought—I just could not keep my eyes open. In front of everyone Bill Oakley started snapping his fingers under my nose and saying, "You can't stay here, Grandpa! Come on!"

TIM LONG, writer/producer, *The Simpsons* (1998–   ): There was a stain on the roof when I walked in, and I remember saying, "What the hell is that?" And someone said, "Oh, I think that's where Conan threw a slice of pizza on the ceiling." And I had two simultaneous thoughts. The first was, Holy shit, I am in one of the Stations of the Cross of comedy—I've really arrived. And the second one was, Wait a second, Conan left five years ago.

When I got into *The Simpsons'* writing room it was like joining the Chicago Bulls at their peak and watching guys hit three-point shots from all over the court. I felt like I didn't belong there, like I should have been selling Amway instead.

I didn't know anything about how animation works, and on my first day we all sat down and watched the show, and I thought, I'm really getting paid to watch cartoons. But it turned out there were a few jokes they wanted to fix. There was a Homer line, and it was too late to change the animation, but we didn't like the joke. So we were pitching jokes that had to fit the syllable rhythm of how he was speaking. It seemed like such a crazy thing to have to do. I just remember these eight geniuses in the room with me, all pitching jokes that had the exact same syllabic format. That was the moment I really began to despair.

How a writer arrives at a particular joke defies description, but the process of contribution, and the very mood that lends itself to a room of writers collaborating on a script, can be fascinating.

RICHARD APPEL: You always felt it if an idea started generating a lot of buzz. If an idea just hangs there, no one has to say, "That's no good." You just know it, if you don't hear that crackle of voices. Any run on the show that makes you laugh started with someone pitching something that got people in the room to laugh and then start pitching on top of it.

The best scripts are rewritten 30 to 40 percent in the writers room. For [the episode when] Alec Baldwin and Kim Basinger were moving into town, we were going through what they call "tabling a script," which is preparing it for the table read. I had put in something about how Homer had been sent a congratulatory muffin basket from the Gersh Agency. The Gersh Agency is one of the most respected and powerful talent agencies for actors. At the time, though, I had no idea who they were. But I always saw these ads in *Variety* with "The Gersh Agency Congratulates . . ."

When we were tabling that, it was in a part of the script where Homer had violated Alec and Kim's trust and told some of their secrets. So I had it that Homer had to confess a secret. And we were pitching on what that secret should be. At one point it was decided that his secret was that he couldn't read. And everyone was cracking up and then there were all sorts of pitches about going through the seasons and all the times Homer had read, and we were thinking, Oh, my God, can we really say that he can't read? And then I burst out laughing, because not only in other episodes had he read, but four lines before, he had read the card from the Gersh Agency. And then George Meyer spit out, in Homer's voice, "I recognized their logo." *That* run would not have happened if it had been only one writer working by himself. Just the crackle of the table, that people were enjoying it, let you know that there was going to be something funny in this area.

BRENT FORRESTER: Then there was the joke about the comedy pants. I remember Mirkin used to think this was quite funny. If somebody pitched something hacky, there was this idea that some kind of old-fashioned clown pants would actually appear on your body. Somebody would pitch a joke, then someone else would say, "Here come the pants!"

TOM MARTIN: One day during a dead spot, we were waiting for something, and it was discussed how many girls each of these guys [the writers]—we called them the millionaire nerds club—had been with. One by one all the guys went around the room and admitted the number of women they had had sex with. Let's just say it was surprisingly low in many cases. And it pointed to the fact that this is a group of people who could solve any mathematical problem, any story problem, probably cure cancer, but hadn't figured out the mystery of how to get laid. That equation hadn't been solved.

TIM LONG: The funniest stuff is unrelated to the show, just crazy stuff about people's dating experiences, or their ridiculous families. One time Mike Reiss was telling a story, that I'm afraid I can't tell, about one of his cousins, and I remember laughing so hard, my face lying on the table, water pouring out of my eyes, and I remember thinking, I have to stop, otherwise I'm going to have a stroke . . . I could die here. I'm six minutes into this laugh and it's not ending. That's not an atypical experience. And I'm not an easy laugh.

In later years, the writers were aware that the show could never come close to what it had been under the supervision of the original writing room (plus Conan, Josh, and Bill). After the original room dissipated, later writers considered themselves less pioneers than keepers of the grail. It was their job to try and keep the show up to the incredible standard established by the first four seasons.

BRENT FORRESTER: There was a sense that it had become the greatest show ever, and that it was our job to be guardians of it. And we felt that we were failing, for the most part. And then sometimes we'd go, "Oh, you know what? That one's up there with the best." There was that sense of, We have an obligation to fans like ourselves to keep this thing at the top of its game. And I did feel that we were doing that, you know, some percentage of the time. Certainly not 100 percent of the time, not even close. Maybe 30 percent of the time, or 25 percent? So that was definitely the big motivating factor. And we felt that we were struggling to do so.

As with any collaboration, where there is passion, there is the occasional conflict, though nothing close to the maelstrom of the early days, with Matt Groening and Sam Simon's war.

DONICK CARY: There were different kinds of writers there. And occasionally there'd be, writers about whom you were thinking, Jeez, I don't like his style, really. But that was the nice thing about the balance of the show. I'm sure there were people who didn't like my style of jokes. But, ultimately, at the end of the show, you have twenty different styles of jokes in there. It's a pretty rich, full, fun thing.

Well, there are a lot of Harvard guys, guys who had been lawyers. But then you'd be talking about a joke, and suddenly you'd realize it's not about the joke anymore—it's about winning the court case. And you're like, "Okay, guys. This doesn't matter anymore—let's get back to work."

TOM MARTIN: It was like big Irish family kind of stuff. I think the first time I met Dan [Greaney], I wanted to punch him in the face, but eventually he became one of my best friends. He can't help himself from being too brutally honest. And most people are pretty polite to George [Meyer] because he's earned it and he's older and he's usually in a place of authority. But Dan would go after George, and I think they have this intense rivalry and intense respect for each other, but it did get very heated at times between those two.

DONICK CARY: I love 'em both, Dan Greaney and George Meyer. Somehow the two of them together had a way of really getting under each other's skin. And, you know, it was definitely like, Oh, Mom and Dad are fighting. Greaney's a former lawyer, and George is a supersmart guy who wants, logically, to argue out a point. And if those two hit on a topic that they disagreed on, we could spend hours of tense talking it through.

TOM MARTIN: I think that they almost came to blows at one point, but again, it wasn't while I was there. While I was there, it was just two brilliant guys trying to one-up each other with hilarious comments.

Another witness, who could not recall the subject of the debate, remembers a time when he was thankful there was a wide table between Meyer and Greaney, because he was certain that Meyer (a dedicated pacifist) was ready to reach across and throttle Greaney. For his part, Greaney is remembered as a pit bull, someone who just could not stand down from a challenge. Once, during his days at

Harvard, a gang of townies accosted Greaney and threw a bottle, which smashed near where he was walking. Greaney could not resist yelling something back. He woke up in the hospital—and has a large scar on his head as a souvenir of the incident.

Former staffers remember the conflicts between Meyer and Greaney as a rivalry that at times got heated, but nothing more, and the two men remain friends. Overall, the atmosphere at *The Simpsons* was occasionally tense, sometimes boring, more often rigorous, and regularly hilarious.

One story that found its way out of the writers room involves a showrunner having to side with his wife, who had mistakenly sent an e-mail to the wife of another *Simpsons* writer, in which the former had called the latter a "cunt." The first writer's wife claimed that she had never written the e-mail, that her e-mail account had been the victim of a hacker from France. Back in the writers room, where the story was making the rounds, the showrunner had to back up his wife's hacker story, which sounded, as a former *Simpsons* writer described to me, like "a crazy lie." The other writers at the show delighted in the affair, dubbing it "cuntgate."

TIM LONG: You kind of get used to it. Like I'll be driving home and I'll think, Well that was just a normal day, but then I'll start thinking about it and I realize there were a couple moments during the day when I laughed until I cried. How many people can say that about their job?

The Simpsons is just the best place in the world to work. Sometimes I remind myself, "I have the best job in North America, and I'm still not that happy a person. What is wrong with me?"

TOM MARTIN: It was like getting on the Lakers, but it was like getting on the Lakers with Kobe and Shaq, but also on the same team were Magic Johnson and Kareem Abdul-Jabbar and Jerry West and Wilt Chamberlain. No one ever left, so it was very hard to get the ball, and that was one of the problems with being a newer guy and not one of the older guys. It's tough to make an impact, though that doesn't mean it's impossible. I mean, Matt Selman certainly did it and Tim Long did it, but it makes it a little tough.

TIM LONG: I'm one of the executive producers. As people stay at *The Simpsons*, their titles get higher and higher, so there is just a tsunami of co-executive and executive producers. It's one of those places that once you get there, there's no point in leaving. What are you going to do after *The Simpsons*? Are you going to write jokes for *According to Jim*?

ELEVEN

Conan

In which a dead bird makes us rethink signs from God . . . a very nervous writer gives a security guard a heart attack and Selma Bouvier a baby . . . and Fox trades the next Johnny Carson for $100,000 worth of hair gel.

If there is a single example of *The Simpsons'* writing room's influence on television, it is its most prominent alumnus: Conan O'Brien. Since taking over from David Letterman as the host of *Late Night* in 1993, O'Brien's 12:30–1:30 hour of edgy, smart comedy has been the best television has to offer, post–prime time. In 2008, it was announced that O'Brien would follow the footsteps of Steve Allen, Jack Paar, and Johnny Carson to succeed Jay Leno as the host of *The Tonight Show.* Conan's sharp yet convivial and self-deprecating style has won him legions of fans, among them many of the celebrities who appear on his show. And like Carson, he's promoted more than his share of young, progressive comedians (Andy Richter, Dave Attell, Will Ferrell, and Demetri Martin, to name a few), developing a reputation as one of TV's most insightful, generous, and genuinely nice people and becoming a true titan of the airwaves.

His unlikely trajectory through Springfield began on a familiar course: the *Harvard Lampoon,* a stint writing on another comedy show (*SNL*), and then *The Simpsons'* writing room. Of course, after his three years with Bart and Homer, O'Brien's path would deviate drastically. "Nobody becomes that famous unless he shoots a president," says his friend and fellow *Simpsons* writer Jay Kogen. It's hardly presumptuous to suggest that O'Brien brought his experience from *The Simpsons* with him to *Late Night,* and then *The Tonight Show,* spreading elements of its unique comedic voice to millions of viewers every night (without discounting O'Brien's amazingly singular style).

O'Brien was fresh from writing for *Saturday Night Live* when he joined *The Simpsons*. When not cracking up his fellow writers and contributing to their scripts, he managed to craft memorable episodes, such as "Marge vs. the Monorail" (a takeoff on *The Music Man*, in which a straw-hatted shyster sells Springfield a dilapidated monorail) and "Homer Goes to College" (Homer lives out his college fantasies, which have been informed entirely by eighties *Animal House* rip-offs). One of his fellow writers ventured that if Conan hadn't left to do *Late Night*, he was a shoo-in to take over as showrunner on *The Simpsons*.

BRENT FORRESTER, writer/producer, *The Simpsons* (1993–97); writer/producer, *King of the Hill*, *The Office*: Conan was famous among comedy writers. He's maybe one of the only guys I've ever known in the writing community who could be famous just as a writer.

CONAN O'BRIEN, writer/producer, *The Simpsons* (1991–93): I was working at *Saturday Night Live*. It was fall of '91 and it was time for all the writers to come back on *Saturday Night Live*, and I just realized I was burnt out. [*New York* magazine reported that, at the time, O'Brien's self-esteem was at an all-time low: a sitcom pilot he'd made had not been picked up, and his engagement to be married had fallen through].

I told Lorne Michaels I couldn't come back to work and I just needed to do something else. I had no plan whatsoever. I was literally in this big transition phase in my life where I decided, I'll just walk around New York City, and an idea will come to me.

And this is one of those stories that aspiring TV writers everywhere must hate, but my phone rang, and it was Mike Reiss and Al Jean, and they said, "We heard that you just left *Saturday Night Live*. Would you be interested in working at *The Simpsons*?" So I said, "Yes!" *The Simpsons* was sort of notorious at the time. I think they had done a couple of seasons. Everyone wanted to be on that show, but they never hired. I think they were still going off the original crew. I told them, "Look, I've never written a *Simpsons* episode. I've never written a sitcom script," but I had a good reputation at that point, so I think on the strength of that they just said, "Well, come on."

It was such a quick thing. I quit *Saturday Night Live* and I went out and bought a '92 Ford Taurus, the SHO (Super High Output), by the way—I don't want you to get the wrong idea—a stick-shift model; the ladies go crazy for it. I had just bought it when the call came, and I thought, Well that's all right. I'll have a really cool time, I'll tell them I can't be there for like five weeks, and I'll do like a cool, Jack-Kerouac-in-a-Ford-Taurus, driving cross-country, and I'll grow a beard and wear an eye patch. I had all these romantic ideas, and they said, "No. We need you here in two days." So I was depressed about that and I remember driving out to Waltham, Massachusetts, and driving the Taurus onto the back of one of those big trucks that will ship it across country, and then getting on a plane.

And when I showed up, Jeff Martin was away doing something and they temporarily gave me his office. I was very nervous about this new job. I knew a bunch of the people on the show, but just by reputation. I had never really worked with many of them. I was self-conscious and worried. Could I do it? Am I going to embarrass myself in front of these people? Because I had never worked with Mike Reiss and Al Jean, I had never worked with George Meyer, Vitti, Swartzwelder. It's an intimidating collection of people if you're a comedy writer.

I was very nervous when I started. They showed me into this office and told me to start writing down some ideas. They left me alone in that office. I left after five minutes to go get a cup of coffee. I heard a crash. I walked back to the office, and there was a hole in the window and a dead bird on the floor. Literally, in my first ten minutes at *The Simpsons*, a bird had flown through the glass of my window, hit the far wall, broken its neck, and fallen dead on the floor. George Meyer came in and looked at it, and said, "Man, this is some kind of weird omen."

WALLACE WOLODARSKY, writer/producer, *The Simpsons* (1989–92): He was already a little bit of a legend, of being one of the funniest people. I think it came from his days at the *Lampoon* and then *Saturday Night Live*.

JOSH WEINSTEIN, writer/producer, *The Simpsons* (1991–97): Some of the best memories from the show are with Conan. Every day Conan was in the room it was like a ten-hour Conan show, nonstop.

CONAN O'BRIEN: In the Dick Van Dyke analogy I might have been Morey Amsterdam. I think when I first got there I stood out a bit because everyone sat still in the room and thought, and it wasn't too long before I was climbing on furniture. I would pitch the characters in their voices because I thought that's just what people did, but then Mike Reiss told me nobody does that.

ROBERT COHEN, production assistant, *The Tracey Ullman Show*, *The Simpsons* (1989–92): He was really smart, and pop culture–wise he knew everything—I just remember he was *so quick*. The guy was lightning fast, and I think infused that room with some great comedic energy.

WALLACE WOLODARSKY: Conan used to do this thing called the Nervous Writer that involved him opening a can of Diet Coke and then nervously pitching a joke. He would spray Diet Coke all over himself, and that was always a source of endless amusement among us.

CONAN O'BRIEN: There were different bits that I would do, and the writers would call for them. There was one where I would go to the refrigerator and I'd get a Coke and I'd fill my mouth with Coke and then I'd start twitching, wildly of course, and vibrating my head and the Coke would foam up and come out of my mouth and it looked like I was having this horrible fit. And I don't know why—it doesn't sound funny—but people really enjoyed it.

   I was sort of the monkey in the room. They would say, "Okay, do that thing!" "Go do this!" or "Go do that!" and I would do it. I was very happy to. "Oh, you want one of those ones? All right, fellas, I'll give it to ya. You want number eighteen? I'll do it." I had a lot of sugar energy; I still do. I wasn't able to sit still.

BRENT FORRESTER: Conan had a number of bits. Late at night in *The Simpsons'* writers room—you know, everybody working late—a security guard would come by and make sure that everything was okay in various offices on the lot. He came by and said, "Okay, everything's good in here? All right, fine." And Conan just happened to be standing by the door. And then, when the security guard turned to leave, Conan said, "Everything's just fine, indeed!" And then he did like a fake double karate chop on the guy's neck. [Laughs] And that was just considered hilarious—like vintage Conan O'Brien. Give the security guard a double karate chop on the neck.

Another famous bit: Conan would pretend to be talking about someone and not want that person to hear—but put his hand on the wrong side of his mouth. That, alone, was considered really funny.

Another of Conan's digressions involved a product named Jub, which he talked about often. He and other writers used to riff about horrible commercials for it, where the people would just say "jub jub jub jub jub jub jub" over and over, as many times as they could before they ran out of time. Or they would have a startling attention grabber, with someone yelling "There's trouble at the school!" followed, of course, by "jub jub jub jub jub." In the fourth season, Selma inherited an iguana from her great-aunt Gladys. In tribute to Conan, the writers named it Jub Jub.

JAY KOGEN, writer/producer, *The Simpsons* (1989–92): He had a small apartment in Beverly Hills, but it was nothing fancy. He had these nice guitars. You'd bring beer or soda, and you'd hang out and there'd be funny people there.

Writers are generally of an ilk, and they tend to make jokes more than communicate their true feelings and emotions. We're not an emotive bunch. We take pride in being silly and making jokes, even at the expense of each other. And that's the relationship, so sometimes we don't know each other on a deeper level. But Conan and I actually had a nice relationship. I feel I knew Conan at a deeper level. We had serious talks.

CONAN O'BRIEN: When I look back at the stuff I did at the *Lampoon*, and I look back at the stuff I did writing sketches for *Saturday Night Live*, I realized that I've always had a very visual sense of humor. Even when I was on the *Lampoon*, I drew a lot of cartoons, and even my written pieces had a cartoonish element to them. I realized later it was always important to me on the *Late Night* show that things *look* funny. Words are important, but I always thought there should be an element of things you do on the show that might be funny even if you had the sound off.

I was very influenced by Warner Bros. cartoons and silly physical humor, the Peter Sellers *Pink Panther* movies and things like that. When I came to *The Simpsons*, that was a big release for me. I finally found myself in an animated world, and people could create what I was talking about. If you had a strange idea for something in Mr. Burns's basement, or a monorail system snaking through the town of Springfield, it could happen. I remember it being a little bit of an aha! moment.

BRENT FORRESTER: *The Simpsons* was not initially cartoony. The first few seasons, it was an animated show about a family that was highly realistic. The conventional wisdom is that the show changed after the monorail episode, written by Conan O'Brien. Conan's monorail episode was surreal, and the jokes were so good that it became irresistible for all the other writers to write that kind of comedy. And that's when the tone of the show really took a rapid shift in the direction of the surreal.

But Conan had a little too much energy for the writers room. When David Letterman announced he was moving to the 11:30 spot at CBS, NBC began looking for a replacement to host *Late Night*. Lorne Michaels thought of Conan.

JAY KOGEN: He'd always said, "I've got this thing with Lorne Michaels, and we're trying to put something together, and I really want to be on TV."

GAVIN POLONE, former agent for Conan O'Brien, *Simpsons* writers; executive producer, *Curb Your Enthusiasm*: Lorne came to him wanting him to produce the show, and in a nutshell we sort of said, "Lorne, this is not the direction he wants to go, to be a producer. He wants to perform." Lorne started talking to him, and while Conan was mulling it over, NBC was talking to different people about taking the job. There weren't that many people they'd want. And at the same time I think a lot of people were also resistant to the idea of taking Letterman's job because they'd be compared to him. So at some point or another we started talking about the fact that Conan would like to host his own show. And Lorne wasn't totally against it. There was some discussion about him doing 1:30 if Greg Kinnear was gonna move up to 12:30. But Greg Kinnear wanted to be an actor, so that didn't fully work out.

WALLACE WOLODARSKY: We had left the show and then we heard that Lorne Michaels was talking to Conan about being the guy to replace Letterman. And it made complete sense to us, because Conan was so funny. We never would have thought of it in a million years, but as soon as you heard it, it made sense.

GAVIN POLONE: We came to this agreement that they would do a test with Conan on *The Tonight Show*'s stage and see how it went. So we furiously put that together. We got Jason Alexander and Mimi Rogers to be the guests, and Conan worked on a monologue—and he did a great job.

WALLACE WOLODARSKY: One of the weirdest experiences of my life was going to see Conan's tryout for *Late Night*, because it was done on the stage at *The Tonight Show*. That was back when Johnny Carson was still hosting the show (the curtain looked a certain way—it was this multicolored curtain), and seeing this friend of yours, this guy that you worked with, walk out from behind that curtain and deliver a monologue was like something you could only dream up that you couldn't ever imagine actually happening.

The whole thing was being beamed back by satellite to New York, where Lorne Michaels was watching and probably other NBC executives.

So Conan came out and did an approximately twenty-minute version of a talk show. And then we all ran down and hung out on *The Tonight Show* stage, because we couldn't believe it, and sat in the guest chair and did all the stuff that a tourist would do.

COLIN A.B.V. LEWIS, postproduction supervisor, *The Simpsons* (1989–97): It was like, They're not gonna hire Conan. He's a writer. Then it happened.

CONAN O'BRIEN: I have to tell you, it was pretty harrowing, and it's a part of my life that I wouldn't . . . I'm glad that part's over. Because it was just such a giant transition.

I remember very clearly: we had just done a script. It was the day we were going to record an episode and we were all sitting around this table. A phone rang and someone said, "It's for you, Conan." It was my agent,

Gavin Polone, and he just said—it was probably like ten o'clock in the morning—and he said, "You're the new host of *Late Night*."

COLIN A.B.V. LEWIS: The day he got hired, Conan came over to hide, basically, in our offices. And he was just lying on the floor, in a doorway, hands over his head, like, Oh, my God! It was just so bizarre.

MICHAEL MENDEL, postproduction supervisor, *The Tracey Ullman Show*, *The Simpsons* (1989–92, 1994–99): He was passed out facedown into this horrible shag carpet. He was just quiet and comatose down there on that carpet. I remember looking at him and saying, "Wow. Your life is about to change, in a really dramatic way."

CONAN O'BRIEN: It was a feeling of, You've just been handed a huge responsibility. It was a little bit like being told, "You've just been designated as the first American to fly to Mars and back." So you're excited, because part of your dream has always been to see Mars, but there's also a feeling that you're probably gonna be killed.

COLIN A.B.V. LEWIS: He's going to be the new Letterman, and I think it just hit him once he got the job. Wow. That was amazing. It was almost like the scene from *Goodfellas*, except that, you know, he didn't get whacked. He actually became a made man.

CONAN O'BRIEN: Everyone heard the news, and John Swartzwelder— he's this incredibly good-looking guy; he looks like a turn-of-the-century constable; he looks like someone who would arrest an anarchist for throwing a bomb at Archduke Ferdinand's carriage—was sitting there and smoke was trailing off his cigarette. He just looked at me and said, "I'd watch your show." And that meant a lot to me, because he's not a guy who will say something he doesn't mean.

And I thought, Well, I got John Swartzwelder, I've got one viewer, anyway. And other than that I remember not seeing anybody too much after that.

I didn't own a suit. I just had a zip-front jacket and three pairs of jeans. So Gavin bought me two suits, 'cause I had to go in and people had to get a look at me. Someday I gotta write it all down. It was a shock to the system, I'll put it that way.

GAVIN POLONE: Conan had a bunch of clothes [before Gavin took him shopping], and me and him were standing out in the parking lot, you know, looking at different sport coats that he had in the trunk of his Ford Taurus.

CONAN O'BRIEN: Some executive at Fox—who I don't remember, and that's probably for the best—said, "No, no, no. He still owes us money on his contract." It was like a year's salary or something. So I think NBC paid half, and I paid half. I actually had to pay my way out of Fox, which always felt a little strange. I'm sure Simon Cowell has that money now. He's using it on hair gel.

GAVIN POLONE: So then, after NBC wanted him, Fox would not let him out of his contract. It was really shocking, actually, because we thought they would. I think it was a guy named Steve Bell, really hard-assed us and I'll never forget it. They actually demanded money. And it wasn't a situation where he was going to compete against them. They could have built goodwill, and they just dispensed with all of that, so they could try to squeeze a writer (who wasn't making huge money to begin with) out of $100,000. It's pretty funny.

BOB KUSHELL, writer/producer, *The Simpsons* (1994–95): I had come in right after he left, but everybody was egging him on, wanting him to succeed, loved him. *Loved him.* But was very critical of him.

Every day at lunch we watched an episode of the Conan O'Brien show—I believe Jennifer Crittenden brought in the tapes of the show from the night before—and we deciphered it, talked about his progress, and I remember vividly everybody yelling at the TV, "Oh, this intro is too long!" And, "You don't have to set things up like that, Conan," because everybody knew him.

And subsequently all of those bad habits that Conan had at the beginning went away. He is so enormously talented at what he does, but just to be a part of the group, his close-knit group of friends watching him go through those growing pains, was very funny and very exciting.

BRENT FORRESTER: You know, Conan had wanted to hire me for his new *Late Night* show. I'd come off of *Mr. Show*. Bob Odenkirk (creator and star with David Cross of *Mr. Show*) was the big writer—the guy we all worshipped—and Odenkirk knew Conan O'Brien. And when Conan started up his new show, he said, "Who are the good writers?" And Bob said, "You should hire Forrester."

And Conan called me up. I told him I'd do it. He just got me fired up—I wanted to work on the show so badly. David Mirkin had taken over as *Simpsons* show runner and was in communication with Conan. And when Conan told him he was going to hire me, Merkin said, "Aha—over my dead body."

They hired me at *The Simpsons* basically to replace Conan. Mirkin poached me. And I felt so bad about telling Conan that I would do his show and then bailing on it to do *The Simpsons*, which was a no-brainer. I couldn't go on this unknown talk show, as opposed to like the greatest show on TV at the time. But I felt that I had betrayed Conan's trust by having said I would. So, as a goodwill gesture, I sent him four ideas that he could do on his show—and two of them he did. One of them was: "When you start your show, act as if you don't have enough money to do live satellite feeds. And then just show a photo of the person you're interviewing and animate the lips." [This became a famous *Late Night* bit.] And, interestingly, they dropped the premise.

And then, of course, the merging of the two heads became a signature bit of theirs. [Conan shows photographs of two celebrities, then combines their worst/weirdest features to see what the couple's offspring would resemble.] What's funny is, to this day, if I submit a list of ideas—story ideas, for example—to *The Office*, I always title them, so that they stand out on a page. And I titled that bit "If They Mated"—M-A-T-E-D. Which, on the page, scans okay—but coming out of your mouth is very ungainly. And always sounds like "If They Made It." But, for some reason, they never changed the name of the bit. And it sounds wrong to me. It's just an example of, If I knew you were gonna use this, I would have given it a better title. And they actually made a book of it. The book is called *If They Mated*. And Conan mentions that I came up with the idea and then wouldn't work on his show.

WALLACE WOLODARSKY: In those early years, periodically we'd go to New York and visit Conan. It took me years to believe he was actually hosting the show. All these years later I haven't fully digested that Conan O'Brien became the host who followed David Letterman. I still don't believe it.

TWELVE

Institutionalized

In which Marge teaches me everything I ever wanted to know about sex but was afraid to ask . . . shockingly, Smithers likes the work of Tennessee Williams . . . nerds like the Internet . . . and very few people like a short, fat, cynical movie critic.

The cooling off of Bartmania might have meant some smaller ratings (and an eventual return to Sunday night, where *The Simpsons* has happily sat since 1994), but it gave the writers an opportunity to take their explorations even farther. Between Seasons 2 and 6, the writing became more jam-packed with jokes and clever allusions, the social satire grew richer, and yet the emotional resonance was maintained and sometimes even deepened. The golden age of *The Simpsons* coincided with the show's expansion into foreign markets, its move into syndication, and the popularization of the Internet—all factors that solidified *The Simpsons* as an institution, not just a hot TV show of the moment. Episodes like "Mr. Plow," "I Love Lisa," and "Flaming Moe's" were widely referenced and quoted, becoming ingrained in the young audience that lapped up the show each week.

GERARD JONES, satirist, media critic: You know, *The Simpsons* clearly seemed to come, to some extent, out of the Reagan culture, the "Let's go back and pretend we are the country we pretended we were in the fifties."

After this flirtation with the fake wholesomeness that people went through, I think it was crucial to George H. W. Bush to stay the course. But he didn't have that same weird charisma of Reagan to make it seem somehow plausible. So it began to shake apart. I think the Bush years were about everybody catching on to the phoniness of the cultural aspects of the Reagan revival, which I think in turn opened us up to buy more of the funny, hip, sleazy charm of the Clintons. They had a weird quality about them that people were open to, especially since things were going fairly well. The cold war had been won, there was no new boogeyman. Americans in general just rolled with our own ease at that point, with our own cynicism.

That made a context where *The Simpsons* felt really mainstream and relevant as opposed to antimainstream and relevant. It felt comfortable and familiar and it could be more of an up-the-middle hit instead of the more troublemaking, out-of-the-urban-left hit it was early on. In the beginning there had been a fairly big anti-*Simpsons* backlash, at least from the conservative end of the media and the culture. Not just conservative in the sense of political right wing, but people who worry about things changing too quickly and in a bad direction, which often includes a lot of liberal psychologists and parents and educators. All of them saw Bart as this sort of terrible role model for kids, and there was a big fear of this kind of stuff.

Pretty soon they certainly weren't worrying about *Simpsons*. By about '94, they probably started watching it and it became wholesome and ordinary.

Personally, from the mid-nineties onward, I cannot remember ever hearing someone being booed without the refrain of "Are you saying 'Boo' or 'Boo-urns'?" following soon after. My peers and I recognized the smell of Otto's jacket, we knew that food could taste like burning, and that things were funny because they were true. We wanted to try "efficient German sex" with anyone who would "Choo Choo Choose us" and were aided and abetted in our efforts by alcohol, which was confirmed as the cause of and solution to all life's problems.

Like *Seinfeld* and *Friends*, as the show progressed, viewers became more attached to the characters. But in terms of plot and setting, animation allowed the characters to go anywhere, anytime, realistically (within *The Simpsons'* world), in a matter of frames. Homer could grow hair overnight, his new appearance catapulting him to the position of executive at the power plant; Bart and Lisa could take over their summer camp with force; we could follow Homer's snowplow business from start-up to success to ruin. Like other sitcoms, "crazy" things could happen each week, with everything going back to normal by the end of the episode, but with greater deftness, creativity, and excess. The writers became expert at portraying the Simpsons' relatable struggles in their increasingly crazy lives: the impotence and alienation of childhood, the drudgery of work, the ills of consumerism and the media that preach its saving graces, the lackluster and faceless institutions that dominate our lives. In other words: they kept it real.

Perhaps animation's greatest asset was that it allowed the characters to remain physically identical from show to show, year to year. If Bart were a real ten-year-old at the beginning of the show, it is hard to believe that his antics could interest us past age twelve. A pubescent Bart is scary, a teenage Bart is depressing, and anything past that is really too terrible to contemplate. Imagine an audience's response to one of Kramer's silly entrances after Michael Richards's racist rant of 2008. How about sweet little Stephanie Tanner's morphing into a methhead in front of our eyes? Real people get old. And unappealing. And crazy. Animated people stay exactly the same, and in so doing solidify their identities within an audience, which parlays into ongoing resonance.

Animation also provided a cover; you could talk about subjects and show content that you couldn't with live-action shows. There were elements of satire on *The Simpsons* that, if they weren't too risqué for other shows—not to mention completely incongruous coming out of the mouth of Urkel, Kimmy Gibbler, or Tim Taylor— were too nuanced. In the episode "Radio Bart," from Season 3, Bart plays a trick on the town, convincing everyone that a boy named Timmy O'Toole is trapped down a well. While Marge is saying grace before the family's TV dinner, she asks God to watch over little Timmy, and Bart bursts out laughing.

> MARGE: Bart! What's wrong with you?
> HOMER: Yeah! That Timmy is a real hero.
> LISA: How do you mean, Dad?
> HOMER: Well, he fell down a well . . . and can't get out.
> LISA: How does that make him a hero?
> HOMER: Well, it's more than you did!

Lisa and Homer's exchange is interrupted by Kent Brockman's news report, which includes a feature on Krusty the Clown's gathering of celebrities, "who normally steer clear of fashionable causes," to record a music video for little Timmy, "We're Sending Our Love . . . Down the Well." The exploitation of local tragedies by the media, celebrities, and citizens would have been difficult to lampoon on any other sitcom; it would be too dark, or too complex, for *Family Matters* or *Home Improvement*. Those shows were made for the people who called well victims "heroes," not those of us who might laugh at that notion. News networks, and not just local ones, are famous for putting victims on display and treating them as people to be celebrated. Whether it's young white women who go missing, trapped miners, or victims of shark attacks, the media relishes these events because they stir up a gut reaction that is quite profound: this could happen to us. The cultural catharsis that takes place isn't so dissimilar to what happens when a joke is told: a deep-seated feeling of dread that we could be the victim, and relief that it is someone else.

There was also elasticity in terms of the show's permissible content, far beyond the violent stranglings of Bart. Season 3's episode "Bart the Lover" opens with Bart's class watching a 1960s-era informational movie about zinc in which a teenager is so despondent about living in a world without zinc that he tries to shoot himself (the gun doesn't go off—the firing pin is made of zinc). No live-action show, then or now, could show a character putting a gun to his head and pulling the trigger. It's too horrific. But not only could *The Simpsons* show attempted suicide, it could get a laugh from it.

In a Season 1 episode, Homer, depressed by the loss of his job and not being able to support his family, tied a large stone to his body and walked toward a bridge, intending to end his life. At the last moment, he was saved by his family. Pretty dark stuff, and really not permissible in anything but a cartoon—Mr. Belvedere may have had his sad moments, but they would never have showed him sitting in front of a bag of sleeping pills and a bottle of Jack.

This sensibility was aided by the long lead time of production, which forced the writers away from topical humor and was conducive to timeless, more intelligent jokes. They stayed far away from the snappy, snarky humor that had become the norm in family sitcoms. A typical scene from *Home Improvement* in 1993 had the father figure, Tim "The Toolman" Taylor, coming home to find out from his wife that his two eldest sons had played a trick on the youngest. Within five lines of dialogue, the father made fun of the mother's cooking and revealed himself as bumbling and gullible, while the mother told her son, "Honey, you're eight years old now, it's time we had this talk: stop being such a sap!" Compare this with a run of jokes revolving around a domestic Simpsons scene from the same period. Homer is lying on the couch watching TV, when Marge enters, sorting mail.

> MARGE: Bills, bills, bills. Oooh! Free sample of Lemon Time.
> HOMER: Oooh! Give it here.
> *Homer begins to drink the sample.*
> MARGE: Homer! That's dishwashing detergent.
> HOMER: (pauses) What are you gonna do?
> *He continues drinking the detergent.*

Silly? Yes. Absurd? Of course. But cheesy? Not at all. Nor was it predictable, safe, or snarky. The scene conveyed Marge and Homer's marital roles: he the incorrigible with an insatiable appetite, unmatched sloth, and less than discerning taste; she the dependable, responsible housewife, both horrified at his disregard for himself and oddly accustomed and attracted to those unorthodox features that made Homer Homer. *Simpsons* episodes were replete with these clever, revealing, ridiculous moments, which were able to make you laugh without cracking jokes about Marge's cooking (The wife is a bad cook! Hilarious! Boo urns).

The end of Bartmania also transferred the focus to Homer, a more wide-ranging, relatable character than Bart (whose proximity to a walking catchphrase was parodied in the "Bart gets famous" episode in Season 5). Homer incorporated many of the impetuous, id-driven behaviors of his errant son, but his age allowed for adult conflicts. Originally Homer was a character not unlike many sitcom dads, an underdog chasing the American dream. During *The Simpsons'* golden age, Homer stayed somewhat anchored to this role but expanded his range of emotions, silliness, caprice, and appetites. It's at this time that viewers began to appreciate in Homer what *Newsweek* called the "most potent ingredient of comedy: the shock of self-recognition."

While it's possible that the writers were simply running dry of Bart stories, Homer was becoming an embodiment of his time, a representation of our nineties selves, Homer became a symbol of our voracious appetites and cultural cravings; our deep dissatisfaction combined with our profound lethargy. More than anything, Homer was a pawn in the chess game of life—he was at the mercy of his job, his cravings, the media, and the pressures of cultural and institutional forces he could not, or chose not to, understand. Giant corporations, lobbyists, and media conglomerates didn't suddenly appear between 1989 and 2000, but in the nineties there was an increasing sense that institutions were growing beyond our control. Bands like Nirvana, books like *The Beach*, and films like *Office Space* expressed a fundamental alienation and helplessness in the culture we'd created. It made a great deal of sense that, after Bart had been a focus of the culture wars during Bush's last years in office, the show would turn to Homer while Newt Gingrich and Rush Limbaugh galvanized the public against gays, immigrants, abortion, and the separation of church and state.

GERARD JONES: I think most Americans don't want anything to do with these culture wars. It was just a couple of small groups battling it out, especially the baby boomers. Most Americans really just wanted to get by, to get along. They may have leaned more to the left or to the right, but really they had no interest in this stuff; in fact, they wanted a relief from it. And that's why I think the show moves to the dopey, apathetic, hedonistic but pretty much nondestructive Homer. I think it's a strong sense of identification. There's all this wild stuff swirling around him, some of which is quite politically pointed, but he himself just kind of stays happily there with his job and his donuts, and his personal dramas.

Additionally, Homer's daily life was so much more varied than Bart's that it allowed greater access to the fantastically rich secondary and tertiary characters Homer interacted with, and story lines incorporating these characters: Moe, Mr. Burns, Barney, Flanders, Wayland Smithers, Apu, Grandpa, and Chief Wiggum.

The expanded cast became institutionalized along with the show. One *Simpsons* writer explained to me on some level how all *Simpsons* characters are essentially stereotypes: the fat, ineffective cop, the crooked mayor, the heartless millionaire businessman, the foreign convenience store owner. But between the writers' prowess and the actors' range, these characters were not only believable; they became an indelible part of Springfield. They were reliably funny without becoming gimmicky or tired (as later additions like Disco Stu, Cletus, Lindsay Naegle, and Gil would become).

One of the richest of all these characters has to be Krusty the Clown, the unpleasant, outdated Jewish clown whose afternoon kids' show is the touchstone of entertainment in Springfield. Krusty came to be Springfield's greatest entertainment celebrity, and its most pathetic hack.

CHRIS TURNER, author, *Planet Simpson*: He plays the role of modern celebrity culture, but he's also a throwback. Like any modern celebrity, his relationship with his audience is completely exploitive. He'll sell anything for any amount of money, and all of his merchandise is shoddy; most of it is actually dangerous. But they managed to give him this backstory, this life offscreen—he's this secular Jew who is estranged from his rabbi father, his show is often on the verge of failure—and you begin to care about him.

Another timeless character is Charles Montgomery Burns, Homer's ancient boss and the greedy, malevolent owner of Springfield's nuclear power plant, who becomes less of a businessman than a business monster, a stand-in for all capitalism. It's hard to say what the inspiration actually was for Burns's character: suggestions indicate an amalgam of Barry Diller, Rupert Murdoch, James L. Brooks, and Charles Foster Kane. Then there's Apu, the owner-operator of the Kwik-E-Mart.

CHRIS TURNER: He is an awful stereotype. The interesting thing is the relationship South Asians have with him, particularly South Asians living in the West. On the one hand, yeah, he's a cartoon. On the other, he's the most prominent South Asian character on TV. He's a great example of how the writing developed, because initially he's a stock character.

But as they realized they had this rich canvas to play on, they decided to get into this idea of being an immigrant, and it was actually really subtly handled.

Ned Flanders is an excellent example of a character who began as stock, was deepened during the golden years, and then became an extreme caricature later on.

CHRIS TURNER: If you watch the early seasons, he's just the annoyingly perfect neighbor. The Christian thing is not up at the front. They revealed Ned's Christianity slowly; Rod and Todd would be playing some weird Christian board game. Eventually, they got rid of everything else and just made him insanely Christian. You had this stand-in for all evangelism.

And then there is Homer's friend and drinking buddy, Barney.

CHRIS TURNER: Barney is a good example of what happens when they tinker too much. Barney was great as just the town drunk. Making him sober falls into the trap of all the stuff *The Simpsons* satirizes, all those simple sitcom narratives where everything is wrapped up in half an hour and everyone learns a lesson in the end.

These are just a few of the steady supporting cast we came to recognize and rely upon (there are approximately two hundred recurring characters in all). There was also Groundskeeper Willie, Martin, the Squeaky Voiced Teen, Dr. Nick, and the list goes on. The supporting cast members not only provided fodder for more and more episodes, but they rounded out Springfield to the point where it was no longer just the town the show was set in. Like the Marvel Universe and Tolkien's Middle Earth, it became a fully formed, imaginary place.

BRAD BIRD: The really fascinating thing about *The Simpsons* that I love is that within that universe of Springfield, there is a counterpart to any type of person you are going to run across in your life. You know a Groundskeeper Willie; you know a Principal Skinner; you know a Flanders. Those guys are all over the place. And I find it really interesting

that as the show went on and on, they kept adding people to that universe, to where now it's pretty complete. And it's the kind of thing that
only TV could really do, because of the volume of things you have to do.

The impressive thing about this period in the show's history is that
while the world around *The Simpsons* was being cultivated, the family became richer, too. As the Simspons became less concerned with
the extent of their dysfunction, Bart's behavior moved away from the
colorful antics of a ten-year-old to edgier critiques of his parents,
school, and lot in life. He came to express a child's version of the
greater nihilism that *The Simpsons* projected. In "Bart Gets an F,"
where Bart's poor academic standing forces him to face the prospect
of repeating the fourth grade, you could really feel his struggling;
Bart the thinking, feeling person really emerged. Lisa, for her part,
became more stoic, less emotional and childish, and her critical
voice was sharpened—and yet the vulnerability of the smart, different middle child was as strong as it ever would be. In "Lisa's Pony,"
when Homer failed his daughter, Lisa's disappointment in her father
was so palpable, and his efforts to regain her love were so sincere, it
is hard to recall a father-daughter relationship as touchingly and
honestly portrayed on television.

And yet there were moments of childish delight in every episode,
like the laughter that followed Bart's prank phone calls, which
heightened the sense that these were actual kids (the contribution
of the actors in making these characters believable cannot be over-
stated). Aiding this was that fact that, compared with the later
episodes, the golden age featured longer, more involved scenes.
There is a sense that the writers weren't afraid of a little space
between jokes, of letting the camera linger on the magic they and
the animators had created.

The early episodes exploited classic movie clichés, not only for
particular scenes and shots (*The Godfather*, Kubrick, and Hitchcock
films were favorites) but also for entire plots, expanding on the
show's riff on the classic sitcom setup by further riffing on classic
film and theater tropes. The writers were uninhibited in their more
blatant references as well, pointing to *Who's Afraid of Virginia
Woolf?*, *The Andy Griffith Show*, *The Old Man and the Sea*, the Al-

gonquin Round Table, *Citizen Kane*, and hundreds of other cultural landmarks. One classic is Season 5's "Secrets of a Successful Marriage," in which Homer teaches a class on relationships. Smithers, the subject of a running joke that he's a closeted homosexual, in love with Mr. Burns, admits to the class that "I was married once— I didn't know how to keep it together." The scene dissolves to a dream/memory sequence, reminiscent of Tennessee Williams's *Cat on a Hot Tin Roof* (with some *Streetcar Named Desire* thrown in for good measure). Smithers, drinking heavily and supported by a crutch, is fighting with a Southern belle who is accusing him of being too devoted to Burns. Smithers smashes the place up, then runs to the window to Mr. Burns, who, in a ripped white T-shirt, is calling him Stanley Kowalski–style. Memory and dream sequences like these would later provide *the* major comic device for *The Simpsons*–inspired *Family Guy*.

This worked because the referential scripts incorporated many different styles—love story, mystery, horror, science fiction—while they simultaneously played with all of these genres. Until the ninth season, the writers managed not to get bogged down in a single trope or genre—they were much more elastic and nimble. "We can also bail on a story any time we want," Matt Groening says with typical flippancy on the Season 5 DVD.

The show wasn't just expanding its own horizons. By 1994, it was reaching whole new audiences through syndication, as kids coming home from school and adults arriving from work could enjoy a rerun from the first four seasons, five nights a week. In many markets, the show was played more than once a night, on more than one station. Fans seeing episodes for the second, third, and tenth time could catch jokes they'd missed in the initial flurry of comedy, or discover new meanings behind the humor and allusions as they became more educated and savvy.

When a show becomes an institution, it becomes something we as viewers rely on, something we could expect every day, like the school bus or a lunch break. Watching *The Simpsons* for many of us became a welcome daily ritual, especially when you compare it to the other syndicated offerings of the period: *Step by Step*, *M*A*S*H*, *Designing Women*, *Murphy Brown*, and *Married . . . with Children*.

When television series reach a certain number of episodes (usually one hundred), a distributor negotiates a fee between the network and television stations to rerun past episodes in a local market, as well as any future episodes the show produces. This is the first round of syndication. Once the show is off the air, there is a second round of bidding, and those deals are renegotiated. With an estimated price of $1.5–$1.8 million per episode,[1] deciding to carry *The Simpsons* was a major decision for any network affiliate (the show's syndication actually marked a reversal in the downward trend in the price for sitcoms[2]).

As a comparison, the hugely successful *Family Ties* cost $1.3 million per episode to syndicate in the eighties (when that deal was struck, its creator, Gary David Goldberg, received a check for $40 million),[3] while *Home Improvement* would score approximately $2.7 million per episode[4] in the mid-nineties (it was a number one show at the time—it has weathered badly). The only series to rival *The Simpsons* in the syndication contest would be *Seinfeld*, which is popular both before prime time and after the ten o'clock news all over the country. *Seinfeld*'s per episode price was above $3 million in 1996. When the show ended in 1998, it negotiated its second round of syndication deals, with two hundred stations, for a record number,[5] as much as $5 million per episode. When *The Simpsons* finally goes off the air, we can count on a new record, as stations all over the world vie for the privilege of accessing twenty-plus years of reruns.

The mid-nineties was also a time when the Internet was finding its way into most homes. Next to pornography, it was hard to find an online subject more popular than *The Simpsons*. Through newsgroups, and then fan sites and web-based message boards, the community of *Simpsons* fans found each other, and a whole new forum to air their praise for and grievances against their favorite show. Finnish Simpsonsphile Jouni Paakkinen has shepherded *The Simpsons'* presence online since the early nineties.

JOUNI PAAKKINEN, administrator, Simpsons Archive: It all started in a newsgroup called alt.tv.simpsons. These so-called Usenet groups were the first global discussion forums on the Internet. They still exist, but the majority of the discussions nowadays take place on web forums. The group was started as early as 1990, and at that time, most of the users studied or worked at academic institutions. Over the nineties, the number of people with access to the Internet grew rapidly, and by the mid-nineties the group had become very active, with dozens of regular posters and probably thousands of lurkers (including even Matt Groening himself). Popular topics were Is Smithers gay? and Where is Springfield? Nowadays it's common for fans to compile this kind of stuff from their favorite shows, but the Simpsons' fans were among the very first to start the tradition.

In the midnineties, alt.tv.Simpsons migrated to this new thing called the web. When the site turned ten in 2004, every month 1.5 million pages were viewed and the site had over fifty maintainers.

JACOB BURCH, administrator, NoHomers.net: In the middle of the week people would ask questions about the episodes on the newsgroup, either things they didn't get or things they wanted further investigation into. On Wednesday—and then Saturday, as the show moved back to Sunday nights—there would be this anticipatory discussion of either what people knew or what had leaked. [An employee of Film Roman was leaking scripts and information to the websites—the word got around Film Roman and he was fired.] And then the day of an episode's airing, the group became a giant reviews warehouse: people loving it, people hating it, people more than willing to point out what was flawed. And that was always the peak.

ERIC WIRTANEN, founder, NoHomers.net: In the mid- to late nineties, on the alt.Simpsons newsgroup, you'd see a new post every three or four seconds. It was ridiculous.

JACOB BURCH: If an episode touched someone a certain way, "Mother Simpson" or "Lisa's Substitute," they would defend it to the death.

JOUNI PAAKKINEN: As it became easier for a regular user to publish web pages, the latter half of the 1990s saw an explosion of *The Simpsons'* fan community on the Internet. Hundreds and soon thousands of *Simpsons* fan sites were available all around the world. When all the good ideas had already been used, even the smallest supporting characters started to get their own dedicated sites. Most of the sites have been short-lived, but some have survived over a decade.

The Simpsons Archive stores information from scripts to celebrity appearances to cultural references—it is a living museum for all things *Simpsons*. Much of the current *Simpsons* debate and discussion takes place on web discussion groups. The most popular of these is NoHomers.net.

ERIC WIRTANEN: It got people together to discuss their love for the merchandise, review episodes. It made them realize that there was a whole world of fans out there just as dedicated as they were.

    The show reached a point where there was this reciprocal relationship, where unlike *Seinfeld* and *The Cosby Show*, there was a wealth of things that could be argued about, things that could be discovered. The level of discourse that it allows is significantly higher than other shows. It created a body of evidence for the creators to note, "Hey, what we're doing is working. Let's do more of it. They like this hidden stuff." It allowed the show to continue because it proved that it worked.

JACOB BURCH: The response on the Internet gave them Comic Book Guy [the overweight überdork who runs the comic book store and has "expert" opinions on all entertainment and media; he is a stand-in for overenthusiastic *Simpsons* fans, absorbing humiliating ripostes to his fanaticism in every scene in which he appears].

As *The Simpsons* entrenched itself into the popular culture of the nineties, it provoked some of the show's veterans to produce animated sitcoms that would avoid the pitfalls of *The Simpsons'* earlier imitators. *The Critic*, created by Al Jean and Mike Reiss and produced by James L. Brooks, lasted twenty-three episodes, on two different networks, before being canceled in 1995. *King of the Hill*, created by *Simpsons* writer Greg Daniels and Mike Judge (of *Beavis and Butt-Head*), has won two Emmys and is entering its fourteenth season on Fox.

    Originally envisioned as a live-action show, *The Critic* followed the life of Jay Sherman, a cuddly (read: fat), balding, divorced film snob who reviews movies like "The Red Balloon Part 2: Revenge of the Red Balloon" and "Crocodile Gandhi," on his weekly New York cable show (using his "Shermometer" as a rating device). I've never understood why *The Critic* did not fare better than it did. Jean and Reiss managed to send up Hollywood, the media that cover it, and life in New York City, while creating a fairly lovable loser out of Sherman, voiced with the knowing cynicism and genuine humility of Jon Lovitz. The look of *The Critic*, more realistic than *The Simpsons*, was simple but elegant, a throwback to old *New Yorker* covers, presenting scenes of a bustling but classic New York City where Gershwin tunes would always be the appropriate sound track.

Critics were bowled over by the idea that someone had finally made a show about them, if not by the show itself. Roger Ebert, who rarely commented on television, devoted a column to it, and Tom Shales called it "the feel-good show of the year. Or at least of the night." Shales went on to say that "Jay Sherman isn't as interesting as any single Simpson" but added that Jon Lovitz "gives the poor schnook not only verve but poignancy." Ultimately, perhaps *The Critic* failed to have enough bite in its Hollywood satire, or enough heart on the homefront, where Jay was confronted by his son, ex-wife, romantic interests, and coming middle age. "Even at its funniest," Howard Rosenberg wrote in the *Los Angeles Times*, "*The Critic* is a sanitized Pillsbury Doughboy compared to HBO's TV-satirizing *The Larry Sanders Show* . . . On the Shermometer, *The Critic* rates about a 7."

Viewers agreed. *The Critic* was not renewed after its thirteen-episode run on ABC. Fox picked it up in 1995 and ran ten episodes before the show was canceled permanently.

King of the Hill took a much less snide, media-savvy approach to the America it was choosing to portray. Drawn in the style (though with much more realism and dignity) of Mike Judge's *Beavis and Butt-Head*, *King of the Hill* introduced us to a normal Texas family, the Hills, living their lives in the suburban town of Arlen. Its patriarch, Hank Hill, a moderately conservative and thoughtful salesman of "propane and propane accessories," is confronted each week with modern incursions into the traditional world of canned beer, football, and pickup trucks. Those challenges revolve around his drinking buddies, who are more redneck than him; his earnest wife, Peggie, a homemaker and substitute Spanish teacher who is discovering alternatives to traditional housewifery; and his chubby, unathletic twelve-year-old son, Bobby, whose dream is to become a prop comedian. "That boy ain't right," is a common refrain from Hank about his son.

"For a cartoon, it's defiantly slow, sometimes a virtual still-life," wrote Tom Shales. "And yet there's something curiously compelling about its utterly trivial everyday goings-on." *The New York Times* was equally impressed and bored with *King of the Hill*'s realism: "It scarcely matters that Hank and his friends are cartoon characters, and that fact suggests the ambition and the problem with *King of the Hill*."

BRENT FORRESTER, writer/producer, *The Simpsons* (1993–97); writer/producer, *King of the Hill*, *The Office*: Their whole goal was to get back to something real, even in animation. And if you look at the designs of the characters, you can really see it. Mike Judge said, "I'm not gonna do google-eyed characters, I'm not gonna do funny characters. I'm gonna go to the mall and look at people and draw them."

And that's what the designs of *King of the Hill* are, and the aesthetic of that show flows from that—actually to a point where Fox was freaked out by the first episode, because Greg and Mike decided they weren't gonna do any close-ups. And that, actually, is very difficult to do in comedy. But they were just like, "Yeah, we're doing all wide shots, man." Reality is in wide shot, but that's actually too revolutionary for comedy. As you sit there trying to laugh at lines, you want to see people's faces. As a human being, you want that information, and so you kind of have to go to close-ups when you're doing punch lines.

If viewers were puzzled at first, they certainly caught on. *King of the Hill* is never derisive or disrespectful toward the sector of America it satirizes—it genuinely appreciates its characters and their struggles, and viewers did the same. "This could easily be a setup for a mean parody about rural life in America," wrote Matt Bai in *The New York Times*, "but *King of the Hill* . . . has never been so crass. The show's central theme has always been transformation—economic, demographic and cultural . . . The real point is not to eviscerate so much as to watch Hank struggle mightily to adapt to a world of political correctness and moral ambiguity."

Later in the decade, Matt Groening would launch his second animated sitcom, *Futurama*, with the help of former *Simpsons* executive producer David S. Cohen. Drawn like a glossier, streamlined *Simpsons* (the overbites and googly eyes are still there), *Futurama* took place in the year 3000, telling the story of a hapless pizza delivery boy who mistakenly freezes himself for a thousand years on the eve of the third millennium. Waking up in thirty-first-century New New York City, Fry must come of age as a delivery boy for his only living relative, the ancient Professor Farnsworth, who operates a package delivery company staffed by a one-eyed, sexy alien named Leila, an alcoholic robot named Bender, and a lobsterlike Jewish stereotype (a "spacejew," one producer called him) named Dr. Zoidberg.

Although it did not premiere until 1999, *Futurama* was, perhaps more than any other series, direct evidence of *The Simpsons'* progenitive abilities. "The way I sold the show was by saying. 'This is *The Simpsons* in the future,' and dollar signs danced in front of their eyes," said Groening.[6] He spent five years researching science fiction before pitching the show with Cohen. To his and Cohen's credit, it is truly funny. Placing the sitcom a thousand years in the future removed many of the restraints on thing like physics and cartoonish exaggeration that Groening had placed on *The Simpsons*. *Futurama* both embraces and parodies its genre, bringing with it the irony, intelligence, and metatheatrical playfulness we'd become accustomed to on *The Simpsons*. Not surprisingly, even though this was Groening's baby, writers Ken Keeler, J. Stewart Burns, Eric Kaplan, Bill Odenkirk, and others carried much of the load, a burden that nearly overwhelmed *Futurama*'s showrunner, David S. Cohen.

BRENT FORRESTER: There are two kinds of comedy people. There are the people who came in because they're kind of like class-clown people, performer energy. And then there're the people who are just very, very intelligent and, frequently, very socially recessive. And *The Simpsons* was mostly the latter. I think, virtually entirely the latter.

David Cohen was no exception there. I mean, he's just a brilliant guy, but when he came to do *Futurama*, he was suddenly sort of thrown to the lions, in terms of him having to deal with the social crises: Whom do you hire? How much did you hire them for? And executive notes and everything.

And, at a certain point in creating *Futurama*, Dave had a bit of what seemed to me to be a breakdown. 'Cause I talked to him, "Dave, how's the show going?" And he said, "Oh, I just told them it wasn't fun anymore. I wanted to keep working, but it just wasn't fun anymore."

He really sounded like he'd been sedated or something. I told him he couldn't just turn his back on this. But, apparently, they got to him; they broke him. And he was out. And so then they came back to him and figured out a way he could do the show. I don't know what psychological compromise they made. But when he came back, he came back as David X. Cohen. I mean, he always uses that X now. And I always think of it like he had a mental breakdown and came back as David X. Cohen. I love that aspect of it.

Futurama lasted four seasons until Fox stopped production in 2003. While critical reception had been varied, but generally strong, it was never really given a fair shot by the network. Fox debuted the series on Sunday nights but then moved it to Tuesdays, while they had allowed *King of the Hill* to build a steady audience on Sunday nights, piggybacking on *The Simpsons* week after week at 8:30, to Groening's chagrin. He lamented to the press how the suits at the network were messing up his show. If he expected the independence and freedom allotted to Jim Brooks with *The Simpsons*, he was misguided. "There's an atmosphere of giving notes, of interference," Matt complained. "When they tried to give me notes on *Futurama*, I just said, 'No, we're going to do this just the way we did *The Simpsons*.' And they said, 'Well, we don't do business that way anymore.'"[7] Throughout its life, the show was jostled around the schedule, often preempted by sports events, making it hard for it to garner a steady fan base. Yet, much like *Family Guy*, it has had such a lively afterlife on DVD and on the Cartoon Network's Adult Swim that it was revived with an additional four *Futurama* films, which have gone straight to DVD in addition to being played on Comedy

Central. While the films have been disappointing and without much humor, Comedy Central officially revived the laughter in 2009 by purchasing twenty-six episodes of the series for its 2010 season, though the good news for fans was stilted by reports that there were disputes with the original cast, with Fox putting out a casting call for new voices. On July 31, 2009, *The Toronto Star* reported that, after tense negotiations, the full cast had signed on for the new episodes.[8]

The *Simpsons* people must be chuffed that their series inspired others. After all, in television, as in life, imitation is the highest form of flattery, that is, next to an Emmy Award. *The Simpsons* has fought a long, disappointing battle with the Academy of Television Arts and Sciences; despite nine Emmys for best animated program, twelve for Outstanding Voice-Over Performance, and two for Outstanding Music and Lyrics, *The Simpsons* has never won the coveted Emmy for Outstanding Comedy Series. For the first few years, Brooks and the producers couldn't even get *The Simpsons* considered in the category—the Emmys would nominate only cartoons for Outstanding Animated Series. "It is a light thrill to beat Garfield every year, but it's getting a little old," said Groening.[9] "It's starting to feel personal," griped James L. Brooks.[10] The academy's argument sounded trifling: allowing *The Simpsons* to compete against *Cheers* and *Roseanne* would set too dangerous a precedent, and could negatively influence the animation awards structure.[11]

Finally, in 1993, the academy relented and changed the rules. The producers submitted "A Streetcar Named Marge" and "Mr. Plow." The show wasn't even nominated. In 1994 they were snubbed once again.* After that, *The Simpsons* went back to battling it out with *Duckman* and *The Flinstones*.†

This isn't to say *The Simpsons* hasn't received its fair share of accolades. It's one of few sitcoms, and the only animated series, to ever win a Peabody Award. It is the longest-running sitcom of all

---

*The academy would finally give animated comedy some acknowledgment when, in 2009, *Family Guy* received a nomination for Outstanding Comedy.

†Not that *The Simpsons* wasn't asking for it. In the Season 3 episode "Brother, Can You Spare Two Dimes?" Homer is given a phony award, the First Annual Montgomery Burns Award for Outstanding Achievement in the Field of Excellence. At the ceremony, noting what a sham the whole affair is, Lisa comments, "This is the biggest farce I ever saw!" Bart retorts, "What about the Emmys?" "I stand corrected," Lisa answers.

time, and in 2009 it surpassed *Gunsmoke* as the longest-running entertainment program of all time. *The Simpsons* has countless Annie Awards (twenty-six, actually), five Writers Guild Awards, and there is a *Simpsons* star on the Walk of Fame. *Time* editor Bruce Handy explained their magazine's decision to name Bart of one of the one hundred most influential people of the past century and in so doing summed up just how *The Simpsons* managed to transcend its faddish beginnings and become something lasting and meaningful.

"You can't talk about twentieth-century art without taking into account pop culture. It's almost what defines the century. I think when people a hundred years from now want to get a sense of what the nineties were like they could do a lot worse than watch *The Simpsons*. It will still be being viewed and enjoyed when a lot of contemporary, serious literature is forgotten. Does anyone think, I don't know, David Foster Wallace is a better satirist than Matt Groening?"

Or Sam Simon? Or George Meyer? Or the people who actually wrote the scripts?

THIRTEEN

The Godfathers

In which the Catholic church scares small children . . . David Letterman nearly goes "Coconuts" . . . George Meyer gets published in *Variety* . . . and John Swartzwelder considers teaching O. J. Simpson the fundamentals of baseball.

While every *Simpsons* episode has a writer—the scribe or pair of scribes who penned the episode's first draft—each final script is the result of input from a room full of writers and many, many edits. When discussing staff writers, two names are repeated constantly, taking on near mythological significance in *The Simpsons'* world: George Meyer and John Swartzwelder.

Meyer, a writer whose status merited a profile in *The New Yorker*, "Taking Humor Seriously: The Funniest Man Behind the Funniest Show on TV," is considered the godfather of the rewrite room[1] (The *Los Angeles Times* called him "the great and powerful Oz behind *The Simpsons*"). While he's never taken the job of showrunner, Meyer was seen as the show's principal architect, before leaving in 2004.

JON VITTI, writer/producer, *The Simpsons* (1989–2004) (to *The New Yorker*, March 13, 2000): A show that you have the writer's credit for will run, and the next day people will come up to you and tell you how great it was. Then they'll mention their two favorite lines, and both of them will be George's.

BRENT FORRESTER, writer/producer, *The Simpsons* (1993–97); writer/producer, *King of the Hill*, *The Office*: In great part, you were pitching for George. If George said something was good, then it was good. That was as close to objectivity as you could get on *The Simpsons*.

David Owen's *New Yorker* profile, which I quote extensively but is well worth reading in its entirety, claims that Meyer has "so thoroughly shaped the program that by now the comedic sensibility of *The Simpsons* can be seen as mostly his."

Meyer was raised Catholic in a large family—he is the oldest of eight—in Arizona. An altar boy, Eagle Scout, and editor of his high school's student newspaper, Meyer was also an avid fan of *MAD* magazine, which other *Simpsons* writers describe as a significant figure in the show's pedigree. Like Groening's, Meyer's own comedic pedigree can be traced back to feelings of subjugation to authority figures. While for Groening it was evil teachers who tore up his drawings, in Meyer's case, it was the Catholic church and its agents.

GEORGE MEYER (to *The New Yorker*, March 13, 2000): People talk about how horrible it is to be brought up Catholic, and it's all true. The main thing was that there was no sense of proportion . . . Once, I was sent to the principal's office, and when I went in my parents were sitting there. They had been summoned somehow. God, that was scary. I would have been very unhappy, but not particularly surprised, if they had said, "This time you have gone too far. Now you must die." . . . That's why one of my favorite forms of black humor is the casual cruelty of bureaucrats and doctors—like, "Here's the rod we're going to put in your spine."

Meyer attended Harvard, where he majored in biochemistry and found like minds at the *Lampoon*. There he was made a staff writer and was eventually elected president (surviving a coup from his fellow Lampoonians, who felt he was not responsible enough to run the magazine).

GEORGE MEYER (to *The New Yorker*, March 13, 2000): I don't think most people like to laugh as much as I do. Most people, sure, they like to laugh, but it's down on their list, like No. 8. At the *Lampoon*, though, people took humor very seriously . . . That changed my life.

Meyer's time at Harvard wasn't all laughs, though. Depression has been a major theme in the writer's life (other writers on the show commented on how "dark" Meyer can be, but never without mentioning his levity and positivity that balanced the darkness), and he admitted in 2004 that for a long period of time while he was at *The Simpsons*, he was suicidal.

After graduating in 1978, Meyer tried substitute teaching, retail, being a *Jeopardy!* contestant, and working in a cancer research lab—he had been accepted to medical school but didn't go. "What Meyer really liked doing was just hanging out with the guys, cracking jokes," noted *Los Angeles* magazine, "and there just aren't that many funny scientists."

In 1981, Meyer was tracked down by producers who were looking for writers for a new late-night talk show hosted by someone named David Letterman. Letterman had heard about Meyer from his *Harvard Lampoon* pals Tom Gammill and Max Pross (who would later write for *Seinfeld* and *The Simpsons*) and was wowed by Meyer's work.

After two years, Meyer left *Letterman* to work on Lorne Michaels's *The New Show*, a doomed attempt to repeat the success of *Saturday Night Live*. After *The New Show* was canceled, Meyer joined the regular writing staff at *SNL* in 1985.

GEORGE MEYER (to *The New Yorker*, March 13, 2000): My stuff wasn't very popular at *Saturday Night* . . . It was regarded as really fringey, and a lot of times my sketches would get cut. Sometimes they would get cut after dress rehearsal, and I would have the horrible experience of looking out and seeing a painter carefully touching up my set and getting it all ready to be smashed to pieces and sent to a landfill in Brooklyn.

Bored with *SNL*, he moved to Boulder, Colorado, to reconnect with "whatever made life worth living."[2] Letterman recommended him to write the script for a film the talk-show host had agreed to star in for Disney, which Meyer is said to have titled "Going Coconuts." Letterman had little real interest in doing a movie and it was never produced. Yet the script is considered a "masterpiece" by those who have seen it.[3]

WALLACE WOLODARSKY, writer/producer, *The Simpsons* (1989–92): We all admired George's work from before, particularly this thing called *Army Man*, which was famous among comedy writers of that generation.

While figuring out his life in Boulder, Meyer printed three issues of a comedy magazine called *Army Man: America's Only Magazine*. It was just a few photocopied pages, with pieces from comedy writing geniuses like John Swartzwelder, Ian Frazier, Andy Borowitz, and Meyer himself, distributed to a few hundred of Meyer's friends and colleagues.

Some examples from *Army Man:*

ARMY MAN #1—
ASTONISHINGLY PRIMITIVE DEBUT ISSUE!

Why I Love America

Why do I love America? Well, maybe "love" is a little strong . . . I mean, I think it's a good country. Definitely. But a lot of that is 'cause I was born here, and haven't seen that many other countries. Canada and Mexico, that's about it. I hear Sweden is really great. Man, I'd move there in a second. Just don't have the bucks.

*   *   *

If God were my co-pilot, I think I'd let Him handle almost all the routine flying. I might do the landings . . . I'm pretty good at those.

*   *   *

Deep Thoughts, by Jack Handey

Dad always thought laughter was the best medicine, which I guess was why several of us died of tuberculosis.

Meyer started *Army Man* out of boredom, and the fact that he wasn't doing very well with women at the time. He thought it would help him get girls. It didn't. A contributor to *Army Man* imitated the typical response to George from women: "What? You run a self-published magazine with two hundred issues every time? No, that's okay."

GEORGE MEYER (to *The New Yorker*, March 13, 2000): The only rule was that the stuff had to be funny and pretty short . . . To me, the quintessential *Army Man* joke was one of John Swartzwelder's: "They can kill the Kennedys. Why can't they make a cup of coffee that tastes good?" It's a horrifying idea juxtaposed with something really banal—and yet there's a kind of logic to it. It's illuminating because it's kind of how Americans see things: Life's a big jumble, but somehow it leads to something I can consume. I love that.

Like the original *South Park* video a decade later, *Army Man* made the rounds of Hollywood, becoming a must-have among comedy writers, including Sam Simon. "Sam got quite a bit of his writing staff from the list of credits of *Army Man*," a *Simpsons* writer told David Owen. "In a sense, that little magazine was the father of the show."

JAY KOGEN, writer/producer, *The Simpsons* (1989–92): I'd always heard great things about George Meyer and I'd read *Army Man*. It was just this weird little magazine. It was almost like a little college comedy paper, ironic little pieces. I thought, I respect anybody who's putting this together.

JOSH WEINSTEIN, writer/producer, *The Simpsons* (1991–97): *Army Man* is like an early genesis of *The Simpsons*. You can see glimmers of what became *Simpsons*-style stuff in that.

GEORGE MEYER (to *The Believer*, 2004): I have no idea how it got so big. I was just trying to find something to do while I was living in Boulder, Colorado, which isn't really a funny town. There are a lot of smart people there, but comedy isn't at the forefront of their minds. For most of Boulder, comedy is just something you see at the multiplex every week or so. To me, it's like oxygen. When the *National Lampoon* entered its slow-motion death, it really hurt me. It was like losing a friend. There were very few publications that were just trying to be funny. Even *Spy* magazine, which was in some ways its successor, was not primarily funny. It was subversive and satirical, but I don't think its goal was to provoke belly laughs. So I tried to make something that had no agenda other than to make you laugh.

Army Man ceased publication after the third issue (Meyer was busy with *The Simpsons*, deluged with submissions from his friends—which he hated rejecting—and was being approached to turn it into something bigger, like a TV show). With the final issue, he included a letter, dated July 22, 1990: "Dear Reader, I have some news for you, and I'm not even going to sugar-coat it. I might varnish it . . . no, I'm not even going to varnish it. Army Man is suspending publication . . . To paraphrase Gen. Douglas MacArthur, 'I shall, if circumstances permit, and no one objects too strenuously, return.' Love, George."

RICHARD APPEL, co–executive producer, *The Simpsons* (1995–99): One thing George does, in any room he's in, is set the bar high just by being in it. One of the best things to have in a writers room is a sense that you're trying to make the best person in the room laugh. And George was always that at *The Simpsons* in my time there, and I don't think it's presumptuous to say that's what he was before I got there and after I left.

CONAN O'BRIEN, writer/producer, *The Simpsons* (1991–93): George Meyer has just such a discerning comedy mind, your biggest fear is saying something hackneyed or contrived.

WALLACE WOLODARSKY: There's a darkness and lightness in George, both of which are surprising. For someone who could pitch such dark material, he also had a kind of hippie lightness of spirit that you wouldn't necessarily think go together.

BOB KUSHELL: There was once an incident where George wrote on a piece of paper a list of everybody on the show and he asked me to number them based on who I thought was the most insane. We were sitting there while everybody else was either breaking stories or punching things up, and we were going through everybody in the room, ranking them based on who we thought was the, literally, most insane, clinically, in the room.

And it was just such a refreshing thing, and for somebody who took the show so seriously, he would have these flights of fancy that were spectacular. I was the crazy, wacky character and George was a real intellectual, I felt. But at the same time he was an intellectual with a kid's heart.

BILL OAKLEY: [when he and writing partner Josh Weinstein were trying to get hired on the show] We talked to George over the phone and he said he would look at our sample material. And we sent it to George and he said it was really funny. But, you know, nothing ever came of it. Four years later, when we were running *The Simpsons*, he was cleaning out his office. He brought our sample material back to me with a note on it that said, "Very funny, you're hired."

BRIAN ROBERTS: A funny little story about George Meyer: He has something like eight sisters and they're all really good-looking, and he was constantly trying to pawn off his sisters on the writing staff. And actually Jon Vitti married one of them.

GEORGE MEYER (to *The Believer*): For me, marriage is a grotesque, unforgiving, clunky contrivance. Yet society pushes it as a shimmering ideal. It's as if medicine came up with the iron lung, then stood back and said, "At last! Our work is done." Men often struggle with their attraction to other women. They don't quite understand why they have to be with the same woman forever. Marriage has a compassionate answer for them: "Oh, shut up, you selfish crybaby." Is it any wonder men have to be pressured into this nasty, lopsided arrangement?

Meyer, who is now in his early fifties, is still not officially married, but he lives with his girlfriend since 1990, TV writer and novelist Maria Semple, whose credits include *Mad About You*, *Ellen*, and *Arrested Development*. They have a daughter. Meyer looks like a scruffy hippie, or Deadhead (which, for years, he was); he's an adherent to vegetarianism, yoga, and environmentalism. If Lisa is the social conscience of the Simpson family, Meyer may have been the conscience of their writers room. "I'm an animal lover who wears leather shoes; a vegetarian who can't resist smoked salmon," Meyer wrote in an op-ed for the BBC News website in 2006. The article was a plea for like-minded folks to join the environmental movement, an acknowledgment that participation in Earth's destruction was no excuse not to try and save it. "Are we really gonna wreck the whole planet? 'Cause that's a big move. That's like something a crazy stripper would do," he continued. He managed to include some of his favorite targets in the critique: "I would enjoy watching dazed stockbrokers and ad men clawing at the dirt for edible roots. I'd remind them that they'd been warned of their folly, right here on the BBC website. And they'd all grunt ruefully, and make me their king."[4]

Despite his work for an industry that makes much of its money from ad revenues, Meyer reserves special contempt for advertising. "I hate it because it irresponsibly induces discontent in people for one myopic goal, and then leaves the debris of that process out there in the culture," he told *The Believer*. "An advertiser will happily make you feel bad about yourself if that will make you buy, say, a Bic pen."

A giant sports fan, Meyer bought Wilt Chamberlain's house in Los Angeles (he has since moved to Washington State). In it he constructed a shrine to Jerry Garcia, whom David Owen described as "the closest thing in Meyer's life to a spiritual figure."

GEORGE MEYER (to *The Believer*): I have a deep suspicion of social institutions and tradition in general . . . I got very good grades in school, I was an Eagle Scout, and I believed in all of it. But I eventually realized that these institutions didn't care about me . . . I do have a baby . . . and that's a religion in itself . . . I was agnostic for most of my adult life, but then Mike Reiss started giving me grief about it. He said, "Oh, come on. Dive in. Go all the way. Be an atheist. The water's fine." I guess I started to realize that being an agnostic was such a wimpy position.

Meyer's disdain for authority extends far past the nuns who persecuted him, and their church. If you look at the episodes he's written, you can see a deep current of his distrust of many of society's institutions, which has become a *Simpsons* institution. For instance, in "Bart vs. Thanksgiving," where Bart, having ruined Thanksgiving dinner by destroying Lisa's centerpiece, runs away, Meyer attacked the Thanksgiving tradition (both the idea of families truly uniting for a day chosen arbitrarily, as well as the spurious roots of the Thanks-giving myth).*

Meyer satirized government corruption in "Mr. Lisa Goes to Washington," where Lisa's winning essay brings her and the Simpsons to Washington, D.C., and Lisa overhears a bribe to a congressman taking place.

And in "Bart's Inner Child," the town becomes enamored with a self-help guru, who holds Bart up as an example and convinces all of Springfield's inhabitants to "be like the boy." The disastrous results pilloried the self-help industry, those who follow it, and the quick-fix, money-grubbing Dr. Phils and Pat Robertsons of the world, who are, depressingly, an institution in their own right.

ROB COHEN: One conversation from back then really sticks out. He was telling me that he was trying to be the largest personal holder of silver in the United States. He definitely is the second or the third. I think it was the Hunt brothers and him. But he was buying up silver at a crazy rate and kept telling me that I should buy silver because it was going to be the new gold.

BRENT FORRESTER: George was investing in gold ever since I knew him. At one point I said to him, "George, by betting on gold, you're sort of betting against humanity, aren't you?" And he said, "Yes." The whole idea was that "if and when all goes to hell, that's when people really go for gold." He had incredibly persuasive arguments for investing in gold. He once made his arguments to [fellow writer] Greg Daniels, and he got Greg so fired up that Greg ran to the telephone to call his broker. He was gonna invest, you know, untold sums in gold. But he couldn't get to a broker in time, and he was gonna have to invest the next day, etc. And then, overnight, gold went through the floor. He would have lost everything that he invested. He was like, "What the hell am I listening to George Meyer for?" But George's day finally came with gold. [In 1995, when the writers would have been having this discussion, gold

*In a lovely aside, while watching the Macy's Thanksgiving Day Parade, Homer tells Bart that if the parade "turned every flash-in-the-pan cartoon character into a balloon, it will be a farce." Meanwhile, a Bart balloon floats by on the tube. Not even the institution *The Simpsons* was becoming was safe from Meyer—that year, a Bart balloon was indeed added to the real parade.

hovered around $380 an ounce. Today it trades at prices near $1,000 an ounce.]

Bob Kushell: I was fortunate enough to share a couch with George Meyer [Meyer later recommended Kushell to the producers of *3rd Rock from the Sun*, who hired Kushell as a top writer]. One night I was leaving the room with George and he was very frustrated with a script. We came out into the parking lot together and he drop-kicked the script into fifty-three flying pages on a windy night and just walked to his car and didn't say anything. He just let the pages spew all over the parking lot. And you know, the passion for what was good and bad, his passion for *The Simpsons* and what it could be, was infectious to everybody in the room.

Michael Carrington: George is just a joke machine. We would be sitting there and he would be firing off jokes, boom, boom, boom, one after another. And no one would be writing them down. And I would be like, Wow, *that* was brilliant. Well, *that* was brilliant too. How come no one's writing? And then I realized he was just getting warmed up. By the time he got to the seventh or eighth joke—that was the twisted one. That's the one that went in. I said, "Oh, I get it now."

And ever since then I've been trying to do that as well. You just toss out those first five or six ones. And you have to remember, if you're writing by yourself, not to think of that first joke and put it in. Just keep going and keep going until you get to one that no one else would think of. And that's what I learned from George.

You can put your finger on some concrete Meyerisms. They include the term "yoink" (it denotes an unexpected snatching), and the Leftorium, Ned Flanders's store for southpaws. Apparently Meyer was once moved, nearly to tears, when he spotted a fledgling store dedicated solely to providing objects to left-handed people. And yet his total contribution to the show could never be quantified.

Bob Kushell: I often wondered whether or not George Meyer would go on to do other things or whether he would just be one of *The Simpsons'* writers for the rest of his life. There really is no place better suited

to George Meyer than *The Simpsons*, where you can literally do anything, and say anything, and have any point of view.

Meyer left the show in 1996. He had had a development deal since
1994, but his efforts to produce his own material were apparently
frustrated by incursions from execs who weren't willing to give him
the creative freedom he required. He had expected carte blanche
and they were "all over him," says one source. As it turned out,
Meyer was not quite done with *The Simpsons* after all. He returned
in 1999, first part-time as a consultant and then full-time in the
room. But by 2002, Meyer was restless again. "I've accomplished all
my goals in the mass media," he told *Los Angeles* magazine. He
wrote, directed, and starred in a play, *Up Your Giggy*, produced by
Maria Semple. *Up Your Giggy* played for only a few nights at West
Hollywood's Court Theatre. Featuring Meyer, Semple, comedian
Dana Gould, and *Mystery Science Theater 3000* creator Joel Hodg-
son in its unpaid cast, Meyer attacked his favorite topics—including
advertising and marriage—with absurd skits and monologues.

BRENT FORRESTER: George would retire several times from *The Simpsons*. The first time he retired, we really took it seriously. We had a
big retirement party for him. And then, as a going-away present, we got
him a brick of gold. What Greg Daniels found hilarious was that, you
know, after a little while, George came back to the show. Didn't give
back the gold brick. I mean, how are you gonna give back a gold brick?
But Greg found that hilarious—that he got a gold brick out of his fake
retirement.

Meyer left for good in 2004, but he did return to work with the
"dream team" of *Simpsons* writers Jim Brooks assembled for *The
Simpsons Movie*.
    While Meyer was always an authoritative voice and often headed
up a room when the staff was divided into writing groups, he never
took on the official job of showrunner. Meyer excels at writing,
not managing, and he didn't deal with the squabbling among
staffers and the nitpicking responsibilities that come with running
a room.

DONICK CARY, writer/producer, *The Simpsons* (1996–99); creator, *Lil' Bush*: George was always best when he was not running the room. Because when you run the room, you have all this extra pressure of tracking the story and making sure everyone breaks at the right time for lunch—practical concerns—rather than just making sure the show is smart and funny. It always seemed best when somebody else was running the room, and George was right next to him, just thinking about how to make this thing smart and funny.

When asked by *The Believer* what his favorite line is that he's written, Meyer said, "Pray for Mojo." (In Season 9's "Girly Edition," Homer pretends to be handicapped so that he can receive a helper monkey to do menial chores for him. The monkey, named Mojo, takes on Homer's personality, becoming drunk and slothful, to the point where he is completely useless. Upon being returned to his trainers—on a wagon—they ask him what went wrong. The monkey's reply is three perfect words typed into a computer: "Pray for Mojo.") "It's almost like an epitaph for Western civilization," Meyer said. "It's this bloated, fucked-out corpse that washes up on a beach, burping up its final breath."

BOB KUSHELL: He thinks so far out of the box that he's in a different box store. The turns of phrase and the ability to connect different things together and form jokes and comedic situations out of it is something I'd never seen before.

RICHARD APPEL: You know how *Variety* always has those punning headlines? When Disney's Michael Eisner fired Jeffrey Katzenberg, one of the writers in the room was just doodling what some headlines for this story could be, all sorts of puns based on "Mouse House" and Katzenberg. And this writer kept on going throughout the morning, pitching these at random moments. At one point, George, who I think was losing some patience with this process, just blurted out, "Katz flees mouse." The other writer loved it. Everyone was laughing, and then we moved on and could focus on the script.

About twenty minutes later, the writer who had been coming up with headlines was on the phone in the kitchen. He popped his head back into the writers room and he said he was on hold with Army Archerd [editor of *Variety*], having just pitched that headline. And the next day in Army Archerd's column, he had something like, "The Katzenberg firing had scribes all over town pitching headlines for *Variety*. George Meyer called in with this one." And George was both mortified and recognized the humor in it. He did say he had a number of phone messages from people saying, "Um, you really called Army Archerd to take credit? This doesn't seem like you."

Not only is George prolific with his jokes, they are regarded as some of the most original that his fellow comedy writers have ever heard. One writer who spent many years with George gave him the most fitting compliment, telling him that he honestly never once knew what Meyer was going to say. Meyer was so touched he replied with a long hug.

Second only to Meyer as the most influential writer in the show's history is John Swartzwelder. Swartzwelder, the author of fifty-nine *Simpsons* scripts, who also left *The Simpsons* in 2004 (he now writes novels), worked in the room only for the show's first few years, appearing on the Fox lot rarely after that to hand in and rework his first drafts. His main role was as the show's premiere first draftsman.

John Swartzwelder is an enigma. No one I interviewed knows much about the man, and unlike Meyer, he has never given an interview or spoken publicly about himself or his work. There is not a single Swartzwelder commentary on *The Simpsons* DVDs (as of this moment, they are up to Season 12). There is even a myth among *Simpsons* fans that Swartzwelder does not exist. A former ad man and writer for *Saturday Night Live* (with Meyer), he has written far more *Simpsons* scripts than anyone else, including such classics as "Krusty Gets Kancelled," "Rosebud," and "Bart Gets an Elephant." According to Matt Groening, Swartzwelder used to write his first drafts while sitting in a booth drinking coffee and smoking cigarettes at a coffee shop in the San Fernando Valley. When California outlawed smoking in restaurants, Swartzwelder bought a coffee shop booth, moved it into his house, and began writing from home.[5] In a nod to Swartzwelder's elusiveness, the writers often place his image or his name in episodes. In the early days, the one-armed military surplus store owner. Herman, was modeled on Swartzwelder. Later on, he appeared more randomly (and had larger hair, a longer mustache, and bigger belly).

BRIAN ROBERTS: Swartzwelder, one of the oddest guys ever to walk the planet. Nice, but odd. Even after he was making a pretty decent salary, he still drove a crappy car to work every day. He chain-smoked too. You could always tell Swartzwelder's car because his dashboard was always full of empty cigarette packets and fast-food shit and whatever.

BRENT FORRESTER: Swartzwelder was incredibly intelligent and just a pure eccentric. I could never have meetings with him in the office because he reeked of smoke so powerfully that, even though he wasn't smoking in the office, his just being in there meant you couldn't be in there for six hours afterward. You would smell like smoke from the secondhand reek of John Swartzwelder.

DARIA PARIS: There was a rule that you couldn't smoke in Jim's office. When we would have meetings in there John Swartzwelder, who is a very talented writer, wouldn't say a word. He couldn't talk without a cigarette.

BRIAN ROBERTS: He looks a little bit like Mark Twain. Everything that's Civil War on *The Simpsons*—if you notice, there's a very big Civil War theme—that's all from John Swartzwelder.

BILL OAKLEY: Swartzwelder—is Mr. *Simpsons*. He's the guy who gave *The Simpsons* its sense of, like, lunacy. But that's more from his first drafts.

HANK AZARIA: Back in the day we all used to look forward to John Swartzwelder's scripts, like seriously look forward to them.

ROB COHEN: Swartzwelder's an enigma. I really like him. He was always incredibly kind to me. He's almost solely responsible for all the Itchy and Scratchy stuff. I remember he had a really old, weird Datsun B210, with one of the windows made out of plywood. His car was even crappier than my crappy car, which was a '76 Datsun 280Z that had multiple different-colored panels on it, so that made me feel good.

Swartzwelder was this big sort of quiet guy—I think he was from Seattle—with a mustache and a mysterious brother nobody'd ever met.

JAY KOGEN: I got to know all those guys over the course of five years pretty well and while I never have been invited over to John Swartz-welder's house, I always used to imagine what it would be like. Stacks of old newspapers, historic newspapers, portraits of people from 1812. One time I remember he bought a picture that Hitler had painted. I was incredulous. "Really, you want to buy a Hitler painting?" But he *loved* historical artifacts. And so [I imagined] he lived with his brother in the valley and they had old newspapers and historical artifacts. I just pictured it being like . . . I don't know if you know who the Collyer brothers were, they actually died under stacks of old newspapers. That's how I pictured their life in Van Nuys.

BRENT FORRESTER: He told us that when he was in advertising it was his goal to spend as much of his money as he could on whatever the newest technology was. So he was one of the first people with a home computer, for example. It was probably enormous and very slow and incredibly expensive, but it was fun for him to have. And, you know, I think he kind of frittered away a lot of his money that way early on.

We would have story meetings with him outside. And I remember distinctly one time being a young comedy writer, and Swarzwelder just happened to be sitting there, smoking a cigarette on the lawn. And I thought, Man, I'm just gonna ask John Swartzwelder a random question and see what he says in return. And I said, "John, what would you do if you had all the money that you could spend?" And without a moment's hesitation he said, "I would buy a battleship and the Empire State Building. With the Empire State Building, I would just let it run down and get decrepit. Because people would say, 'You can't do that! That's the Empire State Building!' I would say, 'No, I can! I *own* the Empire State Building.' The battleship," he said, "I just think it would change people's conversations with me if they knew that I had a battleship."

BILL OAKLEY: The best thing is a Swartzwelder first draft rewritten by people who can sort of bring it down to earth and put in some more emotion. His strength does not lie with emotion, it lies with the jokes that just come out of left field and that no one in history ever could have made up, other than him. If you look at the Swartzwelder scripts, it's like he comes from another dimension. He is a genius. His material is so strange you almost wonder how his brain works. The ultimate Swartzwelder joke that I still remember appears in the episode "Whacking Day." Homer is letting people park on his lawn, and he has a sign that says, "Parking: $10 per axle." And this foreign guy in this crazy foreign car, with like eight axles, drives up, and Homer goes, "Woo-hoo!" and the foreign man goes, "Hooray!" God, it just makes me laugh.

WALLACE WOLODARSKY: Swartzwelder seemed to go directly from being a homeless person to a writer on *The Simpsons*. He was a little bit older than us and had, I think, seen a little bit more of the world, in terms of being up and down. He did have interesting preoccupations. I know for a while he was collecting Wanted posters. Real Patty Hearst Wanted posters.

BRENT FORRESTER: Swartzwelder, George Meyer, and [writer/producer] John Collier were smart about collecting things like R. Crumb stuff before people figured out who R. Crumb was going to be. Or Daniel Clowes and Robert Williams. You know, George Meyer has an incredible Robert Williams collection. The Swartzwelder Museum would be one of the most fascinating places to hang out.

WALLACE WOLODARSKY: He gave me this sage advice once: if you're somewhere, and you see something you really want, no matter how much it costs, just buy it. Which I follow to this day . . . to great success.

Swartzwelder has not written for the show since 2004. Since then he's devoted his time to skewering the crime, western, and scientific genres with novellas such as *The Time Machine Did It*, *The Exploding Detective*, *Dead Men Scare Me Stupid*, and *How I Conquered Your Planet*.

Brent Forrester: He was once a great athlete and tried out for a professional baseball team, was what we'd heard. But by the time I met him, he was certainly a former athlete—a very tall guy, florid red skin in a way that just bespoke some kind of unhealthiness of diet and exercise regimen.

Jennifer Crittenden, writer/producer, *The Simpsons*: He's truly the most eccentric writer I've ever worked with. He wasn't on staff. We'd only see him when we broke his stories. He always wore the same thing: white short-sleeve button-down shirt and beige corduroy pants. Whenever he came, we'd get lunch from the Apple Pan and he was the only writer allowed to smoke in the room. He told me he got his exercise by running from wherever he was to wherever he needed to go. I guess just sort of integrate random bursts of sweaty cardio into his day. Anyway, when I was on *Seinfeld*, I pitched that as a Kramer story, a few times, actually, and no one ever liked it. They always thought it was too crazy, no one would ever do that.

Also, the day of O.J.'s Bronco chase, John didn't show up for work. He told us that he had been walking around Encino with a baseball bat—looking for him.

FOURTEEN

Who's the Boss?

In which *The Journal of Applied Mathematics* is America's most hilarious publication . . . no one can really get on side with the Rappin Rabbis . . . the Internet blames Mike Scully for everything . . . and Jon Lovitz proves much funnier than Kiefer Sutherland.

While it takes a village to raise a child like *The Simpsons*, the humor, atmosphere, and themes of a particular episode are largely attributed to the sensibilities of the showrunner at the time, which is why people will refer to a "Mirkin show" or the "Scully years." With a new showrunner came new staff, different kinds of jokes, and new directions for a series whose writers, cast, critics, and fans were resistant to change.

Al Jean and Mike Reiss, the showrunners for Seasons 3 and 4, very much followed the lead of Sam Simon, who was still supervising from Gracie. The shows stayed sweet and cohesive, and while some writers, like George Meyer, reportedly grated under Jean and Reiss's leadership (his material was more popular with Sam), the group produced two seasons of *The Simpsons'* best episodes.

JAY KOGEN, writer/producer, *The Simpsons* (1989–92): Those years with Al Jean and Mike Reiss running it were pretty darn good. And then the ones after that maybe not so much. Some people ran it better than others.

COLIN A.B.V. LEWIS, postproduction supervisor, *The Simpsons* (1989–97): When Al and Mike came, they recorded so many takes that the days became really long. The actors started saying, "They're recording too much. They're recording out our voices. They're burning us out. It's too much."

Al Jean, for one, is like a machine. When recording actors, he could hold all the takes in his head. Normally, with executive producers, you can say, "This was a good take," and lead them toward stuff you thought was good and move on. But Al would record like twenty takes for a "d'oh," just waiting, because he didn't want to tell the actors how to do it. But he had it in his head, how the line he wrote was supposed to be read. And he would have the actors say the lines over and over and over again until they got it. And then he would say, "Okay, take number seventeen." And he's not writing anything down! Normally when you start building takes, people will say, "Take this line," or "Take the first half of this line," or whatever. Al Jean would be like, "Take the 'T' from take one, take the rest of the word from take five." It was incredible. It was like working with a computer.

There are certain actors, like Harry Shearer, whom you basically can't do that with. Dan Castelanetta comes from improv. He's always trying to think of some other way to do it. He gets caught up in trying to get as much as he can. He's not only okay with doing so many takes, he'll get into a run where he'll say, "Let me do it this way. Let me try it this way." But Harry, on the other hand, will give you three and then he'll just stop. [Other sources dispute that Shearer set any kind of limit on how many takes he would do.]

DAVID RICHARDSON, writer/producer, *The Simpsons* (1993–94): Well, they were brilliant. You gotta realize that these guys—I think I came in year three or four—had done most of the heavy lifting in years one, two, and three, and they knew the characters really well. Al and Mike were just getting ready to start *The Critic*. And so we had them only for a day or two a week, depending on their schedules. And they could just come in on any script and it was second nature to them, like breathing to them.

WALLACE WOLODARSKY, writer/producer, *The Simpsons* (1989–92): We left during the fourth season, and at that point we were already running out of childhood anecdotes. And I think as a result the show got crazier and crazier. Because all the stories we'd experienced, or seen other people experience, had been exploited. And to see the show go on is mindboggling to me.

For the fifth season, Brooks and Sakai brought in an outsider to run the show. David Mirkin originally came from stand-up, though he'd written for *Three's Company* and directed episodes of *The Larry Sanders Show*, and created shows for Fox, like the esoteric *Get a Life*, with Chris Elliott, and a nutty sketch comedy show, *The Edge*. David Mirkin tends to be a popular topic among Simpsons fans, because it was under him that the show began to move from recognizable territory to new terrain. *The Simpsons* had prided itself on how "real" the family was, despite their status as animated characters, and yet under Mirkin, Homer went to space, his barbershop quartet won a Grammy, and Bart became a celebrity.

CHARLEEN EASTON, assistant to David Mirkin: He was fired off of *The Edge* [featuring Jennifer Aniston, Wayne Knight, and Tom Kenny—the voice of SpongeBob SquarePants], which was a Fox show. So he was actually probably just the right guy [to take over *The Simpsons*] because he had the right sensibility.

He was a decent guy. I've been in this business a long time now and I just think he was a decent guy. James Taylor was his idol.

After the fourth season, many of the classic *Simpsons* writers left, including Wallace Wolodarsky, Jay Kogen, and Conan O'Brien (Al Jean and Mike Reiss were busy with *The Critic*), and new writers were brought in to replace them.

COLIN A.B.V. LEWIS: With David Mirkin, it was a different kind of comedy. That's when Homer sort of became stupid. The writers [Mirkin] brought in started to move away from Bart, and the show became very Homercentric, because that's who they could write for. And that, of course, pisses actors off—it makes some actors happy and other actors bummed out. Because before it was sort of a family comedy and there was so much stuff with Julie [Kavner—Marge] and Nancy [Cartwright—Bart] and Yeardley [Smith—Lisa]. Once the shows start becoming all about Homer, the more secondary characters—those people Homer is around away from home—become central. So there's more Harry Shearer, more Hank Azaria. It was a weird dynamic, because they just didn't know how to write for characters like Lisa.

RICHARD APPEL, writer/producer, *The Simpsons* (1995–99): David Mirkin was receptive to having people from other walks of life on the writing staff. He himself had an engineering background, and I had been a prosecutor. He also hired my friend Dave Cohen, who had a degree in applied math.

BRENT FORRESTER, writer/producer, *The Simpsons* (1993–97); writer/producer, *King of the Hill, The Office*: There were two writers, simultaneously, on the show when I was there who had been published in *The Journal of Applied Mathematics*: Dave Cohen and Ken Keeler. I thought Dave Cohen was the smartest guy I had ever met. His response was, "Yeah? You've never met Ken Keeler." One time, Dave was telling us how he'd just had an article published in *The Journal of Applied Mathematics*. And I thought, Holy shit! And then Ken Keeler's says, "What do they pay these days? Is it still, you know, $4 a word or something?"

BOB KUSHELL, writer, *The Simpsons* (1994–95): The group of guys who were writing on *The Simpsons* at that time coalesced under the banner of being Harvard guys. It's not that it was a closed shop, it's just that they all came from a shared interpersonal experience that I didn't. I was a geeky drama major from UC-Irvine who was a playwright and had my own sketch comedy shows in Los Angeles. I was a performer in a lot of ways.

These guys were very different than me, you know? They were literally mathematicians and scientists, and they were brains. Far smarter than I am, far smarter than I ever will be. I was young. So it was even more intimidating. Ultimately, I think they looked at me more as a specimen in a jar that they had to figure out.

I felt like a real fish out of water. David Mirkin, even though I don't know if he'd ever admit it, was maybe feeling the same thing. The pressure was definitely palpable.

BRENT FORRESTER: Mirkin was not a Harvard guy—he came from pure comedy. He is an *incredibly* talented guy. But he came from stand-up; he didn't come from story writing, and he never wrote any episodes. Well, he wrote one, "Deep Space Homer," but it had to be rewritten by other people. And then he never tried again.

CHARLEEN EASTON: I was the one who was in charge of getting all the writers their offices and stuff, so they would confide in me and they would complain to me (about staying long hours, about the direction of the show, that David wasn't the right guy, and that they knew more, that sort of thing). So I did feel like he was an outsider. And he also made certain creative choices that the writers weren't happy with. He was very into heads exploding and stuff like that. Everybody just felt, at first, like he was taking the show in the wrong direction. And then sometimes Matt Groening would want to come sit in the room too—he didn't really offer very much writing-wise, but it added a little bit of tension. David wasn't happy about that. It was kind of like, "Oh, well, let's tolerate him, he's the guy who got lucky basically, hit the lottery."

We could never understand why Matt got so much credit for the show. One of the reasons why we were told was that he was a good front man for *The Simpsons*. He was the guy who would go out and represent *The Simpsons*, and they needed that.

COLIN A.B.V. LEWIS: The mentality of the show changed so much. In the early days, the people in the crew had nicer cars than the writers. I think the nicest car a writer had was a Cressida or something. Then David Mirkin came in, and Mirkin drove an NSX. It's so weird to talk about cars, but it really was evidence of the show changing. Mirkin drove an NSX and all of a sudden you started seeing Beamers and Mercedeses.

And it stopped being the geeky guys from college writing the show and became people who just really wanted to be comedy writers, and wanted to be Hollywood, so they could say, "I work on *The Simpsons*."

HANK AZARIA, voice actor, *The Simpsons*: I love Al, Mike, and David Mirkin as showrunners. I like different things about each of them. David Mirkin, he was really good at combining a lot of elements of the show. Clever is the word that comes to mind with David. I think a lot of the cleverest shows were under David's reign. Specifically, "Deep Space Homer." That's a classic Mirkin show—he'll take a broad idea but make it so specifically funny. Homer literally went into outer space, but David was so aware that the idea was outrageously over the line that he was able to make shows like that work really, really well.

COLIN A.B.V. LEWIS: We'd been doing twenty-four episodes a year, and I think it was Mirkin who said, "This is crazy, we're doing twenty-one." We always hit this point where scripts would just suck. You'd hit a point where people are just burnt, because they're working five or six days a week, like fifteen-hour days. After you get past those initial bunch of scripts, you start getting the second and third ideas from people, and they're not as fleshed out, but there's no time between the first draft and the table read to fix it.

CHARLEEN EASTON: Mirkin just had balls. I remember one time, on *Get a Life*, we were working on a show with monkeys that had to roller-skate around Chris. And we were there till like three in the morning, because the monkey wasn't able to roller-skate and Fox was ready to shut us down. He just didn't care. I mean, they were threatening to fire him. He didn't care, he wanted it the way he wanted it. I just thought that he had incredible balls.

BRENT FORRESTER: Mirkin really knew how to game the system. He was a huge fan of James Taylor and Paul McCartney, and he got them both in the show as guest voices. And with the Paul McCartney one, he managed to convince Fox that Paul McCartney could be recorded only with the showrunner present. Now, why this would be the case, when multiple actors had recorded remotely, is inexplicable. But they flew him on the Concorde, to England, to meet and hang out with Paul McCartney for two days, which was Mirkin's fantasy. He had the mojo to pull that off—so God bless him, man.

CHARLEEN EASTON: There's no way he would go against Jim Brooks or Richard Sakai. They were two people he would never cross.

RICHARD APPEL: David Mirkin delegated a lot less. When I worked there with Bill and Josh, who ran the show after David, and then Mike Scully after that, there were always at least two rooms going. With Bill and Josh, one of them would usually be in a room. They're a very evenly matched partnership, and you don't think, I'm stuck with Bill, I wish I had Josh, or vice versa. Mike Scully would just delegate to me or to someone else to run another room. And so you had a sense of two rooms going. David didn't do that. He liked to have one big room. And I think the shows were great under him.

JENNIFER CRITTENDEN, writer/producer, *The Simpsons* (1995–96): The thing that really stuck me was that there were just so many people. There were so many writers on staff it was crazy. It was a time when there were a lot of consultants, too, so it was like George Meyer, Jace Richdale, Al Jean, Mike Reiss—Mike and Al would consult—Oakley and Weinstein would usually work in their offices but come in occasionally. It was a giant group of people. And we worked in Mirkin's office, which was a little odd, but he had a giant office and it was just couches and chairs all around the perimeter of the room. There could be up to eighteen people in the room.

CHARLEEN EASTON: We would come in the morning and there would be a lot of sitting around because David would read the trades and there was a lot of wasted time during the day. He was really a night owl. So a lot of times we wouldn't even get started on the rewrites until like four or five. We didn't necessarily have to work those crazy hours, but I think David liked to have fun writers and people around him. He liked to be the center of attention. He was always very fair and very generous, but he worked a lot of hours. I think people thought of him as a narcissist.

BOB KUSHELL: David Mirkin sat in front of a room, at a large desk. Visualizing it now, it felt like we were all a little below him. We were all sunken down into these couches and deep chairs and he was kind of the professor behind a desk who was leading the group. And there was an intimidation factor, whether it was intentional or not. I think it was probably unintentional. But there was an intimidation factor and it depressed me. I found the student factor debilitating.

BRENT FORRESTER: I wouldn't say Mirkin's style was "professorial," because that indicates an intellectualism that Mirkin did not bring to the show. It was more that he was a little bit dictatorial. I mean, he really was not one of the guys. He was much more top-down: I am the authority here. But, you know, that actually worked to our advantage in some ways.

There was a giant debate, when I was there—Seasons 5, 6, and 7—almost war in terms of the passions of the people on the show. Some people felt that what was so valuable about *The Simpsons* was that its characters and emotions were realistic, and that David Mirkin was taking it in a direction that was too surreal. And I think Mirkin would agree that he was pushing it more in the direction of pure comedy. I think he really didn't enjoy the human-emotion element of *The Simpsons*, and he drove the show away from there if he could.

I think what happens is, if you're watching a show in which you get something real, it tricks you into being more sensitive and more sensitized. So you couldn't have one character bash another character's head into the ground. In the Mirkin era, you could do that. I specifically remember when Homer has to be Krusty for a while [Homer goes to clown college and begins to fill in for Krusty], there's a scene in which he bashes someone's head on the ground. Homer beats [the Krusty Burger's version of the Hamburglar] to death, crushing his head on the pavement. And there's the memorable line, "Stop, it! He's already dead!" [Laughs] Which was considered the side-busting line.

And I remember thinking, That's never happened on *The Simpsons* before, a man's head being bashed in. But that was kind of the Mirkin sensibility in a nutshell. That was just the most hilarious thing to Mirkin.

Disagreements over these lurches away from the "reality" of Springfield, so carefully constructed, eventually came to a head when the writers were asked to write a crossover episode with Al Jean and Mike Reiss's *The Critic*, which, having failed on ABC, had been resuscitated by Fox, placing it behind the Simpsons in the 8:30 Sunday night spot. *The Simpsons* would be visited by Jay Sherman, who played the title role in the other Fox sitcom, also produced by James L. Brooks.

BRENT FORRESTER: I remember it being controversial. We had a really high standard on *The Simpsons* for not doing things that we felt had already been done in comedy. And unfortunately, the crossover episode began with a set piece that was a parody of the Gregorian monks—who had a popular CD at that time—which involved "Rappin' Rabbis." Now, to parody rapping was considered hacky, and to throw rabbis into comedy was considered hacky. So to open up the crossover show with rappin' rabbis was like [indignant voice], "In the history of comedy of *The Simpsons*, how dare we, in the crossover, do something so mathematically hacky?" That kind of debate was getting people's ire up.

You can't underestimate how fired up people can get over comedy—which might seem, to the outside world, the very definition of trivial.

Some of the more veteran writers had a problem with *The Critic* incursion, but Matt Groening was dead set against it and made his feelings publicly known. Days before the episode went to air, he removed his name from the episode's credits and made his grievances known to the press. "I am furious with Matt," Jim Brooks told the *Los Angeles Times*'s Judy Brennan. "He's been going to everybody who wears a suit at Fox and complaining about this. When he voiced his concerns about how to draw *The Critic* into *The Simpsons*' universe he was right and we agreed to his changes. Certainly he's allowed his opinion, but airing this publicly in the press is going too far . . . This has been my worst fear . . . that the Matt we know privately is going public . . . He is a gifted, adorable, cuddly ingrate. But his behavior right now is rotten. And it's not pretty when a rich man acts like this."[1]

Groening responded: "The two reasons I am opposed to this crossover is that I don't want any credit or blame for *The Critic* and I feel this violates the Simpsons' universe."

Brennan noted that a *Simpsons* episode takes six months to complete. Why was Groening voicing his complaints only days before the show aired? Groening claimed that he hoped Brooks would have a last-minute change of heart (doubtful, considering how much time, money, and effort go into the production and scheduling of an individual episode). Groening's other explanation for his timing—that pieces were appearing in which he was erroneously credited as *The Critic*'s creator—rings equally hollow. I found a single such claim, in a Buffalo newspaper. If there were others, they were not from major newspapers or media outlets. It seemed that Groening's real reason for going to the press was that he had simply not gotten his way; he was having a tantrum.

"My concern is for my professional ethics and reputation," Groening said. "The problem for me is this: In the mind of the public, I created *The Critic* and produced it, or both." (Far be it from Matt Groening to take credit for the work of others—an irony Jim Brooks seemed to appreciate.) "For years, Al and Mike were two guys who worked their hearts out on this show, staying up until four in the morning to get it right," Brooks said. "The point is, Matt's name has been on Mike's and Al's scripts and he has taken plenty of credit for a lot of their great work. In fact, he is the direct beneficiary of their work. *The Critic* is their shot and he should be giving them his support."[2]

Groening did not directly trash *The Critic*, but he didn't have anything nice to say about it either. "Cartoons have their own style," he said, "and I really have nothing to say about *The Critic*."[3] Reiss and Jean were upset but took Groening's bleating in stride, arguing that the cross promotion was minimal, and that *The Simpsons* episode was a good one (to their credit—it is). After all, the episode was already going to air; what sense did it make for them to add anything to the melee? *The Critic* lasted only ten episodes and then died for good, but Jim Brooks and Matt Groening had reached a crisis point in their relationship—which was never that close to begin with—that some say has never been repaired. Rupert Murdoch told me, "Those two can't stand each other."

The crossover brouhaha had reverberations all throughout *The Simpsons*' staff, especially in David Mirkin's writing room.

BOB KUSHELL: There was a big outcry from the writers about doing it. And people just didn't feel like it was right or appropriate. There was a big discussion one evening, and we were all sitting around talking about the validity of doing a crossover episode. And as each individual writer weighed in, it was becoming increasingly evident to David that the writers did not want to do the show. And yet at the same time you could tell that David was feeling a lot of pressure to do the episode and it was probably because Jim Brooks was producing *The Critic*.

BRENT FORRESTER: The higher-level guys [senior writers who were against doing the episode] were arguing with Mirkin, and Mirkin didn't have the clout and/or confidence to fight with them. Bob Kushell was the lowest guy on the totem pole, and Bob mistakenly also threw in some criticism to Mirkin. And Mirkin decided to take it out on Bob.

BOB KUSHELL: Dan McGrath, one of the writers, was sitting behind me and said something about not thinking it was good for the show. You could just see David about to burst. And of course I had to throw my hat in the ring. I remember I raised my hand, and I said, "You know, David, I just think it hurts the integrity of *The Simpsons*." He looked over his desk, and I happened to be sitting on the floor at the time, I couldn't have been any lower to the ground. And he said, "That's why you're an asshole."

And I said, *"What?"*

Remember, I'm only twenty-five years old. I'm on my dream show and I'm—you know—I'm a kid! And here my executive producer is calling me an asshole. The room kind of just stopped. I was thinking, Did this guy just call me an *asshole* in front of all of these guys?

And he goes, "I said that's why you're an asshole."

I said, "Did you just call me an asshole?"

And he said, "Yeah."

I stood up and I gave some crazy guy-in-a-courtroom speech—that had to have been written by Aaron Sorkin—about how you don't call anyone, from the lowest PA on the show to your second in command, an asshole, at any time. It was eloquent and articulate (or I remember it being), and I just let him have it. I laid him low, and I walked out of the room.

As I'm walking out of the room I heard, you know, the room was obviously dead silent, and I heard him yell, "Come on, Bob, you know we talk that way in this room."

We *never* talked that way in this room. That was *never* a way we talked to *anybody*; it was not that type of room. I love rooms where you can call people assholes, but this was not a room where you can call people an asshole, and if you did, it was serious.

BRENT FORRESTER: Bob then made the mistake of acting as if Mirkin and he were on the same level socially, or something, and said, "What you said was really rude and hurtful to me, and I demand an apology." Mirkin just said, "Well, I'm not gonna give you an apology."

Now Bob was kind of over his head: What could he do? So he stormed out of the room, and he said, "I will not ever come back until I get an apology." You know, again he hadn't thought it through. [Laughs]

BOB KUSHELL: And I turned back on my heels, walked back into the room, and just did it again. I made another speech that was articulate and well delivered—I've never been able to reconstruct since, but I remember it was *very* good.

And I left the room. I had just bought a house, and I remember thinking, There goes that, and there goes everything. I was walking back to my office, and I started crying, and I called my wife, and I said, "Karen, either I just fucked up so bad, or I am the hero of the staff." Because I think that everybody had wished or wanted to tell David Mirkin off at one point or another. And she said, "Bob, I support you, whatever you did; I believe that you had to do it, and I support you."

I remember just hanging up the phone and sitting in my office all alone and crying. Just like, This is it. I'm off the show.

And one by one, the writers I guess had snuck out of the room and called me, or came up to my office to see how I was, and everybody thanked me for what I had done. And I remember very vividly that Bill and Josh, who had not been in the room, called me when they heard about it and said that I was their hero.

BRENT FORRESTER: And, you know, like a few hours later, he just kind of slunk back in and went back to his job, and kept working there for a year or so.

BOB KUSHELL: At the same time, you know, of course I was completely fucked because my contract was a pay or play for the rest of the season and my contract wasn't up until December and this was February. I had to persevere on that staff under David Mirkin for the next eleven months after what happened, and it was brutal.

I never got another script, and it was very difficult, and it would have been much better just to have been fired and been able to move on. But my boss was somebody who I don't think could ever get over me having done what I did.

BRENT FORRESTER: You know, Bob's contract was not renewed. Some people say that Mirkin's final indignity to Bob was to make sure that Bob's contract did not get renewed, even though Mirkin wasn't coming back. Why not renew this guy's contract? He wasn't even running the show. So I don't know. If that's true, then what he did was pretty mean. But it doesn't seem to have hurt Bob's career at all.

Bill Oakley and Josh Weinstein, the writing team that took over next, are described as true *Simpsons* fans. Mirkin had been deferential to the pair, allowing them autonomy with their scripts and rewrites not granted to others. When they took over, they tried to bring the show back to its roots as a family sitcom, digging deeper into the characters, but also taking it in wild new directions, further exploring the world of Springfield with episodes like "22 Short Films About Springfield" and "The Itchy & Scratchy & Poochie Show." Bill and Josh were in paradise. For them, it was like they were back in college, hanging out, screwing around, and making each other laugh. Their style produced the last great *Simpsons* seasons, but the clubby atmosphere could rub some of the writers the wrong way. "It was almost like a fraternity. It's like they didn't seem to want to go home. And that's sort of a common thing in a lot of showrunners—they use their work to avoid whatever situation was happening," one writer told me. "Showrunners didn't usually have families, they didn't have girlfriends. There wasn't any reason to go home."

BRENT FORRESTER: The kind of chutzpah and confidence that a stand-up comedian has, you'll find the opposite of that in writers. The writers pride themselves on their tear-myself-apart introspection. That's more the Bill and Josh way. That's what you'll find with people who come at it from writing. And people who come at it from comedy—Judd Apatow, Dave Mirkin—they're bluffing, at first, when they say, "This is the greatest idea of all time." But they just stick to it until, finally, it does become very good. And that's the way comedians work.

COLIN A.B.V. LEWIS: The reason I love Bill and Josh is that they represented a great balance. They worshipped Sam's writing, Vitti's, Meyer's. But they also inherited *The Simpsons* from Mirkin, where stuff was more jokey, so there'd be a lot of jokes. But Bill and Josh went back to really wrapping each episode into a story that was cohesive and made sense.

BRENT FORRESTER: These guys were the ultimate fans of *The Simpsons* in a way that Mirkin was not. I mean, these were the guys who had watched every episode, knew every detail of the show, and believed that the show was the most important thing in America. And now they were running it. You could just feel that vibe from them, that they were the caretakers of something incredibly valuable and important.

JENNIFER CRITTENDEN: They ran the room differently. We went back to what had been the rewrite room. They deliberated a lot more, and I think the tone of the show changed a little bit, but those were all really good seasons. It was different because they would discuss things between the two of them, whereas Mirkin made his decisions on his own.

Part of being a great showrunner is managing the time. And there's something to be said for making quick decisions. It's important to keep the morale of the staff high and *wanting* to be there as long as you need to be there, as opposed to dragging their feet and not wanting to be there at all.

BRENT FORRESTER: Anytime there was anything written anywhere in a script, it had to be a joke. And it took a lot of time to do that kind of stuff. And sometimes it would get hallucinatory. I remember in the show with Sideshow Bob at the air show; there's a character in that episode— it was a general.

So we needed a name for this general. And it's gotta be a funny name, I guess. And it's like eleven at night; it's twelve at night; it's one in the morning! And it's like, "How fucking long are we gonna sit here, trying to think of a funny name for this guy?" And we never came up with something that was satisfying to Bill and Josh.

Finally, somebody came up with a name—Colonel Hap Hapablap. And everyone laughed, but it was kind of a laugh of like, "This is my life? My fucking life is like grains of sand in the hourglass to arrive at Colonel Hap Hapablap?" And we were just all kind of laughing at the waste of our lives, I think.

But Bill and Josh heard the laughter, and it was contagious. And they were like, "Hap Hapablap! Colonel Hap Hapablap!" They just kept saying it, and it just kept getting funnier and funnier. And that's the name of that guy in the show: Colonel Hap Hapablap.

RICHARD APPEL: One night there were five of us working and it was midnight and I was exhausted and I didn't know when we were going to finish this script. And Bill excused himself and ten minutes later he came back having taken a *shower* in the bathroom off his office. And I thought, That's a bad sign, when the showrunner takes a shower at midnight to feel refreshed. And Bill looked around and he said, "Isn't this great? Haven't we re-created the entire sensibility of what it was like to be in college around this table?" And I looked at him, and I love Bill, and said, "Yes, except I've gone on to get married and have a baby, both of whom I'd like to see before sunrise."

BRENT FORRESTER: Bill and Josh really were like, We'll sacrifice all the hours of our life to do this. And the thing that distinguished *The Simpsons* from everything else on TV is the density of the jokes. I mean, I used to count and say, "Wow! Fucking twelve good jokes on a page?" There're barely twelve lines on the page, you know? But if you kept going back, you could go, "Oh, you know what? That straight line could be a joke." And it got to the point where people would try to get two jokes within a joke.

Bill Oakley finally coined one of the great phrases ever in comedy—I use it all the time: "One joke per joke, please." And that was an indication of the way people would try to add an extra joke into the punch line of a joke. It actually ruins it if you go that far. But it would get rococo on *The Simpsons*.

After Bill and Josh, Mike Scully took over for Season 9. Although it's difficult to determine how much blame can be ascribed to Scully personally, he presided over the first seasons after the golden age of the Simpsons had passed. Scully's episodes excel when compared to what *The Simpsons* airs nowadays, but he was the man at the helm when the ship turned toward the iceberg.

RUPERT MURDOCH, chairman, News Corp: The show has had its ups and downs. It had a couple years there where it grew a bit dark, but we sort of got them out of that.

LARRY DOYLE, writer/producer, *The Simpsons* (1998–2001): Mike Scully was running the show all four years I was there. From a boss point of view he was a great showrunner. They had just come off of several years where the showrunners had acted like most TV showrunners: they kind of didn't get around to doing anything until ten o'clock at night. But with Mike it was really important that we kept decent hours and we went home probably by eight o'clock almost every night. Now that seems late to someone who works in a regular office, but to people in TV that's kind of unthinkable.

DONICK CARY, writer/producer, *The Simpsons* (1996–99): Mike Scully is a guy with five daughters and, you know, occasionally liked to get home and see his family. With Mike, you came in and started working— went through the script, took an hour for lunch, and then came back and started working again. It was much more focused.

TOM MARTIN, writer/producer, *The Simpsons* (1999–2001): He is quite possibly the best boss I've ever worked for. I mean, it isn't just that he is a great guy—he is a great manager of people. He had a natural intellect that wasn't institutionalized, but he also had a natural way with people, and he had trust in you. So he would take people and assign them things, and not [hover over their] shoulders, and assume that they would do a good job, and then they would do a good job.

BRENT FORRESTER: My feeling always was that Scully sat there, working under Bill and Josh, thinking, We don't have to be here this many hours. You know, the show will still be really good without this level of sacrifice.

TOM MARTIN: I'll tell ya, when someone's running a room he tends to listen to two or three people, and it's the people he's on the same wavelength with, and then he kind of filters other people out. Scully had this ability to listen to eight or nine or ten people. If somebody said something, he would at least make eye contact to acknowledge that he heard rather than make the person wonder. He was able to communicate with everybody and keep them working. Everybody went after every loose ball.

LARRY DOYLE: I remember that we were there when the Internet decided the show had gone down the toilet, so Mike Scully became kind of a focus for that. I'd like to point out, however, that now, many years later, many of the episodes that were apparently the end of the show are now considered golden classics and are used to illustrate how shitty the show is now.

JACOB BURCH, administrator, NoHomers.net: The notion that the show had been getting worse and worse and worse had been around since the fifth or sixth season. Then the consensus was Season 9, but now I see people naming 10, the idea being that Season 9 was unjustly criticized, though still not great.

TOM MARTIN: There're a lot of complaints on the Internet about Scully and I never quite understood why. He handled it so well. I think it bothered him, and it still bothers him, but he managed to not get worked up over it and not take it personally. He talks about it, but shockingly it doesn't seem to really bother him as much as it would a normal person.

LARRY DOYLE: One of the things that happened is that Bill and Josh seemed to have gotten bored with the Simpsons, so a lot of the episodes from their last two years focused on secondary characters. I think they were really into trying to deepen and explore the world of Springfield— they did the "22 Short Films About Springfield" episode. And Mike wanted to bring it back to the family.

BILL OAKLEY, writer/producer, *The Simpsons* (1991–97): I haven't been in the writers room since the ninth season; that's when they put the conference table in. Everything is very different now. It's not the way you remember it. I like to preserve my memories the way they were.

In 2001, Al Jean once again took the reins and has not relinquished them to this day. Until Scully, showrunners took the helm for two-year stints. While Scully's four-year tenure as showrunner was seen as too long, Jean's Mugabe-like stewardship is nearing a decade. Critically speaking, Scully's last seasons were the worst the show had seen. There was a hope that Jean would bring the show back to some recognizable level of quality. Despite some bright spots here and there ("The President Wore Pearls," for example), he has largely failed. Trying to explain the decline of the show's quality over the past eight seasons, current and former staffers tend to use two words more than any others: Al Jean.

The years Jean and Reiss ran the show together were some of the best, but that was a decade earlier, with a single room of less than a dozen über-talented writers (and Reiss's contribution should not be underestimated). When Jean returned to run *The Simpsons*, the sentiment among the writers, according to one of them, was, "We'll work around it. There're so many writers. I think there was a lot of feeling that the show would be the same as it ever was."

As for the veterans of the room, most of the ex-*Simpsons* staffers I spoke to no longer watch the show. Other than being amazed at its longevity, none of them had much positive to say about it. Many give Jean and the other producers credit for keeping up any level of quality after this many years, which points to Jean's skill as an organizer. Coordinating *The Simpsons* takes a phenomenal amount of organization. As one *Simpsons* staffer put it, it is a twenty-hour-a-day job, twelve months of the year (because the seasons overlap). There are forty steps per episode for a showrunner to manage, and halfway through the year you're on step sixteen of the first show, step twelve of the second show, and meanwhile, you have the shows you wrote last year coming back from Korea, which will be on step thirty, etc. They have massive charts to keep everything organized. You need to be a genius like Al Jean to keep it all straight. Another staffer asserted that this was the key reason Brooks has kept Jean at the helm for so long—the shows might not be amazing, but Jeans makes the trains run on time.

TOM MARTIN: I remember one time we were trying to figure out the national debt and what each of us owed. It was printed on the cover of the *Los Angeles Times*, "National debt is" whatever dollars. And then I said, "Let's say there's 250 million people," and I go, "Hey, Al, let's say it was like 55 trillion divided by 250 million?" And he did it in one second. He literally did this complicated mathematical equation that involved 10 or 12 places, digits, and he solved it in his head faster than a calculator. Yeah, he's a freak.

But the ability to run the show like a well-oiled machine may have had negative consequences as well. One writer attributed the show's decline to the division of the now massive writing staff into two or more rooms. Often, one room doesn't know or care what the other is doing, which leads to a lack of cohesion and can affect story lines, as well as the more touching, subtle, soft, or tender aspects of the show. Jokes are pumped as if they're on an assembly line. Scripts are assembled, tied together by executive producers with solitary visions, which can sometimes mean the stories become chaotic and disjointed.

TIM LONG, writer/producer, *The Simpsons* (1998–   ): I didn't really get a strong sense of the content of the show changing—you have to understand that Mike Scully was working for Al. Whenever anybody stops being a showrunner, he continues to work for the show and for the next showrunner. It's as if Clinton gave way to George W. Bush but continued on as George W. Bush's second in command. The show is this rolling stone that never loses any of its moss. It just keeps growing, and people stay in one capacity or another.

DONICK CARY: It seems like it's gotten a little simpler. It goes a little more topical. And it's a little easy. But, at the same time, they're in Season 18, so what the hell?

Not everyone has been so sanguine about Jean's captaining of the show's prolonged downturn. In 2004, the notoriously vocal Harry Shearer told United Press that he believed the show had run its course. (It wasn't a coincidence that 2004 was the year Shearer and the cast went on strike for more money. That being said, Shearer made these comments in August, many months after the dispute had been resolved.) "It makes me sad," Shearer told the news service. Jean was touchy about Shearer's remarks and seemed more than a little hurt. "I think this past season was great, and I'm just so shocked that he would say that," he told the *New York Post*. "I ran Season 4 and he wasn't happy then." Jean accused Shearer of grumbling because of his characters' lack of airtime, and shot back, "I don't know why I have to defend the quality of the show to Harry Shearer . . . He's a guy who's been a malcontent, in my view," Jean told UPI. "For someone earning millions off the show this year . . . I just think it's unfathomable for him to take a shot at us."

Former writers complain that under Jean, the show is "on autopilot," "too sentimental," and that the shows are "just being cranked out." One of Jean's own producers complained that Jean is "ruining the show." Off the record, others acknowledge that the show has entered a steady decline under Jean and is no longer really funny. While no one would argue with Jean's experience, commitment, and intelligence (he now has a piece of the show), it's clear that he does not inspire the same kind of loyalty and admiration previous showrunners enjoyed. While it could amount to little more than office politics, there is real dissatisfaction with the head writer for the show, which could benefit from a change in leadership. Dana Gould, Matt Selman, and Tim Long were put forward as people who, at this point, could run the show better than Jean.

What has defined the Al Jean era is the show's definitive move into the mainstream of American TV and culture. By now *The Simpsons* is the most successful show in the history of television—it's a long way from the young, mouthy, experimental series on the upstart network. With the show's popularity such a shift was inevitable, and for many reasons it's unfair to compare today's episodes with those from the show's heyday. But it's undeniable that the bite in the satire and social commentary is no longer there.

MATT GROENING (to Terry Gross on NPR's *Fresh Air*): You know, at the beginning, virtually anything we did would get somebody upset. And now it seems like the people who are eager to be offended—and this country is full of people who are eager to be offended—they've given up on our show. So if you're bothered by *The Simpsons*, by now you know to tune out.

DOUGLAS RUSHKOFF, media critic: What you'd have to do [to keep *The Simpsons* relevant] is constantly leverage your financial excess to ratchet up the intensity of your cultural critique. What happened with *The Simpsons* is the more ubiquitous it got, the more regular little kids were watching it, and the more responsible, I think, the writers felt for these little minds. Bart went from being a true prince of irreverence, a true dangerous Gen X slacker catalyst, into a vulnerable little boomer.

The toothlessness of the Jean era is best exemplified with the show's four hundredth episode, a parody of the hit Fox series *24*, with a guest appearance by Kiefer Sutherland (as agent Jack Bauer). They created a *Simpsons* version of the hit program, in which Principal Skinner ran his own CTU (Counter-Truancy Unit), staffed by Lisa and other dorks, and charged with stopping several bullies from setting off a stink bomb. Despite some skilled animation, which cleverly aped *24*'s filming and editing style (and won *The Simpsons* an Annie Award), the episode is little more than a marketing video for both series.

This campy, humorless tribute to *24* was the kind of thing *The Simpsons* would have made fun of in the old days. To make sure they included Sutherland and his character, midway through the episode Jack Bauer picks up a misdirected call from Bart Simpson. "Who is this?" asks Bart. "I'm Jack Bauer. Who the hell are you?" he replies. Get it? That's Bart's catchphrase; the episode was so lame that they could not even find a clever way to mock their involvement—they just referred back to their own show. It was not just a crossover episode, like *The Simpsons* had done with the *X-Files* and *The Critic*, accompanied by some sense of complicity (when Bart met Jay Sherman, he said, "I think all kids should watch your show," and then turned away, saying, "I suddenly feel so dirty"). Instead, this was a full-on hand job to Fox and its most popular drama. It should be added that *24*, aside from being chock-full of McBain-type violence and melodrama, owes its success to the post-9/11 climate of terrorist fear-baiting promulgated by network and cable news (especially Fox), and the Bush administration. *24* unapologetically endorses torture and, less overtly, the Bush administration's erosion of civil rights that accompanied its war on terror. This was precisely the kind of show *The Simpsons* would have taken to task back in the day, with a smart send-up or a clever gibe. Instead, the Al Jean *Simpsons* devoted an entire episode to its further promotion.

While episodes like this indicate apathy in *The Simpsons*' satire, another symptom of the Jean years is the increasingly explicit social and political commentary. We are now clubbed over the head with entire episodes devoted to a single contemporary subject, like electoral politics ("See Homer Run"/2005),* gay marriage ("There's Something About Marrying"/2005), and FCC censorship ("You Kent Always Say What You Want"/2008).

Previously, politics had been mocked with the consistently corrupt and lascivious Mayor Quimby, characterizations of Republicans in episodes like "Sideshow Bob Roberts," and the recurring exploitation of the town's populist leanings, whether against bears or immigrants. Yet 2007's Halloween episode contained a message that was so blatant and facile, a *Family Guy* viewer would have caught it. At the end of a segment parodying the reaction to Orson Welles's 1938 radio broadcast *The War of the Worlds*, the aliens Kang and Kodos, who have destroyed the town and become an occupying force, survey the destruction. Kang blames Kodos, saying that he'd promised they would be greeted as liberators. "Don't worry, we still have the people's hearts and minds," replies Kodos, holding up a human heart and brain. "I'm starting to think Operation Enduring Occupation was a bad idea," says Kang. "We had to invade. They were working on weapons of mass disintegration," Kodos insists, reinforcing the analogy *yet again*. "Sure they were," concludes Kang. "This sure is a lot like Iraq will be." This last line, made available to media on a preview DVD of the episode, was cut for broadcast, because Jean thought the reference was "too obvious."[4]

---

*An episode written by Stephanie Gillis, the wife of Al Jean and a former personal trainer. She has since written two more scripts, to the dismay of other *Simpsons* writers, who see her involvement in the show as a bone of contention with Jean and his leadership.

FIFTEEN

Foxy Boxing

In which Moe, Apu, Principal Skinner, and Homer form a united front . . . Marge and Bart become scabs . . . we learn the difference between the Catholic church and the Catholic league . . . and Rupert Murdoch hates the Internet.

When any single entity, like *The Simpsons*, makes such a heavy imprint on its parent company, struggles over power are inevitable. Fox would emerge in the 2000s as the number one network on television, and in many ways *The Simpsons* provided the foundation for Fox's growth, both financially and as its most recognizable brand (Disney has Mickey Mouse; Fox has Bart Simpson). This role made *The Simpsons* disproportionately powerful—the producers, writers, and actors could make demands that other employees simply couldn't—so they thought.

If compensation was ever an issue for producers, it has never come to my attention—Fox has been more than happy to reward *The Simpsons'* genius writers handsomely, even in consulting roles. The actors are a different matter. It was very much in Fox's interest to keep the identities of the voices obscure for as long as possible to reinforce the notion that they were "replaceable." Their perceived contribution was reflected in their small paychecks: in the first two years, they made $3,000[1] an episode; by the late nineties, that figure had risen to $25,000,[2] with a negligible percentage of the licensing and merchandising revenues. At the same time, the *Seinfeld* cast members were making $600,000[3] per episode, and *Home Improvement*'s Tim Allen had signed a deal giving him $1.25 million[4] per episode. *The Simpsons'* voices were paid one-fiftieth of that, and in their opinion were making an integral contribution to a product that was making untold sums for its parent company.

As far as Fox was concerned, the actors were well compensated; after all, they were making tens of thousands per episode, for only a few hours of work each week. Also, the voices didn't bear the same weight as actors on a sitcom, such as *Friends* or *Seinfeld*, and their lax schedule and virtual anonymity allowed them to pursue other projects in film and TV. In 1998, negotiations for new contracts turned bitter as the cast banded together, demanding more money and a share in the profits. Though showrunner Mike Scully refused to participate, Fox began auditioning replacements.

COLIN A.B.V. LEWIS, postproduction supervisor, *The Simpsons* (1989– 97): There was a day, there was an actual moment, when the actors, who are normally just friendly, sat down and started talking more in depth about contracts. They asked us to give them some time alone, and we were thinking, Alone? You guys don't hang out alone. They literally closed the door.

HANK AZARIA, voice actor, *The Simpsons* (1989–   ): The show has made so much money, in so many ways. Eventually, we just wanted to get our piece of the pie. And Fox is tough. They're very tough negotiators. Their business model is not to give money away. So it got a little intense at times.

Julie Kavner and Nancy Cartwright signed separate deals, but Azaria, Shearer, Castellaneta, and Smith held out. Fox was happy to give them more money, but these four actors wanted points. On most sitcoms, the talent will be recognized as producers after a number of seasons and given a piece of the back end. Fox's refusal even to discuss such an option was a reflection of their belief that the voices were simply not as important to *The Simpsons* as, say, the friends were to *Friends*.

The fact that the voices ended up getting a raise, but not a piece of the action, indicates that Fox was seriously considering replacing them. "If they get all new voices, some people will be upset until they get used to it," a media buying executive told *Variety*. "Some people will say the show's not the same, the voices are different. But I've got to believe the people at Fox are smart enough to get voices that closely approach the originals. There are enough mimics out there."[5]

HANK AZARIA: Even if you can get people to sound a lot like us, it's very difficult to get people who can perform it the same way. Ultimately, you get paid what you're worth. *Believe me*, if they discovered in the course of that process that they could get other people, they absolutely would have done that.

LARRY DOYLE, writer/producer, *The Simpsons* (1998–2001): The actors actually didn't come to work for a while. Their contract expired, and we weren't recording them for I think a month. Fox had started to audition people. The actors got their deal in 1998 because of a last-minute bonus [and a raise to $50,000 per episode for Season 10, $60,000 for Season 11, and $70,000 for Season 12[6]]. But it turned out that they weren't going to get the bonus money until 2005 or something. So it was a real Fox "Fuck you," where the fine print means, "We're going to deliver that, in pennies, after you're dead." So Harry Shearer, for the longest time, came to every table read wearing a T-shirt that said, "You'll Get It in 2005," the suggestion being that he wasn't going to do anything but work to contract.

Oddly, while Gracie Films refused to comment, other than to pledge their hope that things would be resolved, Jim Brooks certainly had a role in all of this too. The voices were officially negotiating with Fox, but Brooks and the other producers ultimately controlled *The Simpsons'* content and held enormous sway with the network. It was Brooks's lawyer, not the actors' representatives, who came in to negotiate the bonus that ended the actors' holdout. (Hence there's an argument to be made that the "fuck you" bonus came from Brooks, not Fox.)

RUPERT MURDOCH: The voices who have been there since the very beginning are now getting very large salaries. I'm not saying whether they're worth it or not or whether you could replace them or not, but Jim Brooks wouldn't hear of that, because they're all his friends.

It is highly unlikely Jim Brooks would take that position—he wasn't really good friends with the actors, and he's first and foremost a businessman. "If he was saying he didn't want to replace them, it was because he thought the show would tank, and I think it probably would have," a former producer says. "Had they replaced Homer, I think that would have been the last year of the show."

HANK AZARIA: I think that Fox, and even our own representation, didn't realize how much these voices couldn't just be replaced. And also, by the way, you don't animate first and then stick in voices. You're animating to the vocal performance, so that means comic timing and inflection and character all come first, and then you animate. Bottom line is: they tried to replace us and couldn't. [The voice actors who do *The Simpsons* in Japan were not so lucky. For the film, the regular voice actors were replaced by Fox Japan with celebrities from television and film. Fans were outraged.[7]]

In 2001, far kinder contract negotiations gave the cast $100,000 per episode for the following two seasons, $125,000 for the third, and delivered their $1 million bonuses four years early[8] (Castellaneta was also given a production deal with Fox).

Things got ugly again in 2004, when the cast demanded more cash and equity positions, and stopped showing up to work until a deal was reached. The voices were clamoring for $8 million each per season (that's $360,000 per episode) and some kind of back-end position,[9] the first time voice actors had demanded to be treated on par with live action sitcom stars. For execs told *The New York Times* that it was "an enormous stretch" for the voices to make this comparison, noting that sitcom actors like *Ray Romano* and *Kelsey Grammer* are forever associated with their television characters, which can affect their future careers[10] (Romano was reportedly receiving $1.7–$2 million per episode[11] for his contribution to the most ironically named sitcom of all time, *Everybody Loves Raymond*. Not everybody. Trust me). Fox again pointed out that the workload for the voices was several hours per week, leaving them time to pursue other opportunities in film, TV, and theater.[12] Jim Brooks and the other producers at Gracie refused to comment.

The actors and their representatives hired a financial analyst who specialized in TV and presented Fox with a report claiming that in its lifetime, *The Simpsons* had made $2.5–$3 billion;[13] it was time they got their share. Fox execs claimed this number was astronomically high and said it did not take into account the high cost of producing an animated show and paying its massive staff. The voices' refusal to come to work stretched toward May, with Fox claiming that the strike would curtail the show's thirteenth season (it didn't), and finally threatening to cancel the series.[14] During the last week of April, Fox put forth a final offer, which the actors accepted, settling on approximately $300,000 per episode.[15] (*Variety* reported that two of the voices had broken ranks, putting pressure on the others to drop their demand for profit sharing. "You're only as strong as your weakest link," a source close to the negotiation told the newspaper.)

The most recent dispute was settled in the summer of 2008, with production being delayed several months as the actors demanded $500,000 per episode.[16] In early June, a deal was announced, giving the cast members, with the exception of Harry Shearer, $400,000 per episode for the coming nineteenth and twentieth seasons, and naming Castellaneta a consulting producer.[17] Shearer hammered out the terms of his contract several weeks later. The show has been renewed to Season 22. The next round of negotiations will take place in 2010.

DONICK CARY, writer/producer, *The Simpsons* (1996–99): They have an hour of work a week—or two hours a week—and, you know, at this point they're bringing in three, four million a year.

Other than Mike Scully, none of the producers, especially the senior ones like Brooks, Sakai, and Al Jean, have ever weighed in on the negotiations or the importance of the cast to their show, a fact that Fox could take advantage of during talks. After all, it became much more difficult for the actors to negotiate if just one of them broke ranks. Not all of them have much else going on in their careers outside of *The Simpsons*. It isn't difficult to imagine that one or several of the voices were afraid of losing their job, no matter how much they stood to make if they held on. Fear, it seems, spreads faster than greed. Without support from Gracie and Brooks, Fox could tell an actor that Brooks was sick of all the BS from them, that it was getting to be more trouble than it was worth. Gracie's silence throughout these flare-ups with the cast speaks volumes about its commitment to the cast.

———

A second issue between the network and *The Simpsons*, where Fox has exerted far less leverage, relates to the content of the show. Network notes are the bane of many a showrunner and writer's existence. The creative content of most network television shows can be dictated by network execs, who want to channel a show's direction to maximize profitability ("The eighteen- to twenty-four-year-olds like it when the cat murders people. Can you add some more scenes with Mr. Meowser?"). *The Simpsons* has long claimed that one of the keys to its success is that, under the protective umbrella of Jim Brooks, it has never had to deal with network notes. While the show is certainly autonomous in a way no other network shows are (cable shows have different standards and controls, which is why most innovative and well-written programming can be found on HBO, Showtime, Comedy Central, etc.), there are some different opinions on how much influence Fox has held.

BRENT FORRESTER, writer/producer, *The Simpsons* (1993–97); writer/producer, *King of the Hill*, *The Office*: Jim Brooks, when he established the show, said, "There's gonna be none of that." And the executives, in fact, are not invited to the table reads. Unheard of—but he had the clout to do that. And I think you can see that it didn't hurt *The Simpsons*.

GARTH ANCIER, former president of entertainment, Fox Broadcasting: My style with someone like Jim—I can't say it's my style with everybody, but my style with someone as talented as Jim—is to give very broad notes. I don't give more than five of 'em (a rule I learned from Brandon Tartikoff, when I was a child in television). If you have to give more than five notes, you have the wrong producer.

LARRY DOYLE: When you have a table read with a regular sitcom, you go in there and there's always a sense of fear, because those people at the network are unpredictable. They can come back and say, "No, we don't want you to do that," and then you'll have a day to write a new script. That never happens to us.

BRENT FORRESTER: [Recently] Mike Reiss finally decided that he was secure enough in his career to publicly say what he'd always thought, which is that executive notes are the bane of television comedy. If people asked themselves, "Why does TV comedy suck?" the simple one-line answer is "executive interference."

That's Mike's opinion. I don't know enough to disagree with him. And I certainly have seen enough to say there's a lot to that.

The Simpsons never had notes—maybe of any kind. Typically with a television show, you submit the scripts, you get notes on the scripts; if they come to the table, you get notes on the table; if they come to the rehearsals, you get notes on that.

JOSH WEINSTEIN, writer/producer, *The Simpsons* (1991–97): Working on *The Simpsons* felt like being in the graduate school of comedy, or a great comedy lab, where you could try and do anything and no one would stop you, as long as it was good or funny. That had an amazing feel.

BRAD BIRD, executive consultant, *The Simpsons* (1989–97); director, *The Incredibles, Ratatouille*: There were discussions with the network, but they were over pretty quickly. I think people felt good being under the titanium shield of Jim Brooks. The studio might get upset and might make notes, but we didn't have to take them unless Brooks said we had to take them.

He was inclined to do whatever was necessary to make the best episode and the best comedy. And he protected his showrunners and his writers and allowed good work to flourish.

I think all of my best experiences, for the most part, have been from behind some sort of titanium shield, whether it's *The Simpsons*, or up here at Pixar, where you don't get affected by the kind of mentality that runs most of Hollywood.

BARRY DILLER, former CEO, 20th Century Fox: Anything with Jim Brooks has a level of independence in it, but it's not exclusionary. Jim's not about being exclusionary, and in this case couldn't be—there was just too much strife going on between Sam Simon and Matt Groening. Were we engaged in the early development of it, Fox network people? Yes. Did we give line notes? Not ever. I never gave line notes in my life.

GARTH ANCIER: You can't produce a show from the network. It has to be that the person who's actually making the show has a vision and a voice to make it. So you know we did kick around, was it possible to make this show? How would we make it? Was it economically possible to make with the lead times? How would we order a back nine* (which is why we started it midseason, so we wouldn't have to worry about back nines and all those kinds of things)? But at the end of the day, I don't think we did give much guidance to Jim and the team because it's Jim Brooks.

AL JEAN (Season 2 DVD commentary): Very early on we had difficulty [with the broadcast standards people] saying "butt" or "ass." And of course *now* NBC's logo is "kiss our ass."

BRIAN ROBERTS, editor, *The Simpsons* (1989–92): I came up with this idea that Marge paints this picture of Mr. Burns and he's got the world's tiniest dick. And when it's unveiled, I said, "The very top of a feather obscures his tiny dick," or whatever it was, and then the last line of the show is "By the way, Marge, thanks for not making fun of my genitalia."

It was at a time at Fox where the envelope was still being pushed and Barry Diller and the network and the studio guys were saying, "We absolutely cannot allow the word 'genitalia' to be on Fox." This was actually kind of a big deal because this was the first time that Fox had tried to control the content on *The Simpsons* . . . I still have this. This is one of my prized possessions. There's a letter.

It says, "Dear Mr. Diller, We respect and support Brian Roberts's use of the word 'genitalia' at the end of 'Brush with Greatness.' We will not remove it under any circumstances." And then it's signed Matt Groening, James L. Brooks, Sam Simon, and the rest of the writing staff. It was at that time that the power shifted and Fox realized that *The Simpsons* was just gonna do whatever it fucking wanted to do and that Fox

---

*The back nine refers to the later nine episodes of the first season. When a network decides that it likes a show that has been on the air for a few weeks, and is going to purchase a full season's worth of episodes, it orders the back nine. With *The Simpsons*, because of the long lead time involved with animation, they couldn't show a few episodes, see if it was a hit or not, and then order up more episodes if it was. They had to order the back nine at the same time they gave the pilot the green light.

was the recipient of a whole bunch of good luck. It was a really great compliment that they backed me up and stood by me.

Al Jean has said that, in the episode where Bart was hired by Fat Tony and became a mobster, the broadcast standards people had a huge problem because they believed it would influence children to join a gang. "But this is an Italian, mafia gang,"[18] Jean told the network folks, who were afraid the gang Bart was joining would be like the Bloods or the Crips. At the time, Jean was apoplectic that they had to spend so much time meeting with the network on this topic—there were six pages of notes on that episode alone.

DONICK CARY: There was this one joke where Homer's making new inventions, and one of his inventions is a whore gun. It's basically a gun you point at your face, and then pull the trigger, and it blasts makeup onto your lips and eyes. The combination of "whore," "gun," and "point a gun at your face" drew some red flags at Fox legal. And then we got to the point where we all really, really loved the whore gun, and the feeling was, No, they can't take that away!

Essentially, on some level you're dealing with a bunch of class clowns. So as soon as someone tells you you can't do something, it becomes even more imperative that you do it. As soon as they say, "We don't really like the whore gun," the response is "Yep—the whore gun's gotta stay."

TOM MARTIN, writer/producer, *The Simpsons* (1999–2001): My Super Bowl episode, we wanted to do a joke about the silly commercials they have and how weird they are. And so we did this commercial where a guy's driving down the road, and you can see the heat coming off of the asphalt. The guy pulls into an abandoned gas station and runs over the thing, *ding, ding,* and it turns into this sort of ZZ Top commercial where all these beautiful girls come out and they clean the car and they pump the gas and it's really sexually suggestive, and then it zooms in on one girl's cleavage, and there's a crucifix there, and then the voice-over says, "The Catholic church. We've made a few changes."

And then they cut to Marge and Lisa watching the Super Bowl at home and saying, "I don't get these commercials. They're getting stranger and stranger." We thought we were making a joke about the type of attempts they make to make an impact with their commercials on Super Bowl Sundays. What we didn't realize was there was this organization called the Catholic League, I believe, that was going to organize forty thousand e-mails and letters from fourth graders and third graders and second graders to say this was offensive to them.

Mind you, there was no official Catholic institution that was offended—it was the Catholic League, which is a lay organization. And it worked. For the rerun, they insisted that we take out the part about the Catholic church, and Fox wanted us to say, "the church. We've made a few changes." Mike Scully just refused. He wasn't going to do it. And I think that, on the first rerun, someone at Fox dipped the volume down during "Catholic." Since then, I don't know what's happened with that episode.

But what struck us as strange was that of all the Catholic countries love *The Simpsons*; there were no complaints from anywhere in South America or France or Italy or Ireland or any of these other places. But the Catholic League in America thought this joke was offensive, and Fox buckled.

One of the great episodes would not have existed without network interference. For "A Streetcar Named Marge," in which Springfield's community theater puts on a version of Tennessee Williams's *A Streetcar Named Desire*, the writers originally merely had Marge and the other actors performing scenes from the play. Naturally, the Williams estate wouldn't let them rip off entire scenes from the copyrighted work, so the writers had to change it. Even though they couldn't replicate the play, they were allowed to parody it. Hence: *A Streetcar Named Desire: The Musical*. Unfortunately, that episode still managed to land *The Simpsons* in trouble. In opening number of the musical, New Orleans is referred to as a "town of drunks and whores."

In New Orleans, where Quincy Jones owned the local Fox affiliate, *The Simpsons* was pulled off the air for several weeks. Bart Simpson, who was supposed to be the king of the Mardi Gras parade that year, received a death threat. Someone from New Orleans called up Mike Reiss and told him, "When your friend Bart comes down here, we're gonna kill him." Reiss informed the real-life

Sideshow Bob that there was in fact no real Bart Simpson, and that the Bart Simpson in the Mardi Gras parade would be a midget in a foam and rubber costume. "Well," the man replied, "we're gonna kill him."[19]

Around the world, when it is played in different languages for wide-ranging cultures, foreign audiences often appreciate *The Simpsons* as a satire of American life. Yet when other countries are satirized on the show, they can have less of a sense of humor about themselves.

The Simpsons was also pulled off the air in Japan and condemned in the Australian parliament. When *The Simpsons* went to Rio de Janeiro in 2002, the show was sued by the Brazilian Tourist Council. According to Mike Reiss, their complaint was "When *The Simpsons* came to Rio, they encountered grinding poverty, rat-infested slums, pickpockets, kidnappers, and wild monkeys. There are *no wild monkeys* in Rio."[20]

The tiff with Brazil, which had just spent $18 million on a tourism promotion campaign, was smoothed over when Jim Brooks said, "We apologize to the lovely city and people of Rio de Janeiro, and if that doesn't settle the issue, Homer Simpson offers to take on the president of Brazil on Fox's *Celebrity Boxing*."[21] Since then, the Simpsons have gone to Africa (where they were chased by a hippo, engaged in tribal dancing, and witnessed political strife), London, and Toronto without incident.

COLIN A.B.V. LEWIS: David Mirkin was the first showrunner who said, "Why do we have to change it? We're *The Simpsons*. We're in control because they want their hit show, and I will get to Saturday night and I won't deliver them a show, and then they will have to air what I give them." I remember episodes where they gave us a list of changes to make and where stuff needed to be cut, and Mirkin's telling me, "No. Don't change it. Colin, do not change it."

For Mirkin, taking a stand against the network didn't end with censorship.

BRENT FORRESTER: One of the things that Mirkin was most proud of was that we were allowed to eat at the most expensive restaurants, always. Mirkin really felt that was something cool he had done for us. He would brag about it, saying, "They told me I had to bring this food budget down. I said, 'Well, you know what, then? The scripts will be a week late. 'Cause I cannot deliver the script on time if my people are not fed with the most expensive food.' " And they caved. Or maybe he was lying about that, but that certainly was the myth he created about himself.

The Simpsons' people see these victories as major, but speak to the execs and you get the idea that, for them, the important thing was to let the writers *think* they were getting away with murder.

Rupert Murdoch: What happens with every show is the producers and different people discuss and debate things and the people on the cutting edge of the product side are always saying, "I'm carrying around the network, and they bring in suits, and aren't they horrible," but that's all right.

When *The Simpsons* made fun of Fox News with a scrolling banner that included such fake news items as "Rupert Murdoch: Terrific Dancer," "Study: 92 Percent of Democrats Are Gay," and "The Bible Says Jesus Favored Capital Gains Cut," the writers were forbidden from ever doing it again. According to Matt Groening, the network was afraid people would think the news items were real.[22]

The Simpsons' "subversive" brand of humor was ultimately very profitable for Fox. Rupert Murdoch would broadcast Marxist propaganda if the ratings were high enough. The volume at which *The Simpsons'* staff broadcast their relative freedom betrays their tacit knowledge that their content fits right in with the Fox system, and that the decision to leave them alone comes from News Corp, not the Gracie bungalow. For the last ten to twelve years, the point has been nearly moot; the content of the show has hardly been racy, even for network TV. If the network had the power to interfere with the show, and I believe they do, they wouldn't need to. *The Simpsons* people are falling over themselves to make episodes promoting *24*— what reason would Fox have to censor *The Simpsons*? More than ever, they're playing for Fox's team.

As they demonstrated by green-lighting *The Simpsons* and then leaving them alone, occasionally network executives make smart decisions.

MATT GROENING (to *Rolling Stone*, November 28, 2002): It's tough to run a network these days, but just to show how misguided they are: I pitched a spin-off of *The Simpsons*—imagine the idea of Teen Homer or Li'l Homer's Adventures. Fox wasn't interested, which is baffling . . . Rupert Murdoch might not have been happy with his henchmen, if he knew about it.

One forum where Fox has been able to effectively assert dominance is the Internet. Like most television, film, and music executives, the suits at Fox failed to catch on to how they could use the Internet to their advantage. They saw it only as a new way for people to infringe on their copyright, pursuing the smallest fan sites for using sounds or images from the show. While Fox has relaxed in recent years, realizing the benefit and free advertising the web has handed their products, they are still vigilant and resolvedly behind the times. While all of *South Park*'s episodes are offered for free online viewing by Comedy Central, Fox still aggressively prohibits YouTube and other video-sharing services from showing even *Simpsons* clips, never mind entire episodes.*

JOUNI PAAKKINEN, administrator, The Simpsons Archive: Fox did not greet this fan enthusiasm [on the Internet] with pure joy. In fact, they started to send out cease-and-desist letters, demanding site owners remove all the material they considered infringing. Usually this meant multimedia, especially video and sound clips, but sometimes even links to other *Simpsons* sites were regarded as illegal. This action left many sites crippled. For a while, the atmosphere was really grim and fans didn't feel that they were appreciated at all.

ERIC WIRTANEN, founder, NoHomers.net: I had a huge fan site from 1998 to 2002, and I received probably seven cease-and-desist letters. The wording in some of those letters was just so frightening I eventually

---

*During the writing of this book, Fox began to allow recent *Simpsons* episodes to be viewed on Fox.com.

had to give up. I had screen grabs, sound bytes, wallpaper. Gradually I removed everything, bowing to their wishes, but they just kept going after me until I couldn't take it anymore. They forced me to remove the advertisements I had on the page, which kept it afloat. I wasn't making any money; I had no other way to pay for the site. I did not want to be involved in a lawsuit, being a poor college student. I had no choice but to take it down.

JOUNI PAAKKINEN: Eventually, instead of banning everything, Fox laid out some ground rules and the sites that have followed them have lately been left in peace.

Wirtanen's current site, NoHomers.net, the go-to discussion group for *Simpsons* fans, has had no such problems. The only letter he received was due to *Simpsons* fans posting screen grabs with their comments, a problem quickly addressed by the webmasters, who had not even seen the offending post. The more interesting aside here is that Fox is obviously monitoring for the most minute infringements. They are literally scanning discussion forums on the web, to see if a fan is posting an unlicensed image of Bart with his or her comment on an episode.

Beginning with the fact that Fox paid for the show, nowhere is the notion of *The Simpsons* as a collaboration stronger than in its relationship with the network; the two were a match made in heaven. Fox was young enough, edgy enough, and smart enough to let *The Simpsons* run wild in its earliest, most successful, years; in turn *The Simpsons* became synonymous with Fox. That brand would become so inextricable from the network (and probably just as important financially) that, at different times, Fox would need to concede huge amounts of money and battles over content to keep different elements of the collaboration happy. But those concessions don't mean that the actors or the writers somehow beat out the network. The question of whether the voices are worth what they're paid, or whether it made sense for Fox to let *The Simpsons* writers do whatever they wanted was best answered by Rupert Murdoch. When I asked Murdoch how much *The Simpsons* has made him, in total, he smiled and said, "Let's just say it's a lot."

SIXTEEN

The Guest Stars

In which Albert Brooks finds himself in the trunk of a stranger's car . . . *The Simpsons* depresses Tom Wolfe . . . and Mel Gibson is nice to Jews.

A pleasant side effect of being everyone's favorite show is that "everyone" includes celebrities. No other series has had as many guest stars or featured guests as extraordinarily famous as *The Simpsons* has. During the first season, the show relied on friends of Jim Brooks (Penny Marshall, Al Brooks) for guest voices, but as the show hit it big with the kids, Hollywood parents (and Michael Jackson) soon came clamoring.

ALBERT BROOKS, guest voice, *The Simpsons*; comedian: I think it's different once you have children. You're sitting alone as an adult, watching yourself as a cartoon, and you don't have much feeling for it. But if you can watch any cartoon with a child, it's always fifty times better.

Season 2 guests included Tracey Ullman, Danny DeVito, and Dustin Hoffman (who played Lisa's substitute teacher crush, in one of the single greatest episodes ever written). Since then, *The Simpsons'* writers have gone to town, pulling everyone from legends of television (Johnny Carson) to their favorite athletes (Ken Griffey Jr., Mark McGwire) to musicians (two Rolling Stones and the three living Beatles, though not all at once) to a prime minister of Great Britain (Tony Blair). Stories of these appearances range from the absurd—Elizabeth Taylor telling Matt Groening to "fuck off"—to the downright cool—the Ramones calling David Mirkin up several times, after their appearance, with detailed questions about the show.[1]

By the fourth season, guest appearances on *The Simpsons* were already an institution in their own right. In December 1993, *Spy* magazine published an article called "Homerphobic—The Simpsons Voice-Over Curse." The article pointed to the post-appearance career nosedives of Michael Jackson (poor album sales, accusations of pedophilia), Dustin Hoffman (he made the film *Hero*), and Darryl Strawberry (arrested for hitting his pregnant girlfriend). Never one to pull its punches, *Spy* added Liz Taylor to the list. Their evidence that she was cursed: "Remains married to Larry Fortensky."[2]

ALBERT BROOKS: I had been friends with Jim Brooks forever and *Broadcast News* was 1987 and he and I would speak often during that period and at some point he asked, "Would you come over and do this?" And I think that's really how it happened, just as a friendship thing, in the first year.

BRIAN ROBERTS, editor, *The Simpsons* (1989–92): He was the RV salesman. That was his first role. And then he was the bowling instructor [whom Marge almost has an affair with].

Al Brooks has returned to play motivational speaker Brad Goodman, gentle but power-mad supervillain Hank Scorpio, former fast-food addict and fat-camp supervisor Tab Spangler, and EPA head Russ Cargill in *The Simpsons Movie*.

ALBERT BROOKS: The favorite one I did, just in terms of voice, and the one I think I liked the most was the bowling instructor. I like it because there had never been—and I don't know if there's ever been since—a cartoon character who might have had an affair. And that was just "Whoa." That was unusual. That was a great story line, "Gee, is she going to leave her cartoon husband for this guy?"

BRIAN ROBERTS: Mike Mendel went out to Brooks's house with a DAT machine, and it was him and Julie Kavner, and they basically riffed on this character. I had three hours of material for what amounted to two scenes. I remember turning to Sam and saying, "Somebody should release an album. This is the funniest three hours of material." I had real trouble because I couldn't cut it down. We sat around and took different swipes at it until he came down to the minute or so he's on screen.

ALBERT BROOKS: I don't know where all that stuff is, probably in the same room as the music from *I'll Do Anything* [Jim Brooks's failed musical starring Nick Nolte, from which he removed all the musical numbers before releasing it].

Dan Castellaneta also get special kudos from masters like Albert Brooks for his ability to improvise with the best.

ALBERT BROOKS: Dan's great . . . they're all great. They know their characters and, you know, you're just riffing. These guys can go with you. Dan doesn't shy away; if you throw something out, Dan will answer that new thing you give him as Homer. You're not going to be able to throw him. So that part's fun.

I like all those people. I've known them forever. As a matter of fact, one of the most fun things about the movie was actually working again with Harry Shearer, whom I hadn't worked with for years and years. That was the high point of the movie for me, just to be in a room with Harry.

Hank Azaria, another master improviser, also gets his props, in some cases making the showrunners second-guess their need for a guest star at all.

NANCY CARTWRIGHT, voice of Bart, *The Simpsons* (in *My Life as a Ten-Year-Old Boy*): We were going to have a guest star play Frank Grimes in "Homer's Enemy." Hank, at the table read, just filling in, created such a beautifully crafted character, beautifully psychotic, that no one was used to replace him.

Recurring guests like Al Brooks, Phil Hartman, and Kelsey Grammer were always welcome additions. Hartman, who was shot and killed by his wife in a freak incident in 1998, voiced two of *The Simpsons*' most memorable recurring characters: the slimy, incompetent, yet

affable discount lawyer Lionel Hutz, and the washed-up actor Troy McClure. The versatility, comic timing, and understated brilliance of the characters that he'd brought to *Saturday Night Live* and *Newsradio* were on full display at *The Simpsons*. From Season 3 to 9, McClure and Hutz provided the series with some of its best moments. No one could lampoon the moral indifference of an ambulance chaser, or the desperate shilling of a has-been like the genial and gently ironic Hartman. When he died, Hartman was sincerely mourned in and outside of Hollywood; Steve Martin called him "deeply funny."[3]

RICHARD APPEL, writer/producer, *The Simpsons* (1995–99): We all got into the table read, and about half the people were in a really good mood and half the people in the room were seemingly in a terrible mood. And then Mike Scully came in and said that Phil Hartman had just been murdered. So the table read was canceled. Everybody loved Phil. He was great.

Kelsey Grammer has had two successful sitcom runs with his sophisticated and snobbish character Dr. Frasier Crane, first on *Cheers* and then with his own show, *Frasier*, which ran from 1993 to 2004 and won thirty-seven Emmys. Yet Grammer brought bombast to a level of near perfection on *The Simpsons*, giving voice to Krusty's revenge-obsessed former assistant, the maniacal, faultlessly refined Yalee, Sideshow Bob. One annoying facet of Sideshow Bob's highbrow wit is that Grammer actually is that smart. The writers pen many incredibly high-minded, obscure references for Sideshow Bob, and according to one writer, Grammer gets them all.

The most famous *Simpsons* guest is also its oddest. Michael Jackson was a huge *Simpsons* fan and was eager to do the show. When celebrities first started coming on the show, they didn't appear as themselves in the credits, as they did in later shows. (Dustin Hoffman was Sam Etic. Semitic. Get it? It's a Jewish thing.) Jackson (credited as John Jay Smith) was depicted as a four-hundred-pound bald white mental patient who is convinced he is Michael Jackson and who shares Homer's room in a mental hospital when Homer is deemed mentally unfit after wearing a pink shirt to work. The King of Pop had some ideas of his own, which made for a very unusual table read.

It all started with a phone call. According to Brooks, Michael Jackson called him, told him that he loved Bart, and said he wanted to give the youngster a number one single.[4] (Jackson ended up writing "Do the Bartman.")

BRIAN ROBERTS: So Michael Jackson agrees to do this show and he wants to play himself. And whatever anybody sort of says, I think Sam just sort of goes the other way. He's like, "No, you can't play yourself. You have to play another character." So they came up with this idea that Michael Jackson would play an insane asylum guy who thinks he's Michael Jackson.

WALLACE WOLODARSKY, writer/producer, *The Simpsons* (1989–92): We did the table read at Jackson's manager's house, which was unheard of—we never left the studio—and it was a crazy environment where we were all served food by Sikhs in white robes and turbans.

HANK AZARIA, voice actor, *The Simpsons* (1989–   ): I remember having to make conversation with Michael Jackson. That had to be one of the freakiest moments of my life. This was more than fifteen years ago, so he wasn't quite the figure he's become today, but still, I remember even then, staring at his nose, and it was all about Don't Stare at His Nose.

Back in the early days, they did a second table read before the record. This one took place on the Fox lot.

BRIAN ROBERTS: Michael walked in, dressed in the big epaulettes, the whole nine yards. And as luck would have it, the only available seat is right next to me. I literally didn't want to look at him. I just sort of had my head in my script. We were touching elbows and shit. So I get my head buried in the script, and then at one point in the script he sang "Man in the Mirror," and I said, "All right." How many times in your life are you sitting right next to Michael Jackson and he's singing "Man in the Mirror"? I just gotta look.

So I looked over to Michael Jackson, and he wasn't singing. He had a sing-along guy next to him who was actually singing for him. I couldn't believe it. I was like, What kinda weird shit is this?

So they did the table read. Michael goes whatever, and later on the story is that Michael did sing some of the parts in the show, but to this day, I don't know whether it was actually Michael Jackson singing the "Man in the Mirror" part. I know that he did the "Happy Birthday, Lisa."

Matt Groening claims to have heard versions of the song that Jackson did himself, and that Jackson's version may be the one in the episode, but Al Jean says that *The Simpsons*' music editor assured him it was the imitator's version that made it on to the show.[5]

Jackson's appearance wouldn't be the only surprising encounter with a megastar. In 1992, Elizabeth Taylor agreed to speak Maggie Simpson's first word—"Daddy." "We did twenty-four takes, but they were always too sexual," Matt Groening told *Playboy*. "Finally Liz said, 'Fuck you,' and walked out."[6]

The first of these guest appearances gave the writers some opportunities to take the show to some different places and cover some of the parts of everyday life, like infidelity and gay issues, that regular shows refused to portray. In Season 2, when Homer grew hair and became an executive, openly gay Broadway and film star Harvey Fierstein played his assistant—dashing, competent, statuesque Carl.

HARVEY FIERSTEIN, actor; guest voice, *The Simpsons*: I think what we played with was that he was the first openly gay cartoon character. He was also Homer's first male kiss. Also, did I slap his ass or something? [Before a big presentation to Mr. Burns and his fellow execs, Carl gives Homer a motivational speech, kisses him, and slaps him on the behind.]

Right, well the thing was, Matt Groening was sketching me a little bit. And I said to him, "What are you doing?" He said, "You're gonna look wonderful as a Simpson." And I said, "No, don't make it look like me." He said, "What do you mean?" I said, "No, no, no, no, no," I said. "You need to make him"—cuz I'm often called a caricature of homosexuality. I've been accused of that, but let's face it, I'm the exact opposite of a gay caricature. "Make him blond, and tall, and gorgeous, and skinny, and give him a beautiful place to live. If you're gonna do a gay cartoon character, make him a gay cartoon character." So that's why Carl is tall and blond. I mean, if a *Simpsons* character can be said to be good-looking, I guess he's sort of good-looking, and he lives in this beautiful apartment and has beautiful things around him, but that was because I said, "Don't make it look like me. I don't look like gay people, how they're supposed to look. I'm Jewish and fat and . . ."

When we were actually doing the recording, I got so into everybody's acting that I actually started to make a suggestion, and then caught myself. And everybody's staring at me, like, What's the new guy over there giving notes for? It's one of those embarrassing memories that actually make you clench your fist. But I was so excited by the incredible amount of talent in that one circle. I mean, those people are all so wonderful, each in his own way. A cartoon is a cartoon, but as I stood in that circle of actors reading the script, what struck me is that these writers could do absolutely anything, and these talented people, these voices, would pull it off. There's a certain morality in those performances. They don't question those characters; they just accept them exactly as they are.

Years later they contacted me when they wanted Carl to return. But I didn't really like their approach. It had nothing to do with my character. Homer and Marge have a fight, and she throws him out and he has no place to stay, and he runs into Carl, who sets him up with a pair of gay men. All they needed me for was to introduce him to these gay guys. But the script was basically just a lot of very clever gay jokes, and there wasn't that *Simpsons* twist. Jim Brooks and Matt Groening and those writers have always added that extra something beneath the surface, and it just wasn't there. Basically, Homer just had a lot of fun hanging out with gay men, and drinking in bars, and dancing at discos, and all that, and there was nothing—there was no commentary there. Every restaurant had a silly gay name. The gym had a silly gay name. They were all double entendres, obviously. And I said, "Anybody could do this. You're the fucking *Simpsons*. Do something we have never seen before."

And let me say that it was very flattering that they asked me to do it. Jim Brooks said, "You know, you're the very first voice we ever asked to come back and do it again." I was surprised. I asked, "Why do they need me to introduce them to this gay couple? Why wouldn't he move in with

Carl and his partner?" Then I started thinking, Maybe they just wanted my stamp of approval on it because it was just a bunch of clichés.

So I called Jim Brooks and said, "You know, it looks to me like you're only asking me to do this to okay this episode, since my character doesn't do anything. I don't understand why you want my okay unless you think there's something wrong with it. But it seems to me that it might be more interesting if this gay couple he got set up to live with"— I think it was sort of a take on when Giuliani got thrown out of his home and lived with a gay couple—"are raising children, a parallel of him and Marge, and that he learned from this gay couple how to be a better parent and a better partner to his wife. Wouldn't it be funny if it took a gay couple to teach them family values?"

Jim Brooks said, "I think that's an interesting, fun idea. Would you mind telling it to one of our head writers?" And so I did, and he said, "Oh, thank you so much," and I never heard from them again.*

Musical guests have been popular throughout the show's history. (Writers are also music dorks, who would have known?) Aerosmith was the first.

STEVEN TYLER, lead singer, Aerosmith; guest voice, *The Simpsons*: *The Simpsons* was one of the first comedic endeavors to be a little risqué. They took the piss out of people and situations. And when they asked Aerosmith to be there, with Moe, to drink a Flaming Moe, it was perfect. I had done overlays and shit for movies in the past, but when the actual voicing cast came in, I freaked! I heard all these voices, like Marge Simpson, so I was pretty blissed out. Hank came in, and when I did my speaking part—it wasn't a hell of a lot—he was on one microphone, and I was on another one, and it was fuckin' hilarious.

Believe me, I riffed a little, and they didn't use everything I did, but I said, "Keep it in the tank." What was written, of course, we elaborated on with voice, because you can say everything nine ways, "What the hell

*John Waters appeared in Season 8's "Homer's Phobia" as John, Homer's new gay (though unbeknownst to Homer) friend. The episode was so successful, Waters and the episode's director, Mike Anderson, were commissioned to make a pilot of a series called *Uncle John* for MTV based on the same character. MTV never aired the pilot, neither did another network that had asked to see it, but Waters says it may make it to TV "someday."

are you talking about? *What* the hell are you talking about? What *the hell* are . . ." And then when they drew me, you don't have to guess what appendages they would make bigger on my face. Looking back at the characters [on TV], I'm not dead, I'm just drawn that way, you know what I'm saying?

We were elated, because it's a you-know-you've-made-it-when moment. You're this lowlife rock-and-roll band, just raping and pillaging from town to town—I say that loosely, not literally—a rock band that's throwing parties for twenty thousand people a night, and then you see yourself on television on the biggest cartoon of its time. It was the height of the insanity of the cartoon era, for me the equivalent of when we did "Walk this Way" with Run-DMC during the beginning of that era of rap. We always tried to get in on the ground floor of these things, and we were blown away that we were asked to do it.

It's pretty much a cookie cutter of the time, when all of this was fresh and new, and we just ripped it another asshole.

Aerosmith was pretty major, as were U2 (all Bono asked for was a giant glass of vodka—a PA was sent out to fetch him a bottle) and The Who (who played Springfield just before an army of angry badgers lays siege to the town in Season 12), but the biggest coup came in Season 14, where Homer went to band camp, hosted by the world's biggest rock stars: Mick Jagger, Keith Richards, Elvis Costello, Lenny Kravitz, and, uh, Brian Setzer.

Later, when Dan Castellaneta was being interviewed by Conan O'Brien, he recounted how he'd noticed a particular rock-and-roll hierarchy among the superstars. "In terms of lateness you would have Mick Jagger and Keith Richards coming in about forty-five minutes late," Castellaneta said. "And then Elvis Costello, thirty. Tom Petty, maybe twenty-five. Lenny Kravitz, twenty-three. Brian Setzer, right on time. Michael Bolton came early. And he wasn't even on the show." Castellaneta went on to describe Richards—after slurring his way through his lines, tumbler of vodka and OJ in hand—acting totally cordial and offering to take pictures and sign autographs. He signed Castellaneta's wife's album "Old Band, Old Part, 2002." When she asked him why he's added the year, he replied, "I never thought I'd live to see 2002."

HANK AZARIA: They sent me down to greet Mick Jagger when he arrived to record his part, and I said, "Hey, Mick, we're all thrilled to have you here." And he kind of blew right by me like I was the greeter, and went [dismissively], "Yeah, we'll get it." I knew it was going to get awkward, because I was about to walk upstairs and record with him. And it also made me a little bit annoyed. So before I even thought, I went, "No, I don't think we'll get it—I'm just glad you're here." And he kind of turned around and looked back at me like, What the fuck did you just say to me? And I was just like, "Hi, I'm Hank. I'll be recording with you." So that was slightly awkward.

There was room for bands that had yet to reach rock-and-roll's pantheon, including some writers' favorites. Mike Scully agreed to let Donick Carey's friends, the members of Yo La Tengo, recorded a version of *The Simpsons* theme for the closing credits of the episode where Homer decides he's a hippie and ends up infusing the town's favorite beverage with hallucinogenic drugs.

DONICK CAREY, writer/producer, *The Simpsons* (1996–99): They came in and recorded a great psychedelic version of the theme music. And we put it at the end of the show, which was really fun. Then a couple years later I was touring around with the band and we were in Barcelona. They opened the show with *The Simpsons* theme done psychedelic style. The crowd in Spain went nuts—they loved it. And I thought, Wow, this thing is really universal.

Other musical guests have included Phish, Ted Nugent, Smashing Pumpkins, Peter Frampton, Sonic Youth, Tito Puente, Shawn Colvin, *NSync, R.E.M., and inexplicably, on two separate occasions, the Baha Men (of "Who Let the Dogs Out?" fame).

   During Season 13, an episode called "I Am Furious Yellow" was devoted to comic books.* *The Simpsons*' writers' inner dorks could not help themselves, and the grand master of Marvel Comics, Stan Lee himself, was called in. Lee actually has the episode's funniest

*As opposed to an episode from the second season, "Three Men and a Comic Book," which used the comic book to explore the nature of friendship, "I Am Furious Yellow" was a series of plot twists written to the end of Homer transforming into a parody of the Incredible Hulk.

moments (he stops by Comic Book Guy's store and never leaves), especially when he approaches a young nerd carrying a Batmobile (Batman is a creation of Marvel's rival, DC), asks if he wouldn't prefer an exciting action figure, and despite the child's protests, stuffs a The Thing figure into the Batmobile, effectively destroying the toy. When the nerd complains that Lee has broken it, Lee responds, "Broke? Or made it better?"

STAN LEE, former president, Marvel Comics; guest voice, *The Simpsons*: To begin with, I'm something of a ham. I love doing cameos. Plus, *The Simpsons* has always been one of my favorite shows. So when I received the offer to do a cameo there was no way I was gonna refuse!

The experience knocked me out. However, nothing is perfect. The drawing of me didn't look quite as much like Brad Pitt as I had expected. The thing that impressed me most was the size and the quality of the creative staff. There must have been more than twenty people around a huge conference table—writers, actors, and producers. And when it was my turn to read my lines, I was in puppy heaven! Honestly, there was so much genuine talent gathered around that table you could have cut it with a knife. I spoke to many of the writers and was pleasantly surprised to find that they were as familiar with my work as I was with theirs. A short time later, Al Jean called and we had a great lunch together. At least, it was great for me. Considering he's one of the show's top producers, he's one of the nicest, most unassuming guys you could hope to meet. Of course, I probably said something wrong to him, or maybe he didn't like my table manners, because I haven't been invited back for another guest shot. But hey, one lives in hope.

Of course, boys being boys, the real draw was always the sports figures.

LARRY DOYLE: The biggest hullabaloo was when Mark McGwire came in. That was when loads of people who didn't have any reason to be in the recording booth ended up there. All the girls and all the guys were there. He seems like a nice guy, but he looks like a monster. His arms are as big as your legs—that's not an exaggeration. Interestingly, the line he had the most trouble with was "Hi, I'm Mark McGwire."

DONICK CARY: There's just certain people. Like, you can work with Mel Gibson* or Barbra Streisand where you're thinking, All right, just do the lines and get outta here. And then, suddenly, you're working with John Madden, who coached the '76 Raiders! You can barely talk, and it's . . . [Laughs] you know, like I'm like a kid in the candy store. But that was really fun. He's clearly out of his mind.

Next to sports figures, nothing got the writers excited like recording a comedy legend. Bob Hope was no exception. Conan O'Brien believed that you didn't want to be in the comedy business without having met Bob Hope, so when the opportunity came to travel to Hope's house in Toluca Lake and record his Season 4 appearance, Conan leapt.† In a wood-paneled room, featuring photos of JFK and Patton, he and fellow writer Jeff Martin waited for Hope, with Conan resisting the temptation to rifle through his drawers. "We were there for about forty-five minutes," remembered Conan, "and we'd spent thirty minutes of that waiting for Bob Hope." Hope did his takes, then made a quick exit. "But then I heard him out in the hallway, headed toward the stairs," said Conan. "One of the people who works with him said: 'I just got a call from the veterinarian. It's time for Junior to be neutered.' Bob Hope paused on the stairway, and he went, 'Ah, gee, better let me tell him.'"[7]

In Season 15, Prime Minister Tony Blair became the first sitting head of state to ever be a voice on *The Simpsons*.

AL JEAN, writer/producer, *The Simpsons* (1989–present) (to *Entertainment Weekly*, July 27, 2007): I was lucky enough to direct Tony Blair. He wanted to promote tourism. We had a thing where he was going to give out dogs to people in the airport but they said, "No, no, people call him Bush's poodle, that's going to look bad."

---

*Gibson appeared in the Season 11 premiere, "Beyond Blunderdome." This was before Gibson's *The Passion of the Christ* or his 2006 DUI, where he blamed "the fucking Jews" for "all the wars in the world." Those who worked with Gibson for his guest appearance on *The Simpsons* report that he seemed very nice, in control, and didn't appear to have any issues with the Jews in the room.
†Writer Jeff Martin, who went with O'Brien, has said that he's not sure if he can say they really "met" the comic, because he doesn't believe that Hope could see or hear them.

The Simpsons' writing room being what it is, how could they resist inviting the world's smartest astrophysicist, Stephen Hawking?

LARRY DOYLE: I was the one who got Stephen Hawking on the show.* When I was at *New York* magazine, Lucy Hawking [his daughter] was my intern. Even though we could have just typed his script into the computer and read it off the computer, because it's the same program, we went and did an actual recording of his chair, which they had programmed his stuff into.

I flew up to Santa Barbara; he was at some conference up there. And I remember going to lunch with him. It's really strange having a conversation with him, because you're talking about something and then he comments on it about five minutes later. Everybody in the room was sort of used to that happening and sort of had the mental playback machine in their head so they could immediately register what he was commenting on, but I got lost sometimes.

His family seemed to have a sense of humor with him. One of the things he apparently likes to do is tell his driver to slow down. And so his kids once reprogrammed his chair so that when he tried to do that, instead he said, "Go, you bastard! Go!"

And then there are the intentionally odd guests, those stars who are more cultural relics than out-and-out celebrities: Gary Coleman, Gary Busey, Mr. T, and Adam West.†

TIM LONG, writer/producer, *The Simpsons* (1998–   ): I had an incredible experience when Mr. T was on the show. He was telling me about the scenes in *Rocky III* where he lost. The reason he lost was that his mother needed money for an operation, and so he was paid to take a

---

*In Hawking's first appearance (there have been four in all), he makes an eloquent, enlightened speech to a group of Springfieldians, Homer among them. During the awed silence that follows, Homer, inspired, yells out, "Larry Flynt is right!" Homer's confusion of one famous man in a wheelchair for another is the best single joke, in terms of a guest star and their relevance, that *The Simpsons* has ever come up with. (A close second is Mr. Burns telling Smithers to "Have the Rolling Stones killed" after C. J. Ramone of the Ramones tells Mr. Burns to go to hell at the old bastard's birthday party.)

†Hats off to *Family Guy* for taking West's absurdity, and his solemn monotone, and making him into a regular source of hilarity as Adam West, mayor of Quahog.

dive. And I said, "Well, I don't remember that in the movie." And he just looked at me right in the eye and said, "Things you don't see!" And I thought, Well that's an interesting way to look at it. He sort of invented his own movie that happened behind the scenes of the actual movie to sort of justify his behavior. He could have been fucking with me, but I was so besotted with him. It was just a magical moment.

I said to him, "I remember you put out a record called *Mr. T's Commandments.*" And somehow he heard that as "Mr. T, please sing 'Mr. T's Commandments.'" So he sang me the whole song. And I thought, If I'm killed by a sniper tonight, well, my life would have ended beautifully, because I have been sung to by Mr. T.

HANK AZARIA: Gary Busey came in to record, and there's a line in the script where he says [in Busey's husky, psychopathic drawl], "I'm Gary Busey." And the stage direction said "crazy insane laugh." And so Gary Busey comes in to record and he says, "Now why does it say 'crazy laugh'?" And the guy who wrote it—you can imagine how terrified he was at this moment—he said, "Well, it's just kind of like, you know, 'cause you're Gary Busey . . . you're so . . . you're Gary Busey, man . . . you're so happy you're Gary Busey. You're just overjoyed by it." Gary kind of stared at him for a few seconds and went, "Yeah, okay, sure." He was happy with that.

In Season 17, *The Office* creator Ricky Gervais was asked to write an episode, the first time a guest performer had been asked to do this.

RICKY GERVAIS, guest voice, *The Simpsons*; creator, star, *The Office, Extras*: It started when I won the Golden Globe. I was called for an audience with Matt Groening the next day. I went along to Fox studios. And I knew Matt was *The* [UK] *Office*'s sort of first industry/celebrity champion. In one of the first interviews I'd done, a journalist said her friend Matt Groening had bought a DVD player that could play British DVDs because he saw an episode of *The Office* on the plane. So I knew he was a fan.

Then when I met him, it was an hour of mutual backslapping. "You're the greatest!" "No. No. You're the greatest." [Obviously I am right and they are the greatest.] And there's no doubt about that. We had a lunch with Matt and Al Jean and all the writers and producers and everything, and at the very end, I was doing the nerdy thing, asking Matt to draw me a Homer. I've never asked for an autograph in my life, except that one. He did it on the back of an envelope, which I've got framed in my office. (I was jealous of Moby's. I saw a *Cribs* and it was Moby, and he said it was his prized possession. I think it was the first *Cribs* where you actually saw a bookshelf.) And he said, "Would you like to be a guest voice?" And I said, "What are the hours?" And he said, "The hours are really good." I went, "Of course I would."

And we chatted about that, and I said, "Well, I'm not famous enough to be me, and I don't want to be David Brent," because it's not my favorite thing to do a fictional character in a fictional program. So we thought we'd come up with an homage to David Brent, but with a new character, which is what we did.

I was waiting for the call. And I got to know Al Jean, and I got to know Matt better, and one day I was talking to Al about it and he went, "Have you got any ideas? Why don't you write it?" And I thought, Oh, my God. That's one of those jobs where you say yes first and worry about it later.

It was my girlfriend who said, "Have they done wife swap?" I checked, and they hadn't, which was nice, because I thought that would really be a mutual ground there: documentary, reality, game shows, TV itself, because I know *The Simpsons* has done that brilliantly and most of the stuff I've done is around that area. And it involved it family unit as well. So I sent some ideas off. I must say it's a cowrite. Really the only thing that's wholly mine is the song. I just wrote the song and sent it off to them, the very rough sketch, but it went into their mill and came back a complete episode. And they gave me the credit for it, but I can't take the credit for it.

The fact that I got a song in *The Simpsons* is amazing. Because they do the best songs as well, and I always try to crowbar a song into everything I do, somehow. And it was easy in *The Office,* because I just made David Brent a frustrated, failed musician like myself, and with *Extras* we had to think outside the box a little, but then cowriting a song with David Bowie is okay too [laughs].

The literary community has also embraced *The Simpsons*. Writers are a snobby bunch, and until *The Sopranos*, few regarded anything

on television as worth watching, except, of course, *The Simpsons*. In September 1998, the American poet laureate, Robert Pinsky, wrote an editorial in *The New York Times Magazine*, "My Favorite Show," declaring that "there is something about *The Simpsons* that penetrates to the nature of television itself." Arguing that television is at its most powerful when broadcasting live events, Pinsky saw *The Simpsons'* effectiveness in its mastery of the opposite sphere. "It isn't simply that these characters are not live—they were never alive. Repeatedly, the show mocks and embraces its own genre. It even mocks disruption itself." Ten years later, Pinsky remains a fan.

ROBERT PINSKY, United States poet laureate, 1997–2000; guest voice, *The Simpsons*: Not the type to get immersed in lore and what people call "trivia," not a nostalgist for past glory, not fond of philosophizing or high-flown analysis, I do continue to enjoy and admire the show. It remains an effectively funny, antibullshit device.

A precursor of the excellent *South Park*, Jon Stewart, Colbert stuff—the beginning of a golden age for American comedy.

A gag that never wears out for me is when the characters need to be reminded of hundreds of past episodes—Mr. Burns musing "Simpson, Simpson . . ." trying to recall him. Instead of the sitcom jumping the shark, it demonstrates that it knows the shark is artificial. In a mark of successful satire, the show will be funny even after the sitcoms it parodies are long dead and forgotten—like those forgotten bad poets, pretentious leaders, and bullshit parsons of the eighteenth century mocked by Swift and Pope.

The episode where I play a pompous poet named Robert Pinsky was taped on September 10, 2001. I flew out that day on the same flight that went down twenty-four hours later. On September 12, the producers invited me to a table read. On that occasion, we all laughed, then parted with nothing said about "national tragedy," etc. I haven't figured it all out, but it remains in my mind a classy response to that event that came to be exploited in certain ways, by politicians and others.

I don't know what to make of my 9/11 experience being tied up with the show—it's a personal oddity or conundrum that I think about. And I do think of those writers and actors and directors as admirable, nonbullshit practitioners of civilization.

The show has featured a number of great literary figures, including Thomas Pynchon, Tom Wolfe, George Plimpton, and Maya Angelou. In Season 18, a poem Lisa helped Moe to write landed him at the Bread Loaf Writers' Conference, alongside Michael Chabon, Jonathan Franzen, and Tom Wolfe. Unbeknownst to Moe, Wolfe had actually made an appearance as a Simpson years before (they hadn't needed his voice) for a sight gag that paid tribute to Wolfe's unique sartorial style.

TOM WOLFE, guest voice, *The Simpsons*; author: I appeared in one [episode] without knowing it. I didn't even know they were going to do it. Lisa wants to go to the book fair and nobody else does. She seems to be the entire brains in the family. And so they're there with Maya Angelou. One of the characters at this book festival buys a hot dog, and suddenly there I am in a white suit, and he squeezes the hot dog and the mustard goes all over my suit. And I immediately take off my suit and I have exactly the same suit on underneath. My son was watching it and he said, "Dad, come here! Come here! It's you." I didn't know what he was talking about. And I just managed to catch a bit of that. I don't have any lines, it was just me.

The Simpsons was one of the few shows that children loved and adults loved because there were so many layers of humor. Now a child watching that, having no idea who this Tom Wolfe might possibly be, is gonna be entertained by this mustard going all over the suit and the fact that this man has another suit underneath the first one. But if anybody happens to have heard of me, they'll know that the white suit has a special significance for me, and also must wonder, If somebody has all those suits, how does he keep them clean? And it would be very funny if he doesn't keep them clean. He just throws them away if they get dirty.

It's one of the only shows on television that dares not have a laugh track. And I cannot stand laugh tracks. It's what I always resented about *Seinfeld*. You know, if you're funny—let's see if you're funny. He is so much better in a stand-up comedy routine where he can't order the audience to laugh than in that canned laughter situation. I just won't watch it. Who knows whether *Friends* was good or bad. I know my children loved it, I think my wife loved *Friends*. But I couldn't watch it. I just refused to be cued that way and to be told what is funny.

The Simpsons also managed to make a virtue out of bad draftsman-ship. The characters are really terribly drawn, but they are so stylized that it doesn't make any difference any longer. I mean, every type of human being is rendered in that child's style of drawing but put to a very sophisticated use.

I must have a very low threshold when it comes to humor. I mean *The Simpsons* has often reduced me to tears of laughter. If I'm really feeling down, *The Simpsons* makes me feel worse. If I'm feeling bad, in a depressed mood let's say, I can't really stand to watch *The Simpsons* because there are so many people being humiliated. You may not follow that logic, you would think it would be the opposite, but it's that real to me. There're constant situations where every character is humiliated, and humiliation is one of the most powerful forms of humor. I mean, everybody loves to see somebody else humiliated. But if you're feeling down, you might think, God, that could happen to me.

SEVENTEEN

On and On

In which Homer Jay Simpson finally has something in common with Arthur Herbert Fonzarelli . . . Matt Groening faces yet another divorce . . . and the Dream Team of *Simpsons'* writers can barely hit a free throw, never mind three-pointers.

They drove a dump truck full of money up to my house. I'm not made of stone!
—*Krusty the Clown (on selling out)*

As the golden age of the Simpsons wound down, and the quality began to vary to greater degrees, some viewers began to abandon the show. Many others kept watching, with new feelings of anticipation that they might just see some sign of its return to former greatness. It never came. Viewership varied from 10 million per week[1] in the mid-nineties to slightly less than that[2] in the early 2000s, to approximately 7.5 million[3] in the late 2000s. But more important than the numbers is what was happening onscreen and in the writers room.

While the show doesn't simply fall off a cliff between Season 8, the final year of Bill and Josh's tenure as showrunners, and Season 9, the first year of Mike Scully's,* this moment does mark the end of the remarkably high-yielding creative run that began in 1991. "One of the things that emerged was that they began to rely on gags, not characters, wherever that switch got flipped, whether it's the ninth or tenth season," says *Planet Simpson* author Chris Turner. "For example, Mr. Burns would show up, make his antiquated refer-

---

*Indeed, some episodes from Scully's first years, Seasons 9 and 10—"The Wizard of Evergreen Terrace" and "When You Dish Upon a Star"—are superior to episodes from Bill and Josh's Seasons 7 and 8, such as "22 Short Films About Springfield" and "Bart on the Road."

ences and say a couple of evil things, but there wasn't the same robustness to those characters."

Ironically, *The Simpsons* presaged its own downturn. In Season 8's "The Itchy & Scratchy & Poochie Show,"* network executives at Itchy and Scratchy studios attempt to retool Bart and Lisa's favorite cartoon by adding a new character, Poochie, voiced by none other than Homer Simpson. Poochie is a ridiculous amalgam of disposable trends, network notes, and corporate buzzwords ("I feel we should Rasta-fy him by 10 percent or so," one exec offers). Upon his debut, he is immediately loathed by *Itchy & Scratchy*'s devoted fans, leading to Comic Book Guy's famous declaration, "Worst. Episode. Ever." At a decisive moment in the episode, Lisa shares an observation *The Simpsons*' writers hoped would be heeded: "The thing is, there's not really anything wrong with the *Itchy & Scratchy Show*. It's as good as ever. But after so many years, the characters just can't have the same impact they once had."

While Groening has said that the episode was his answer to Fox's attempts to meddle in his show over the years (at this time, apparently, the network wanted them to add a new character, one that he described as being more Bart than Bart), the episode was about much more than that. "Poochie" is a perfect parody of network interference, the TV business, corporate culture, and obsessed fans. The episode is a metacelebration, a tongue-in-cheek rebuttal to everyone who claimed that the quality of *The Simpsons* had declined over the years. And yet while *The Simpsons*' writers were parodying the notion of a beloved series jumping the shark, "The Itchy & Scratchy & Poochie Show" came at a time when their own series was doing just that. Mike Scully's turn as showrunner, and the beginning of the end, were just around the corner.

The show's quality certainly declined under Mike Scully's four-year stewardship, and things went from bad to worse when Al Jean took over in Season 13, though he didn't seem to think so. "A good episode from Season 14 can be switched with one from Season 4 pretty interchangeably,"[4] he said in 2004. Critics saw things differ-

---

*The episode aired on February 9, 1997, marking the year *The Simpsons* could be viewed in every major television market on the planet.

ently. "Put a fork in 'The Simpsons' because this show is done," wrote the *New York Times*'s Adam Buckman in 2005. "Gone are the rich details and inventive storylines that characterized this beloved show for so many incredible seasons. In their place is a sitcom that is seriously showing its age."[5]* Touting the show's brilliance up to Season 9, *New York* magazine concurred: "Perhaps it was inevitable that *The Simpsons* couldn't sustain forever such a high-wire mix of hilarity and humanity."[6]†

Even though Jean has presided over the show's worst years, to blame a single head writer for the show's decline is unfair. *The Simpsons* is, and always has been, a giant collaboration. Speaking at Northwestern University in 2004, Mike Reiss, Jean's longtime writing partner, made reference to the show's apparent decline. Reiss told the audience that when viewers tell him that the show is not as good as it used to be, he offers the following explanation: "Go fuck yourself!"[7] Belying Reiss's joke is the fans' disappointment, which by the early 2000s was palatable, not only in the critical response or the decreasing numbers in the ratings, but in *The Simpsons*' community at large.

JACOB BURCH, administrator, NoHomers.net: I've never ever heard anyone say the show is better than ever. There are varied opinions on whether or not it's still *good*. In an interview Matt Groening referred to us as "spurned lovers." Well, most of us have divorced *The Simpsons* by now. Some just stick it out. It was such a big part of their childhood that they feel this devotion, they feel they have to continue to subject themselves to *The Simpsons*. Some people will watch eighteen episodes of a show they now hate, and rate them "FFFF" [the lowest rating for an episode on NoHomers], and some people are more positive.

The debate became, "Is the show getting worse? And if it is, is it now

---

*Such articles tended to be as plaintive as they were critical. After writing that *The Simpsons* was done for, Buckman immediately added, "And that is one of the saddest things I've ever had to report."

†That isn't to say there wasn't criticism in the mainstream press before this. After Mirkin took over in Season 5, which I and many others consider very much part of *The Simpsons*' golden age, the *Los Angeles Times* wrote that "lately . . . there are no layers. What you immediately see and hear is everything you get. The show's bratty Bart and once bankable Homer humor are flatter, the gags often labored and belabored, and the characters inconsistent."

a *bad show*? Should they have stopped?" That's the only debate. The only time I would see the old kind of fervor is when someone who was still obviously clinging to the hope that the show would get better, or find some sort of second wind, would write a give-up post. Those are the most emotional posts I've seen, people who have an honest grief at losing this part of their life. They feel shameful saying they're a *Simpsons* fan. Once a week we'll see a die-hard fan change his or her username from something totally *Simpsons*-related to I'm-Giving-Up-I-Don't-Want-to-Be-Associated-With-This-Show-Anymore-Make-It-My-Real-Name. People just stopped caring.*

Matt Groening has managed to pinpoint a potential source of fans' dissatisfaction.

Matt Groening (to the *Los Angeles Daily News*, July 27, 2007): You always hear that the show isn't as good as it used to be . . . But people always compare the new shows to the memories of their favorite episodes, back when the show surprised them. You've got to have an open mind, and for some people, it's impossible. Nostalgia clouds their thinking.

Unlike fans, critics, and many writers, Matt Groening seemed perfectly comfortable with the show's status. In 2004, he told NPR, "You're trying not to repeat yourself, you're trying to surprise the audience . . . As a result, the show has gone off in some very particular directions . . . I was thinking, 'Oh, my God, we can't do this. We can't do this,' and then it turned out to be OK. It's funny, it's crazy, and the show is so fast-paced . . . It's really still a lot of fun."[8]

And there's one very important voice who seems to support Groening and Al Jean's appraisals. "I can't say I've watched every episode, but I watch it at every opportunity," says Rupert Murdoch, "and I think it's still as brilliant as ever."

While flagrant and unforgivable in the eyes of many hard-core

---

*It's interesting to note that the "off-topic" message board on NoHomers.net is now the most popular section of the website. *Simpsons* fans who came together because of the show are now talking to each other about other things, a genuinely positive social externality, like members of a church discovering they share an interest in college football or the same sexual fetish.

fans, *The Simpsons'* downturn was a relative one. The show has maintained, when compared to other network sitcoms, its status as a reliable laugher. Back in the fifth season, *The Simpsons* reached the hundred-episode mark, the point where, for most successful sitcoms, syndication can begin, the bucks start rolling in, and the producers can relax. Yet *The Simpsons* has managed more than four hundred episodes, with no end in sight. How has it kept going so strong, especially if the quality has dropped so noticeably?

GEORGE MEYER (to *The Believer*, September 2004): My feeling is that we'll probably get bored with it before the audience does. We have to spend more time with it and immerse ourselves in this weird little universe. If it's completely dried up, I think we'll know it. I hope so, anyway.

Meyer left later that year.

One major factor keeping the show alive is Homer, thanks in no small part to the performance of Dan Castellaneta. No matter how dull one week's episode might be, or how close to sitcom catchphrasery *The Simpsons* slips, Homer Simpson is so beloved, and still so surprising, we will tune in to see what he will say next.

DONICK CARY: I think we got to times where it felt like Homer was just being dumb. It was like, literally, he's on the floor eating out of the garbage. And you're asking yourself, Hmm. Is this really the best . . . [laughs] the best place to take this character?

As the golden age was winding down, Season 8's episode "Homer's Enemy" gave viewers special insight into this complicated character and provided a probing exposition of his role within the world of *The Simpsons*.

After seeing a news report on an unlucky man named Frank Grimes, who has had to work extremely hard his entire life (as a child he worked delivering gifts to more fortunate kids), Mr. Burns hires him as an executive vice president at the plant. But after Burns sees a heroic dog on a subsequent news report, the dog becomes VP and Grimes lands in sector 7G, alongside one Homer Simpson. With his blithe disregard for professionalism, safety, and hard work,

Homer annoys Grimes no end. Grimes is incredulous that his coworkers and fellow Springfieldians neither notice Homer's idiocy nor seem to care. He becomes so tortured by the contrast between his and Homer's existence, he actually goes mad, committing suicide by grabbing high-voltage wires with his bare hands.

GEORGE MEYER (to *The Believer*): Grimes's cardinal sin was that he shined a light on Springfield. He pointed out everything that was wrong-headed and idiotic about that world. And the people who do that tend to become martyrs. He said things that needed to be said, but once they were said, we needed to destroy that person. I'll admit, we took a certain sadistic glee in his downfall. He was such a righteous person, and that somehow made his demise more satisfying.

Grimes was an interloper, and an earnest one at that, who showed us that Homer is, for all intents and purposes, not a very attractive character. He is boorish, incompetent, lazy, uncaring, unintelligent, and destructive. That being said, the Homer that emerges during this period, and is expounded upon later, is also the opposite of all those things. At any given moment, Homer can be sweet or bitter, angry or happy, smart or stupid, driven or apathetic, bemused or intrigued, gay or straight. And he can switch between these effortlessly within a few frames of animation. Homer has evolved past the everyman. He is both the everyman's fantasy and his nightmare—a symbol of what we all strive for and what we should avoid. He is no longer simply sympathetic and relatable; Homer can be whatever you want him to be, at any time. As a character, he has very few limits.

Yet even a comedic character as perfect as Homer has not been able to save *The Simpsons*. There are a few sitcoms that stayed interesting and funny for more than a decade. They relied on the emotional investment of their audience. Would Sam and Rebecca end up together? Would Ross and Rachel? Daphne and Niles? *The Simpsons* couldn't manage the same feat. It was decided at the beginning of the series that these characters would never age, that each episode would begin again at zero, never allowing plotlines and emotional arcs to extend beyond a single episode, to the great benefit of the early seasons. It's possible this format ended up limiting the series' potential, further hindered by the problems of repetition and staleness inherent in any entertainment's extended longevity, compounded by the lack of any new direction from its showrunner.

GARTH ANCIER: I had lunch with Jim [Brooks] a couple of years ago, and he was saying to me, and this was going into the seventeenth season, he says, "I really need to shake the show up. It's just gotten stale, you know?" I go, "Jim, seventeen years! No one's ever made a show for seventeen years." He still cared so much about it, and cared how good it is. I'll give you another example. He was comparing it to *South Park* and saying, "Gee, I just feel like we're not as fresh as *South Park*." Here's someone who's done arguably the most profitable show in the history of television and is still concerned that the quality isn't quite at the top of its game. You gotta admire someone like that.

SETH MACFARLANE, creator of *Family Guy, American Dad*: It is still funnier than any live-action show that's on television right now, let me put it that way. If I did *Family Guy* for eighteen years, I don't think it would be as good as it is now. There's only so much you can do with a certain group of characters. *The Simpsons* has sustained better than *South Park*.

Further evidence of *The Simpsons'* decline is the show's overshadowing by its own progeny: *South Park* and *Family Guy*. These shows currently provide the hilarity, subversiveness, and relevant social commentary that *The Simpsons* once did. One could argue that the bluntness with which *Family Guy* and *South Park* excoriate their subjects actually makes them less potent than *The Simpsons*, that the loudest voice does not always win the day. But there is something to be said for *South Park's* continued ability to shock and entertain, as well as *Family Guy's* obscene, lyrical, and preposterous look at family life (on an episode-by-episode basis, both elicit more laughs than *The Simpsons*). These upstarts are able to take more risks and aim for a lower common denominator. And while it's true that both series benefit from the groundwork laid by *The Simpsons* and that neither has been on as long—hence they are inherently fresher—it is also possible that they've been able to stay more in touch with today's audience, what it considers taboo and what it expects from comedy. A joke, as Matt Groening pointed out, is what you don't expect.

The Simpsons can rest easy in the knowledge that South Park and Family Guy, not to mention King of the Hill, Futurama, and scores of other shows, would not exist without the foundation they laid. And yet with each passing season, as other comedies—both animated and live action—become bolder, smarter, and more attuned, The Simpsons slips farther into irrelevance. Compared to Two and Half Men, Reba, and My Name Is Earl, The Simpsons still looks pretty good. But after watching postmillennium live-action shows like Arrested Development, 30 Rock, and The Daily Show, and animated series like Family Guy, as well as Adult Swim's avant-garde programs ("Tom Goes to the Mayor," "The Venture Bros.," "Harvey Birdman"), it's difficult to return to The Simpsons, especially in its current lackluster state.*

One area where The Simpsons still rules is in reruns, available at least once an evening in every TV market in the United States. Simpsons episodes hold up remarkably well against shows like Friends and Will and Grace, which have aged with all the grace of the video rental stores that once sold their seasons in giant box sets. But while the older episodes were enjoyed over and over by older fans, the show's then-current producers had to reach out to new ones by injecting a dose of the medicine most often prescribed for shows on the wane: the celebrity guest star. Over the last few seasons, celebrity guest voices have become a feature of every episode, along with the unfortunate side effect of plots being geared toward those stars, no matter what the cost to the show and its story lines. Drew Barrymore's appearance as Krusty's daughter in Season 12, for example, focused on a father's selfishness toward his daughter (the theme of every Homer/Lisa episode), and even reused a previous setup—the loss of a child's musical instrument, her prized possession.†

---

*"I like Family Guy," said Mike Reiss in a speech in 2009 at the 92nd Street Y in Tribeca. Reiss then related a well-known story, how Family Guy's creator, Seth MacFarlane, was scheduled to be one American Airlines Flight 11 on September 11, 2001. Because MacFarlane's travel agent had given him the wrong departure time, MacFarlane narrowly missed the flight and watched on the airport TVs as his plane crashed into the North Tower of the World Trade Center. "The point," said Reiss, "is that I may like Family Guy, but God fucking loves Family Guy."
†A few of the guests from the last eleven seasons are Tony Hawk, J. K. Rowling, Steve Martin, Ray Romano, Kiefer Sutherland, Reese Witherspoon, Fallout Boy, Anne Hathaway, and Matt Dillon.

After several hundred episodes, the writers have explored every plotline imaginable. Having a celebrity can provide some understandable relief, as can dedicating an entire show to a topical issue. Season 16's "There's Something About Marrying" addressed gay marriage by having Marge's sister, Selma, come out of the closet and decide to marry another woman. In an interview, showrunner Al Jean pointed to this episode as an example of how the show is still relevant and edgy, and yet the episode was in fact a long-winded and lame exploration of the topic.

The Simpsons has become such a staple of the mainstream and is so lacking in controversy that even conservatives embrace it. In 2000, an article in the *National Review*, William F. Buckley's great bastion of conservative thought, said, *"The Simpsons* celebrates many, if not most, of the best conservative principles: the primacy of family, skepticism about political authority, distrust of abstractions." The series still does manage to irk some people, though. In 2008, a Venezuelan TV station pulled the show, declaring it inappropriate for kids. In its place ran *Baywatch: Hawaii.* In 2006, China banned *The Simpsons* from prime time, though that had more to do with promoting cartoons made domestically than any content issues.[9]

Perhaps it was the show's complacency that spurred Jim Brooks et al. to bring *The Simpsons* to the big screen in 2007. The producers had discussed the possibility of doing a film with the "Kamp Krusty" episode, back in 1992, but had eventually canned the idea. Groening had also expressed interest in creating a Simpsons musical tribute to *Fantasia*, called "Simptasia," which never came to fruition. "We probably could put out just about anything and some people would come," Groening told *Newsweek* in 2001. "But we want to honor the fans."[10]

JAMES L. BROOKS (to Jim Lehrer on the *NewsHour*, July 27, 2007): Well, the idea of doing a movie had always been there, and we'd always said no. And then, about four years ago, we didn't say no. We had a weird contract negotiation.

After Fox Filmed Entertainment brought in Tom Rothman as chairman in 2000, Brooks and the other producers were able to arrange a deal where their film was basically green-lit in perpetuity. Fox would pay them to write the script, and they could take as long as they wanted to complete the writing. And if they weren't happy with the result, they could bail on the film altogether without the studio saying, "Wait a minute, you owe us a movie." Helping things along was a new contract, signed by the actors after their holdout in 2001, in which they pledged to do three features.[11]

In 2003, work on the actual script began, with a "dream team" of writers assembled by Brooks (including John Swartzwelder, George Meyer, Al Jean, Mike Reiss, Jon Vitti, Ian Maxtone-Graham, David Mirkin, Mike Scully, and Matt Selman), with each writer taking responsibility for approximately twenty pages of the first draft.[12] Over the next four years, the script went through more than one hundred rewrites,[13] with noises emanating from the writers room suggesting there was more than a little discontent. The writers didn't work together as well as they once had, especially under Brooks, who it appears inserted himself into the writing process and by all accounts no longer really understood *The Simpsons*. The reason Marge is such a focus of the film (when, in the best *Simpsons* material from the past, she usually took a backseat to the other characters, especially Homer) has to come down to Jim Brooks's influence. He had often been the one to insist on finding an emotional center in the scripts, though now it felt forced.

Ultimately, the result of all the disagreements was a long, drawn-out process that wasn't even much fun. The film was neither funnier nor more coherent than an above-average current episode (the plot's cliff-hanger involves a literal ticking time bomb; that this room could not come up with a more creative trope is stupefying). *The Simpsons Movie,* which cost less than a $100 million to make, grossed over $526 million worldwide.

But why do a film now? It was a question posed to Brooks and Groening with every interview they did. One answer they gave is that a number of factors came together: they finally had the time, Fox had agreed to their conditions, and they managed to get the team of writers together. All this might be true, but there is also Jim Brooks's ego to consider. *Spanglish,* his previous effort as a writer/director, had not been a success, commercially or critically. Costing nearly

$100 million and reaping just $55 million worldwide, *Variety* called it "a problematic attempt at contempo social comedy from an insular point of view . . . short on real drama and incident and long on tedium . . . *Spanglish* actually feels like the work of someone trying to escape the Bel-Air bubble in an academic way but remaining trapped within it all the same."[14] Before this, his only real bomb was *I'll Do Anything* in 1994. Someone close to the legendary writer/ director made the suggestion that after *Spanglish*, Jim Brooks— being called old and out of touch, and feeling it—desperately wanted a hit film. And how could *The Simpsons Movie* not be a hit?

The Simpsons Movie's writers had been working on the script for some time when *Spanglish* tanked, at which point it appears that Jim Brooks decided to rededicate himself to the film. According to sources close to these events, the feeling in the writing room was, What? What do you mean? We've been fine without you. Brooks launched himself back into *The Simpsons Movie* with gusto, which disconcerted his dream team. He had new drafts written every week, threw out entire acts, and changed scenes right up to the final minute before the movie's release. It was described to me as "chaos."

If the writing process frustrated Al Jean, he certainly didn't let on. "It was vital for James Brooks to be involved," he told the press upon the film's release, paying full lip service to the man who'd kept him in charge for the past decade. "He has that movie-making experience which is so vital for a project like this."

The marketing for *The Simpsons Movie* was an event in itself. All over America, and in one location in Canada, 7-Eleven stores were converted into Quick-E-Marts, while most of 7-Eleven's six-thousand-plus locations sold the movie's patented pink-glazed donut with sprinkles, alongside Squishees, Krusty O's, and Buzz Cola (some converted stores saw a 30 percent lift in sales).[15] In New Zealand, in the tiny town of Springfield (pop. 219), Fox erected an enormous pink-glazed donut, measuring nearly twenty feet in diameter. In Dorset, England, next to the location of the Cerne Abbas Giant (a 180-foot-tall hill figure from the seventeenth century, cut into the bedrock so that his formidable body, phallus, and club are outlined by the underlying chalk), a similarly massive Homer Simpson, holding a donut, was painted on the same hill. The Pagan Federation, which worships what they see as a fertility symbol, was not amused. On top of this, Todd MacFarlane designed action figures; a game was released for Xbox 360; Homer made an appearance on Jay Leno; Burger King had *The Simpsons* in their commercials and released a new line of *Simpsons* toys. Even Ben and Jerry's got in on the act, marketing the beer and donut ice cream flavor Duff & D'oh! Nuts. Perhaps the most clever piece of advertising took place online, where fans could go to *The Simpsons Movie* website and, with a collection of heads, bodies, noses, and accessories provided by *Simpsons* artists, make their own *Simpsons* avatar. You could finally see yourself as a *Simpsons* character; it was *Simpsons* dork heaven.

The movie was greeted warmly by critics and audiences, but no one was over the moon. Even with *The Simpsons*' top dogs in the writing room, and all the time in the world, they could not approach the brilliance they had achieved nearly two decades earlier. The movie is ninety minutes of (occasionally very funny) throwaway jokes, some forced and schmaltzy emotional scenes (Marge leaves Homer, for good, again), and a plot that is more zany than captivating. A longtime associate of Brooks's told me that he avoided him for weeks after the film was released—so he would not have to tell Brooks what he thought. Unlike the golden age episodes, there is practically zero replay value (my only repeat laughs involved Homer and his pig). Brooks and company were obviously out of touch with what had once made the show great. Symbolic of this, for bigger, glitzier, more expensive additions, the producers ditched longtime *Simpsons* composer Alf Clausen in favor of Hans Zimmer to compose the film's score. Of the decision, Clausen said, "Sometimes you're the windshield, sometimes you're the bug."[16]

The altogether satisfactory *The Simpsons Movie* should be the nail in coffin, if for no other reason than it was just satisfactory. But maybe for Jim Brooks, Matt Groening, and Al Jean, satisfactory is more than enough (purposely left off this list David Silverman—the film's director—because the animation of *The Simpsons Movie* was nothing short of brilliant). Why keep *The Simpsons* going?

BILL SAVAGE, editor, *Leaving Springfield*: The Simpsons *and the Possibility of Oppositional Culture*: Well, here's an interesting question about the nature of creative people. Why, why don't they stop? They don't stop 'cause it's just the compulsion of creativity. Well, maybe they can't stop. We didn't ask, you know, why didn't the impressionists stop. Some of those guys did a lot of paintings that were, "Oh, another set of water lilies, great."

And they're making a ton of money.

No one except Fox knows exactly how much money *The Simpsons* has made, but a fair guess is around $3 billion. *The Simpsons* is seen in over ninety countries and, since 1996, has engaged in a marketing relaunch that has placed Homer on everything from talking bottle-cap openers to KFC packaging in the UK. In 2002, Burger King launched a new promotion with *The Simpsons*, marking the longest fast-food-chain tie-in of all time.[17] Merchandising revenue for 2004 alone was $1.65 billion (actual gains for Fox, probably 8– 10 percent of that). Renewed through its twenty-first season, with reruns syndicated in nearly every television market in North America, commercially, *The Simpsons* is more than just a show, it's an empire, justifying current producer Tim Long's statement that Matt Groening is "kind of the Walt Disney of our time."

Even if *The Simpsons* ended its run tomorrow, the show wouldn't die. *The Simpsons* is by now so deeply entrenched in our pop culture that its brand is akin to that of Disney's Mickey Mouse, Donald Duck, and whatever that cretinous mutant Goofy might be. Though there aren't any plans for Simpsonsland, an entire theme park dedicated to *The Simpsons* is not difficult to visualize.* The resonance of *The Simpsons* brand is so strong that it's easy to imagine Fox and Gracie continuing with *Simpsons* products long after the death of the series, and even after its creators are long gone.

MATT GROENING (to *LA Weekly*, July 19, 2007): Sometimes, you know, I go, "Is my work redundant? . . . [But] I get to be on the scene where these brilliant people are making this amazing show, and, Oh, yeah—I created it!

---

*In 2008, the Simpsons Ride opened at Universal Studios—one step closer.

If all *The Simpsons* needs to do to be enormously successful is produce moderately well-written material, within a paradigm (as one
could argue it does now), there is no reason it can't keep going. And
that is both a tribute and a slight to Groening and Brooks. Very
few people ever get to see their creation reach the masses, and no
one, except perhaps DJ Kool Herc, has lived to see something he
invented reach an audience the size of *The Simpsons'*. For that to
continue, especially past its point of relevance, is a remarkable
achievement—for a brand. If *The Simpsons* is something more than
a brand, if its goals are genuinely about more than making money,
then its creators should have retired it, triumphantly, some time ago.

And yet for all this, can Groening and *The Simpsons* really ever
be accused of selling out? While subversive in tone, the series has
rarely pretended to be about anything more than humor and constantly pokes fun at itself for being a shill for their giant, bottom-
feeding corporate overload, News Corp. Maybe Groening made his
point fifteen years ago, inserting his worldview, his malicious frivolity, into the culture at large. Why shouldn't he sit back and enjoy the
fruits of his victory?

MATT GROENING (to *LA Weekly*, July 19, 2007): I'm one of those people who gets more credit than I deserve . . . So do I feel guilty? Yes. Do I
admit it? Yes. And then I move on.

EIGHTEEN

Under the Influence of Duff

In which I cut and paste the dictionary . . . Bart and Nietzsche make peace with the Christians . . . *The Simpsons* are the Beatles and the Rolling Stones and Nirvana . . . and Homer suffers the fate of Ouranus, Cronus, and many lesser gods.

CONAN O'BRIEN, writer/producer, *The Simpsons* (1991–93): For the last fourteen years of doing my show, I've been working hard on this comedy, but it's pretty disposable. I could light my arms on fire on the show tonight and you might see it for a couple of days on YouTube, but then it's gone. I'm constantly, no matter where I go in the world, running into people who know which episodes of *The Simpsons* I worked on, and they're quoting lines to me. I think long after my *Late Night* show is gone, the *Simpsons* episodes I worked on will always be in the ether. People will be watching them on some space station, like, two hundred years from now. That's a nice feeling.

The Simpsons has been hugely influential in television, but the show's reach has gone so much farther than just that medium. If you look around, you can see the evidence, but as with any truly powerful cultural force, you can never see it all—it's buried too deep. There are the obvious examples, shows like *King of the Hill*, *Family Guy*, and *South Park*. And then there are those entities which, over the years, have been developed and staffed by *Simpsons* alumni, shows like *The Office*, *Late Night with Conan O'Brien*, *Frasier*, and the digitally animated films of Brad Bird (*The Incredibles*, *Ratatouille*). But there is also the show's less direct influence to consider, how it revolutionized television comedy, how Jon Stewart speaks *Simpsons*, as have the writers of *Seinfeld* and *Saturday Night Live*.

Moreover, examples of the show's profound influence abound outside the cable box, from "doh" becoming officially part of the English language to the use of *Simpsons* phrases on the cover of the *New York Post* and *New York Daily News.** As Chris Turner put it in *Planet Simpson*, "The Simpsons has become the new repository of the West's common metaphors, the wellspring of its most resonant quotes, the progenitor of its default tone . . . the parlance of our times."

That parlance, at times, can be quite literal. In 2005, *Verbatim: The Language Quarterly* published an article about the embiggening of our language by *Simpsons* words, such as "cromulent," "surrender monkey," "yoink," and of course, "D'oh!" Added to the *Oxford English Dictionary* in 2001, along with "Bollywood," "clubbing," "full monty," "six-pack," "street cred," and "mullet," the entry of this Fox trademark reads:

> Doh, *int.*
> *colloq.*
> Expressing frustration at the realization that things have turned out badly or not as planned, or that one has just said or done something foolish. Also (usu. mildly derogatory): implying that another person has said or done something foolish (cf. DUH *int.*).

BRAD BIRD, executive consultant, *The Simpsons* (1989–97); director, *The Incredibles*, *Ratatouille*: I think that the show encourages people to know more about the world around them. The show refers to things. And it's very facile about it. But it refers not just to the pop hit of the last two or three years, but to Kubrick films and Orson Welles. It gets into jokes about Russian literature, and it encourages you to go out and know more about the world and experience more in terms of art and culture, because the writers are so smart and well read.

---

*"Surrender Monkeys," a phrase coined by Groundskeeper Willie, was the headline on the *Daily News*'s cover on December 7, 2006—the conservative tabloid's response to the Iraq Survey Group's suggestion that some brigades begin withdrawal from Iraq in 2008—with panel members' faces Photoshopped onto monkey bodies.

JONATHAN GRAY, author, *Watching with The Simpsons*; lecturer on media, Fordham University: Parity and satire are inherently forms that ask you to examine the underside of things. They're about taking the clothes off the emperor and showing you what's underneath. And so when you engage in good parody and satire you are always going to be requiring that your audience think about the world.

BRENT FORRESTER, writer/producer, *The Simpsons* (1993–97); writer/ producer, *King of the Hill, The Office*: I well remember somebody pitching a joke that I just didn't get. You know, unfortunately, I only went to Columbia University, not Harvard. And so when somebody pitched "Monticello, I thought you said 'Montebello,'" I realized: I don't know what that means. You know, that kind of stuff. And so there were a lot of smart references, and a feeling of like, Oh, it's cool to be smart. That's the great legacy of the show.

MATT STONE, cocreator, *South Park*: It's probably too big a statement to say it's made us smarter, but *The Simpsons* doesn't ever promise to do anything more than make you laugh. There's social satire in it, social commentary, deeper themes in it, but what's great about *The Simpsons* is it says up front, "All we're gonna do is make you laugh." That's a purely noble cause, I think. It somehow doesn't make you totally *dumber* by doing that. Most things that promise just to make you laugh don't have any other redeeming qualities, and *The Simpsons* seems to.

GARY PANTER, friend of Matt Groening's; cartoonist: *The Simpsons* and *Life in Hell* speak to your average Joe, but at a really high level that makes your average Joe agree with it and share values with it. And it's a lot more of a liberal slant than what the average Joe probably thinks he'd agree with. So I think it's persuasive and it's humanistic and enlightened, and psychologically aware. Americans aren't as stupid as they would like to pretend to be. And you see that in its embrace of *The Simpsons*.

DEBORAH GROENING, Matt Groening's ex-wife: Well, that's the genius of their humor—they're socially aware. We're all products of the sixties in our age group, and I think we haven't forgotten that idealism. It's just that there's a kind of cynicism attached to it, so it's idealistic without being naïve. To quote Matt, we're "sneakily subversive."

One group that has accepted *The Simpsons* as an eye from which to see the world is academia. *The Simpsons* as a cultural critique and as an institution has been endorsed by professors and schools all around the globe. Aside from the hundreds of papers and theses with the Simpsons as their topic, there are collections of essays, including *Leaving Springfield:* The Simpsons *and the Possibility of Oppositional Culture* (Lisa as feminist) and *The Simpsons and Philosophy: The D'Oh! of Homer* (Bart as Nietzsche). There is also *What's Science Ever Done for Us? What* The Simpsons *Can Teach Us About Physics, Robots, Life and the Universe.*

At Berkeley, in 2003, a philosophy course (student led, but for credit), The Simpsons and Philosophy, was offered.

TYLER SHORES, creator and former instructor, The Simpsons and Philosophy: I was a student at Berkeley. This was in 2003. Berkeley had a certain gist or open-mindedness that was perfect for a class on *The Simpsons* and philosophy.

The premise of the class came from a book, *The Simpsons and Philosophy*, edited by William Irwin. The purpose of the class was never to find the philosophy of *The Simpsons* but to be a philosophy course that had *The Simpsons* in it. There's a philosophy topic, let's say Nietzsche, for instance, and there would be an episode that would fit that particular topic, and during the lecture I'd play clips that would illustrate what we were trying to discuss.

There was definitely a buzz that first semester when it came out, which I've never seen or heard since. I can't imagine it happens that often in academia. Everyone knew about it: faculty, students. It was supposed to be a small class; I thought I'd be lucky if twenty students showed up. But it wasn't twenty or fifty but five hundred students on that first day, and we managed to fill that school's largest auditorium for that first class. It was really, really something. The *San Francisco Chronicle* ended up doing a little feature article on it. CNN asked about visiting us. The Swedish national news station actually came all the way to visit us and take the class.

It's in its sixth year now. It's still a pretty good-size class.

Mainstream publications have also used *The Simpsons* to inform their readership on everything from beauty ("Marge Simpson Tells All," *Glamour*), to wrestling ("The 'Bart' Foundation," *World Wrestling Federation Magazine*), to fashion ("The Simpsons Go to Paris," *Harper's Bazaar*), and politics ("Bart for President," *The New Republic*). *The Simpsons* has been the focus of magazine articles on art, dance, feminism, fitness, pornography, math, and music. It's appeared on the cover of everything from *Mother Jones* to *Screw* (also *National Employment Review, Esquire, Spy, LA Salsa, Rolling Stone, Contingency Planning and Management, Adweek*, and many more).

JONATHAN GRAY: If you look at the ways people talked about television in many of the preceeding decades, a lot of the discussion was at the level of how bad television is for us. Things like Neil Postman's *Amusing Ourselves to Death* and these endless suggestions that school shootings and any kind of violence that happens in the street must be due to television. Television was this very culturally degraded object.

And so I think *The Simpsons* is a good outgrowth of that dual tension: being heavily critical of television and television culture and yet doing so with a sense of love (each episode brings in many, many references to different movies and TV shows). It's clearly criticism coming from a knowing place, rather than the kind of criticism from people who were talking about television as horrific and yet it was quite clear that they had very rarely watched television. The same thing happens today with video games. You hear people talking about video games being awful and it's very clear that they've never actually played a game. They just sort of have heard that it's bad.

JOHN ALBERTI, editor, *Leaving Springfield*; professor of English, Northern Kentucky University: I think there's something to it being part of an evolution of TV comedy—like *Saturday Night Live* was taking *National Lampoon*, sixties underground humor, to network TV. But that was on at 11:30 on Saturday night. There was still a kind of off-the-radar aspect. But *The Simpsons* was prime time, and its influence has been directly seen in *South Park* and *King of the Hill* and all the other kind of animated shows, but I think it's also very connected to the *Daily Show* or the *Colbert Report*. Jon Stewart is name-checking them all the time and bringing the same sort of sensibility. And what's interesting about it is that it's ideological but not partisan, if that makes any kind of sense.

And the writers, of course, will always claim neutrality, but also will acknowledge that Lisa is the point of view of the show, which I guess could be called liberal—but it's not liberal like John Kerry's liberal; John Kerry's liberal in a way that doesn't seem at all funny or entertaining— in the way Jon Stewart is liberal.

There is a historical context in which to interpret *The Simpsons* and its place in culture as well.

BILL SAVAGE, contributor, *Leaving Springfield*; lecturer, department of English, Northwestern University: *Steamboat Willie* was the first sound-synchronized cartoon. It was like a technological marvel. So they had this thing where they do "Turkey in the Straw" playing on an animal of some kind. And audiences said, "Holy God! The sound matches up with the action." But early Mickey Mouse was not what we think of when we think of Mickey Mouse today. Early Mickey Mouse was raunchy and counterculture, and people complained it was obscene just like they did with Bart Simpson. There's a real parallel there.

The show that was once a target of the Christian right is now held up as an example of the values they are crusading for (if you didn't already know, the Simpsons belong to the "one true church," the Western Branch of American Reform Presbylutheranism); Britain's archbishop of Canterbury referred to the show as "generally on the side of the angels."[1] As well, the Family Research Council's Robert Knight* has commented that *The Simpsons*' reality is a moral one, and PRISM, the Evangelicals for Social Action's monthly publication, has called it "the most pro-family, God-preoccupied, home-based program on television."

Orlando journalist Mark Pinsky wrote a book in 2001 called *The Gospel According to The Simpsons*, which examined the moral and religious quandaries addressed by the show. Later, along with a pas-

---

*Knight spends much of his energy trying to promote legislation dictating marriage that can occur only between a man and a woman, as well as directing movies about "recovered" homosexuals.

tor, he produced a prayer guide, which can be used at Bible study and Sunday school to teach kids and adults the lessons of the Scripture through *The Simpsons*. In the UK, rumors of a Cult of Ned Flanders prompted a report by the BBC about a group of Christians who, while not necessarily worshipping the nerd-a-rino next door, were tremendously influenced by the Simpsons' neighbor.

STEPHEN GODDARD, co-editor, Christian comedy magazine *Ship of Fools* (on ABC Australia program *Enough Rope*, April 21, 2003): Well, we discovered that Ned was a bigger popular icon than any other major Christian personality—bigger than Billy Graham in the States, the pope or even the late Mother Teresa . . . We couldn't believe this, but we wanted to test it out, so we ran a Ned Flanders night, a tribute to the man and his green jumper . . . And we had 2,000 people turn up.

JONATHAN GRAY: That's one of the things I think is really interesting about *The Simpsons*—you can see whatever you want to see in it.

HANK AZARIA, voice actor, *The Simpsons*: I think It's pretty safe to say that we are from a fairly leftist, Democratic slant, which makes my heart sing. Look, they'll evenhandedly take on whatever seems hypocritical or nonsensical—but one of the things I love about the show is that it has a really good conscience. And I think it's incredibly ironic that a show with such a leftist, Democratic slant is one of the *cornerstones* of Fox News Corp financially. It never ceases to amaze me.

DOUGLAS RUSHKOFF, media critic: That's the way you look at it. It's just a justification for doing countercultural media, even if it's going to give some money to Rupert Murdoch. But you would argue that Rupert Murdoch's business now is being used to undermine his values of mainstream corporate culture [through *The Simpsons'* subversive satire] instead of promoting them, so it's a net good.

And maybe for four or five years, it can be, but the problem is that after four or five years you've communicated the message. You've sort of said the same thing and it slowly tips toward just really contributing more money to corporate coffers rather than to making new statements or creating progress. The longer Bart stays alive as part of Fox empire, the more neutralized he is. First, just because he exists so long, he's an institution, so he's part of the thing. It's like Ralph Nader or something. It's like, Who's really afraid anymore?

You need new stuff to keep it dangerous. And second, the longer he exists, the more the Bart property is leveraged toward the benefit of the corporate conglomerate and gets away from the subversive effect on youth. So other things, maybe *South Park*, replaced *The Simpsons* as the more culturally provocative, dangerous thing. *The Simpsons'* economic reality was to create a conservative media infrastructure [aka Fox News], which, in a sense, far outweighs anything that its content does.

BILL SAVAGE: What people tend to forget is that all that capitalism cares about is the bottom line. I mean, Rupert Murdoch will appear as a character on *The Simpsons* as a greedy, billionaire scumbag if the ratings are good enough and they make money on it. That's all that matters. I don't think any capitalists feel particularly threatened by leftist ideas.

JOHN ALBERTI: I think it's significant that *The Simpsons* started with the machine on the Fox TV network, so there's a kind of awareness from the beginning that this isn't some Utopian space that's uncontaminated. And *The Simpsons* keeps pointing it out: "Hey you're watching Fox TV." There might not have been Fox News if it hadn't been for the success of *The Simpsons*, which really helped to establish Fox as a network.

AL JEAN (to Douglas Rushkoff, 1992): The thesis of *The Simpsons* is nihilism. There's nothing to believe in anymore once you assume that organized structures and institutions are out to get you.

TIM LONG, writer/producer, *The Simpsons* (1998–   ): I'd like to think that we prevented the president from invading Iraq and we kept Bush from being reelected. Oh, whoops, we didn't do any of those things. You can overstate the importance of comedy. At best I think comedians tend to be like that guy standing in front of the tank in Tiananmen Square— you're flattering yourself if you think you're actually affecting anything.

Viewed in more than ninety countries—it is most popular in the UK, Mexico, Germany, Spain, and Scandinavia—the show is sometimes tweaked to fit in with a particular culture's norms. In 2005, Homer and Bart finally made it to the Arab world, but as Omar and Badr Shamshoon (voiced by some of the Middle East's most popular actors). Omar had to give up his love of beer and donuts for soda and kahk (Arab cookies).[2] While the show did poorly, it's an illustration of *The Simpsons*' universality—and its influence.

SETH MCFARLANE: It's like what sci-fi fans say about *Star Trek*: it created an audience for that genre. And I think *The Simpsons* created an audience for prime-time animation that had not been there for many many years. It created what you could classify as a wholly new medium. It really is like no other television or feature animation that came before it. It's just wholly original. In the same way that *The Honeymooners* created a genre for live-action comedy, I think *The Simpsons* created a genre for animated comedy that paved the way for many, many other shows to work essentially in that new medium they came up with.

It was the first sitcom to heavily reference elements of pop culture. The TV and movies we watch and the products we buy are big parts of daily life, and yet prior to *The Simpsons*, I don't think you saw a lot of that referenced in pop culture. Everything was more generic. And *The Simpsons* was the first show with the balls to deal with specifics and make fun of actual television shows, products, movies, elements of pop culture that previously had been genericized.

WALLACE WOLODARSKY, writer/producer, *The Simpsons* (1989–92): I see it in a continuum that starts with Martin and Lewis, *Your Show of Shows*, *Honeymooners*, early Carson, early Letterman, *Get Smart*, early *SNL*, and just keeps moving. I don't see it as a revolution. I see it as a natural continuum of all the stuff we really loved.

BILL OAKLEY, writer/producer, *The Simpsons* (1991 97): *The Simpsons* has transplanted *MAD*. Basically everyone who was young between 1955 and 1975 read *MAD*, and that's where your sense of humor came from. And we knew all those people, you know Dave Berg and Don Martin—all heroes and unfortunately now all dead. And I think *The Simpsons* has taken that spot in America's heart. The humor is a fusion of the people who grew up reading *MAD* and mid-eighties Letterman, *SNL*, and also the *Harvard Lampoon*.

DONICK CARY, writer/producer, *The Simpsons* (1996–99): It certainly opened the door for Adult Swim; it opened the door for *Family Guy*, obviously, *South Park*, Comedy Central. And I think, in some ways, it also opened the door for the animation craze in feature films.

BRAD BIRD: My agenda almost as long as I've been working professionally is to try to reinforce the idea that animation is not exclusively for kids. And so, for me, *The Simpsons* was a wonderful way to get on board a ship that was flying in the face of that. The problem with a lot of animated films that aren't aimed at kids is that they try to declare their "adultness," and it's an adolescent way of announcing that you're not aimed at kids. It's not truly an adult way. What I liked about *The Simpsons* was that besides it being really funny, it was smart. It ran the gamut from really base, the occasional butt-crack joke, and then talking about Susan Sontag or something in the next sentence. It has affected things very profoundly. But I think, unfortunately, a lot of people have taken the wrong lessons from *The Simpsons* and just done the butt-crack jokes, and not picked up the smart ball.

Bird didn't name any names, but one could assume he was referring to *The Simpsons'* disobedient stepchildren, *South Park* and *Family Guy*, which, for better or worse, picked up the rebellious animated comedy reins.

   South Park's birth was akin to *Army Man*, in that it was originally samizdat (albeit a video version), which circulated Hollywood. The series focuses on four foul-mouthed fourth graders: Stan, Kyle, Cartman, and Kenny. As with *The Simpsons*, *South Park* played with the classic comedy tropes (a set group of characters based in a single locale go on weekly adventures and learn a lesson), except that its creators went to much greater lengths to undercut these standards, beginning with the killing of Kenny in each episode. *South Park* was truly crude, and there was no topic it would not directly attack: abortion, racism, mentally and physically challenged people, Scientology (something *The Simpsons* has not dared approach, because Bart's voice, Nancy Cartwright, is a devout member).*

---

*In 2009, Cartwright made a Robocall, which went out to people in Los Angeles, asking them to attend a Scientology event. The *Simpsons* producers hit the roof: it seems that Fox owns the rights

The extremes *South Park* is willing to go to (two handicapped children engage in a "cripple fight," while the townspeople gleefully observe; Cartman is nearly molested by members of NAMBLA) create stiff competition for "The Simpsons are going to London!" And while *The Simpsons* have courted celebrities, *South Park* mercilessly slaughters them. On that series, Tom Cruise and John Travolta are closeted homosexuals; Barbra Streisand is a power-mad, Godzilla-like monster; Paris Hilton is a "rich, spoiled whore"; and Al Gore is an attention-seeking fabulist.

As *The Simpsons* did for Fox, the enormously successful *South Park* would brand Comedy Central, flooding the fledgling network with ad and merchandising revenue. Depending how you choose to see it, the series either built on *The Simpsons*, taking it to new heights, or rebelled against *The Simpsons'* middling good behavior and created an animated sitcom that threw accepted ideas of iconoclasm, animation, and good taste right back into people's faces.

South Park has framed itself as the anti-*Simpsons*. While *The Simpsons* is somewhat democratic with its scorn, if a little liberal, *South Park* is virulently libertarian, even conservative. And while *The Simpsons'* weapons of irreverence include wit, subtlety, and a good grounding in the liberal arts, *South Park's* repertoire contains the tools of shock and awe: racial epithets, controversial subject matter, and extreme situations (taking revenge on an older boy who tricked him out of $10, Cartman murders his parents and feeds them to the teen). And yet it is unfair to attribute *South Park's* success solely to its risqué content. While it may rely too much on shock value—its more problematic crutch may be its constant reliance on filmic parody for plot structure—this is a show with some excellent writing. It offers a scathing criticism of contemporary society that is absolutely original, even if *The Simpsons* served as a stepping-stone to getting it on the air.

MATT STONE: *The Simpsons* is the bane of our existence. It has done so many parodies, tackled so many subjects, and had so many episodes.

---

to Bart's voice, not Cartwright, and Al Jean issued a statement. Cartwright had given $10 million to Scientology in 2008, earning her that organization's Patriot Laureate award, and making her their most generous celebrity donor (her contribution doubled that of Tom Cruise's).[3]

"Simpsons did it!" is a familiar refrain in our writers room. Because *South Park* and *The Simpsons* are both animated, Trey [Parker] and I are constantly having our little cartoon compared to the *best* show in the history of television, *The Simpsons*. Why can't we be compared to *According to Jim*? Or *Sister, Sister*?

In the world of twenty-two-minute comedy shows, even in the world of television, I think it's the best show that's ever been on TV. It's not like every episode is the best thing on TV, because there have been four million episodes, but its batting average is pretty high. As a body of work, I think it's unrivaled, I really do.

The density of the joke writing is unbelievable. In my life, it seems like comedy has gotten denser. Like Pixar movies and other animated shows, it feels like we have this goalpost of density of animated jokes that you have to get to. We try purposely not to do that, because you can't compete on that level with *The Simpsons'* writing room. Other shows do it, but they don't succeed; they seem to make you dumber. *The Simpsons* is just this machine-gun fire of jokes, and it doesn't talk down to you; it's like a smart machine-gun fire. It's frustrating that we're always compared to *The Simpsons*, but on the other hand, it's an honor.

The same credit for originality credited to *South Park* cannot be awarded to *The Simpsons'* other famous spawn. No less funny than *South Park*, *Family Guy* is a slightly derivative though faster-paced product than *The Simpsons*, geared toward a younger, hipper audience. Its focus is Peter Griffin, the obese, coarse, and cretinous head of a family that includes his lovely, Waspy wife, Lois, his dimwitted son, Chris, his unattractive daughter, Meg, a matricidal talking baby named Stewie, and a hard-drinking, perspicacious talking dog named Brian. Based on shorts for the Cartoon Network made by then-twenty-four-year-old wunderkind Seth MacFarlane, who is also a writer, voice actor, singer, animator, and composer, *Family Guy* is a gestalt of sex and bathroom jokes, pop culture references, musical numbers, celebrity bashing, and random cutaways. In terms of allusions, the show is like *The Simpsons* on methamphetamines.

Family Guy isn't about tackling social issues, or about letting you know how smart its writers are with allusions to high culture; it is all about the laugh. While the Griffins stay consistent, the family isn't meant to approximate a real one in their speech or deeds. Nor are their neighbors, like the hyperaggressive, paraplegic policeman Joe, sexual predator and best friend Glenn Quagmire, the old pedophile who lives down the street, or the sporadically appearing Greased Up Naked Guy. A typical episode has Meg pretending that Stewie is her crack-addicted baby to earn sympathy and tips as a waitress, while the adults accuse each other of stealing a prized trophy. It ends with Rod Serling, from *The Twilight Zone*, revealing that it was the talking dog, Brian, who took the trophy so he could bury it in the backyard, resulting in Brian assaulting him with a shovel and then burying the body.

It's easy to see *The Family Guy* as a frat boy version of *The Simpsons*: bigger, ruder, and meaner. But, like *South Park*, there is more going on than easy jokes—the show has captured the imagination of millions with its hyperallusive, kinetic approach to comedy. If *The Simpsons* was a cartoon for adults in 1989, *Family Guy* was that for 1999 and beyond. Its popularity—on DVD and on the Cartoon Network's late-night showcase, Adult Swim—among millions of college kids and twenty-somethings caused a true first: in 2005, after a two-year hiatus, Fox uncanceled the series, bringing it back on Sunday nights, where it regularly trounces its forebear. It has gone on to spawn two more cartoon series: (the god-awful) *American Dad* and (the as-yet-to-be-seen) *The Cleveland Show*, and continues its strong DVD sales. In May 2008, Fox signed a $100 million deal with MacFarlane, keeping his shows until 2012 and making him the highest-paid writer in Hollywood. The entire *Family Guy* operation is now valued at over $1 billion.

SETH MACFARLANE: Early on, when I was in college, I had decided that I wanted to work for Disney 'cause they were sort of the biggest thing happening in animation at the time, because of their resurgence. Then *The Simpsons* came on the scene and completely eclipsed Disney in sophistication. I would watch *The Simpsons* and just go, "Wow, these guys are opening up a whole bunch of new doorways for animation with some bite to it." So much of feature animation is geared toward kids— and to me animation is so often at its best when it's got some teeth to it. *The Simpsons* sort of opened the doors: characters could swear.

[*The Simpsons*] is still funnier than any live-action show on television right now. I'll watch *The Simpsons* before I watch a live-action sitcom any day of the week. I think the show, in its prime years, is up there with *All in the Family*, with *Mary Tyler Moore*, with *Dick Van Dyke* as one of the great sitcoms of all time. It deserves its place of honor on that list, as far as I'm concerned. It's been eighteen years. So it's a different show, obviously.

I'm always walking on eggshells with this issue, because I can't stress enough how much respect I have for that show as a series. In some ways the stories tend to be a little bigger nowadays. They tend to be a little more out there; whether that's a good thing or a bad thing really depends on the taste of each particular viewer. Tonally, every sitcom evolves in one way or another, and I think that *The Simpsons* is tonally certainly very different than it was four hundred episodes ago.

If I did *Family Guy* for eighteen years, I don't think it would be as good as it is now. There's only so much you can do with a certain group of characters, and I think that for a show that's been on eighteen years, *The Simpsons* is doing as great a job as anyone could, after that long, of keeping it fresh.

It just depends on the episode. They aren't doing quite as many of the smaller, quieter character stories anymore. I think that's what that show does so beautifully and I would love to see them get back to that.

Among fans, much has been made of the rivalry between *Family Guy* and *The Simpsons*, which take the occasional shot at each other.

SETH MACFARLANE: I've had some interaction with Matt Groening and I've found him to be a really terrific guy. And obviously very, very talented. Just a good guy, in addition to everything else. I don't know Jim Brooks, but Mike Scully, who ran *The Simpsons* for a number of years, is a friend of mine, and he's a hysterically funny guy. I don't know all those guys; I know enough of them to have sort of a relationship with that show.

For me there's sort of a glaze over all of the back-and-forth gibes that you see on TV between the two shows. I have yet to meet one person on the writing staff of *The Simpsons* who isn't pretty cool to hang out with. There is the belief among a lot of the fans that there's a harsh rivalry between us and *The Simpsons*. The gibes are never really *discussed* between us, because I think it goes without saying that, yeah, we're going to take jabs at each other because we both take jabs at everything else. I think sometimes, onscreen, they can get a little mean-spirited, but for me it doesn't stick, because it's all in good fun.

Even when you consider the gigantic success of *The Simpsons*' offspring, no series has come close to *The Simpsons*' level of influence. Seinfeld is comparable, in terms of money, and even how often its referenced, but only within a certain bourgeois American audience. *Friends* was, for years, a religion, but its popularity was passing and resounded barely past the nineties. *Family Guy* and *South Park* are somewhat in the same universe, in terms of annual financial revenues, and laughs per minute, but nowhere close in terms of syndication, smarts, or scope. With broadband, the increasing prominence of cable, DVR, and the increasing number of alternatives to network TV, it is unlikely that any television series will ever have *The Simpsons*' success, import, or resonance.

MICHAEL MENDEL, postproduction supervisor, *The Tracey Ullman Show*, *The Simpsons* (1989–92, 1994–99): My big fat opinion about it is there seem to be fewer Jim Brookses and Steven Bochcos and David Kelleys and those kinds of people who can get a show on the air with their vision intact. That doesn't exist in the way that shows are made these days.

JOHN ALBERTI: My daughter once referred to *The Simpsons* as the Beatles of television. Everything kind of starts with *The Simpsons*, and they are a little more mainstream than, say, punk rock, but still everybody still likes the Beatles, especially the classic Beatles. And now maybe *The Simpsons* have stretched it into the Rolling Stones because the Rolling Stones are so corporatized now it's really hard to imagine that they were ever subversive or edgy or countercultural. It seems like they're beating a dead horse to pick up a paycheck. So everybody was sad when the Beatles broke up, but now you look back and you think, Maybe it's not quite so bad that the Beatles broke up, before they did anything really awful and embarrassing, just kind of hauling out that name because people would respond to it. So maybe that's it. Maybe they've gone from the Beatles to the Rolling Stones.

ROBERT PINSKY, United States poet laureate, 1997–2000; guest voice, *The Simpsons*: All due respect to the Beatles, *The Simpsons* never went through the equivalent of a cute, mop-top, harmless, and charming period. The show never represented "youth." On the contrary, it represented an irritable, anarchic impatience with cornball, pretentious ideas like "youth." Like the Beatles, the show represents a watershed, but its spirit, its attitude is more like David Byrne.

RICKY GERVAIS, guest voice, *The Simpsons*; creator and star, *The Office*, *Extras*: I imagine its influence is as a paradigm of excellence. By definition, excellence is rare. People go, "Would that pass in *The Simpsons*?" What I like about *The Simpsons* is that it's timeless and universal. And that's something I've always aspired to. I don't want to do a joke that people in my backyard get, that (1) won't travel and (2) won't be funny in a year's time because you'll forget the cultural reference. *The Simpsons* does that brilliantly. But I don't know if it's influenced people, because they are still rubbish. I don't know if it's changed the way people make TV. I don't know if many things do that outside technology and law. But I imagine it's made a lot of people go, "Oh, my God!" You ask any comedians, "What's your favorite thing?" "Well, let's talk about what our second favorite thing is, because we'll all agree that it's *The Simpsons*." That's it. *Simpsons. Simpsons* is king.

In the end, explaining how *The Simpsons* managed to accomplish what it did is as futile as explaining how a joke is funny. It is said that talking about music is like dancing about architecture. Perhaps talking about *The Simpsons* is like laughing about biochemistry. If that's the case, as with all of the above, *The Simpsons* could say it better than I can.

JAY KOGEN, writer/producer, *The Simpsons* (1989–92): We thought we were writing these really funny, smart, special shows that were chock-full of jokes every few seconds. And then someone showed us this study Fox had done. The number one reason people liked *The Simpsons* was "all the pretty colors," and they liked it when Homer hit his head. We were writing the show for ourselves—we always made it funny for ourselves. But who knows why America likes it. Maybe they do like the pretty colors and when Homer hits his head. But I hope there's more.

Notes

Introduction: "Hi, Everybody!"
1. Wayne Walley, "Fox Rates Look from Advertisers; Fourth TV Network Rebuffs Skeptics," *Advertising Age*, December 14, 1987.
2. Chris Turner, *Planet Simpson* (Cambridge, MA: Da Capo, 2004), p. 120.
3. Quoted in Gary Budzak, "Cracked Humor, Creative Freedom Keep 'Simpsons' Going," *Columbus Dispatch*, March 2, 2004.

1: The Matt Groening Show
1. Thomas J. Meyer, "To Hell and Back," *Northwest Magazine*, March 25, 1990.
2. Neil Tesser, "20 Questions: Matt Groening," *Playboy*, July 1990.
3. Quoted in Joe Morgenstern, "Bart Simpson's Real Father," *Los Angeles Times Magazine*, April 29, 1990.
4. Paul Andrews, "The Groening of America," *Seattle Times*, August 19, 1990.
5. "Best Colleges," *U.S. News & World Report*, February 13, 2009.
6. Quoted in Jim Lynch, "2 Schools of Thought Compete at Evergreen," *Sunday Oregonian*, June 10, 2001.
7. Tesser, "20 Questions: Matt Groening."
8. Mark Rahner, "Matt Groening to Give Grads Bart-like Wisdom?" *Seattle Times*, June 9, 2000.
9. Meyer, "To Hell and Back."
10. Quoted ibid.
11. Quoted in Andrews, "The Groening of America."
12. Tesser, "20 Questions: Matt Groening."
13. Ibid.
14. Jenny Eliscu, "Homer and Me," *Rolling Stone*, November 28, 2008.
15. Morgenstern, "Bart Simpson's Real Father."
16. Quoted in Andrews, "The Groening of America."
17. Tesser, "20 Questions: Matt Groening."

2: THE KING OF COMEDY

1. Hilary De Vries, "The Director's Long Shot," *Washington Post*, February 12, 1994.
2. Quoted in Steve Daly, "What, Him Worry?" *Entertainment Weekly*, November 12, 2004.
3. Patrick Danaher, "Simpsons Producer Plans to Take World's Funniest Family to Ireland," *Sunday Tribune* (Dublin), March 2, 2008.
4. Aljean Harmetz, "Coming to Terms with His Success," *New York Times Magazine*, April 8, 1984.
5. "James L. Brooks," *Current Biography* (Bronx, NY: H. W. Wilson, 1998).
6. Daly, "What, Him Worry?"
7. Ibid.
8. Mark Seal, "The Man Who Ate Hollywood," *Vanity Fair*, November 2005.
9. "In Hollywood, a Nouveau Royalty Made by Mergers," *New York Times*, March 1, 1992.
10. James B. Stewart, "The Milken File," *New Yorker*, January 22, 2001.
11. William H. Meyers, "Murdoch's Global Power Play," *New York Times*, June 12, 1988.
12. "Fox Lines Up 79 Independent Affiliates," United Press International, August 4, 1986.

3: WHEN BART MET TRACEY

1. Gary Panter, "The Rozz Tox Manifesto," garypanter.com/2004_05_16_archive.html.
2. James Lipton, "The Cast of *The Simpsons*," *Inside the Actors Studio*, Bravo, February 9, 2003.
3. Ibid.
4. Ibid.
5. Ibid.

4: SAM "SAYONARA" SIMON

1. Morley Safer, "Dog Nut," *60 Minutes*, CBS, July 15, 2007.
2. Quoted in A. O. Scott, "Homer's Odyssey," *New York Times Magazine*, November 4, 2001.
3. Quoted in Howard Rosenberg, "The Simpsons; A Google-Eyed Guerrilla Assault on TV," *Washington Post*, March 18, 1990.
4. Roland Barthes, *Image-Music-Text*, Hill and Wang, 1978.

5: WELCOME TO SPRINGFIELD

1. Quoted in Daniel Kimmel, *The Fourth Network*, Ivan R. Dee, Chicago, 2004.
2. Quoted in Ken Auletta, "Barry Diller's Search for the Future," *New Yorker*, February 22, 1993.
3. Quoted in Jefferson Graham, "Aaauggh! He's Gone, Man: In a Surprise Move, Barry Diller Resigns as Fox Chief," *USA Today*, February 25, 1992.
4. Ibid.

6: THE ROOM

1. World Series of Poker, player profiles, worldseriesofpoker.com/players/playerPro file.asp?playerID=9703.
2. World Series of Poker, player profiles, worldseriesofpoker.com/players/playerPro file.asp?playerID=4470&pagecolor-FFFFFF.

7: THE FIRST EPISODES

1. Joe Morgenstern, "Bart Simpson's Real Father," *Los Angeles Times Magazine*, April 29, 1990.
2. "Some Enchanted Evening," *The Simpsons: The Complete First Season*, Vol. 3, supplementary commentary by Matt Groening, DVD, 2001.
3. Ibid., supplementary commentary by James L. Brooks.
4. Ibid.
5. Ibid., supplementary commentary by Matt Groening.
6. "List of Week's TV Show Ratings," Associated Press, December 28, 1989.
7. Ibid., May 1, 1990.
8. Kenneth R. Clark, "The Simpsons Proves Cartoons Are Not Just for Kids," *Chicago Tribune, TV Week*, January 14, 1990.
9. Michael Kingsley, "For the Life of the Party, Call Roseanne," *Los Angeles Times*, June 30, 1990.
10. Tom Shales, "The Primest Time: Sunday Night Television," *Washington Post*, March 11, 1990.
11. Richard Zoglin, "Home Is Where the Venom Is," *Time*, June 24, 2001.
12. Morgenstern, "Bart Simpson's Real Father."
13. Quoted in Kleinfeld, "Cashing in on a Hot New Brand Name."
14. Tom Shales, "They're Scrapping . . ." *Washington Post*, October 11, 1990.
15. Quoted in Jian Ghomeshi, "A Feature Chat with Bill Cosby," *The Q*, CBC Radio, broadcast July 13, 2009.
16. Joan Hanauer, "Cosby Edges Simpsons Across U.S.," *Los Angeles Times*, October 16, 1990.
17. Rick Du Brow, "Cocky, Freewheeling Fox Falls on Its Face," *Los Angeles Times*, December 11, 1990.
18. Deborah Hastings, "The Simpsons Finally Beats Cos," *Associated Press*, November 28, 1990.

8: BIGGER THAN JESUS

1. Linda Shrieves, "Bart: A '90s Kind of Hero; The Coolest Simpson Has Become America's Hottest Kid," *Orlando Sentinel*, May 4, 1990.
2. Kevin Goldman, "Major Networks Are Calling the Toons to Animate Prime Time TV Ratings," *Wall Street Journal*, January 14, 1991.
3. Michel Marriott, "I'm Black Bart and What About It?," *New York Times*, September 19, 1990.
4. Ibid.
5. Quoted in Ruben Castaneda, "Bart Simpson: Children's Hero, Educators' Menace," *Washington Post*, May 29, 1990.

6. Scott Williams, "Bart Simpson—Cultural Icon or Rebel Without a Clue," Associated Press, May 22, 1990.
7. Matt Neufeld, "Cowabunga, Dudes! T-Shirts of Bart Shaking up Schools," *Washington Times*, September 20, 1990.
8. Donnie Radcliffe, "Marge to Barb: Don't Have a Cow, Ma'am," *Washington Post*, October 12, 1990.
9. "Drug Czar Says He Was 'Just Kidding' in Chiding Bart Simpson," Associated Press, May 24, 1990.
10. "Good Night, John Boy; Hello Bart Simpson," *Seattle Post-Intelligencer*, August 21, 1992.
11. Matt Roush, " 'Simpsons' Creator Puts Loony in 'Toons,' " *USA Today*, January 12, 1990.
12. John Ortved, "Simpsons Family Values," *Vanity Fair*, August 2007.
13. Matthew Grimm, "A Smash Cartoon Hit Called 'The Simpsons' Hits Licensing Paydirt," *Adweek*, March 5, 1990.
14. "Ullman Suit Charges Fox Cut Her out of 'Simpsons' Profits," *Chicago Sun-Times*, April 21, 1991.
15. Anita Gates, "Groening's New World, 1,000 Years from Springfield," *New York Times*, January 24, 1999.
16. *Late Night with Conan O'Brien*, October 7, 1994.
17. Charlie Rose, "A Conversation About *The Simpsons Movie*," *Charlie Rose*, PBS, New York, July 30, 2007.
18. Rod Dreher, "Bart Used by Extremists," *Washington Times*, May 13, 1993.
19. Marla Matzer, "Simpsons Sales: Halving a Cow," *Los Angeles Times*, September 25, 1997.

9: FALLOUT BOYS
1. Quoted in Dennis McDougal and Daniel Cerone, "Ullman Has a Cow over Simpsons," *Los Angeles Times*, April 19, 1991.
2. "Jury Rejects Tracey Ullman's 'Simpsons' Lawsuit," Associated Press, October 21, 1992.

12: INSTITUTIONALIZED
1. Tom Shales, "The Groening of America," *Washington Post*, May 13, 1993.
2. Jim Benson, " 'Simpsons' Surprise Syndicated Success," *Variety*, November 28–December 4, 1994.
3. Shales, "The Groening of America."
4. Benson, " 'Simpsons' Surprise Syndicated Success."
5. Cynthia Littleton, " 'Seinfeld' Set to Earn Record Syndie," *Variety*, January 12, 1998.
6. Quoted in James Sterngold, "Bringing an Alien and a Robot to Life: The Gestation of the Simpsons' Heirs," *New York Times*, July 22, 1999.
7. David Bianculli, "Animation King Takes a Swipe at Fox," *New York Daily News*, April 8, 1999.
8. Sam Salem, "*Futurama* Cast Members Ink New Deal with Fox," *Toronto Star*, July 31, 2009.

9. Quoted in "Simpsons Just a Cartoon to TV Academy," *USA Today*, February 21, 1992.
10. Quoted ibid.
11. Ibid.

13: THE GODFATHERS
1. David Owen, "Taking Humor Seriously: The Funniest Man Behind the Funniest Show on TV," *New Yorker*, March 13, 2000.
2. Eric Spitznagel, "George Meyer," *The Believer*, September 2004.
3. Owen, "Taking Humor Seriously."
4. George Meyer, "Welcoming Homer the Tree-Hugger," BBC News, August 3, 2006, news.bbc.co.uk/2/hi/science/nature/5237038.stm.
5. "Grade School Confidential," *The Simpsons: The Complete Eighth Season*, Vol. 4, supplementary commentary by Matt Groening.

14: WHO'S THE BOSS?
1. Quoted in Judy Brennan, "Groening Has a Cow Over 'Critic' Television," *Los Angeles Times*, March 3, 1995.
2. Ibid.
3. Ibid.
4. Quoted in Adam Buckman, "Homer's Baghdad of Tricks," *New York Post*, October 23, 2006.

15: FOXY BOXING
1. Bernard Weinraub, "Negotiations Are Stalled for Voice Actors in 'The Simpsons,'" *New York Times*, April 14, 2004.
2. Michael Fleming, "'Simpsons' Gang Sees D'Oh," *Variety*, April 30, 2001.
3. Weinraub, "Negotiations Are Stalled for Voice Actors in 'The Simpsons.'"
4. Scott Williams, "Tim Allen: TV's $1.25 Million Man," *New York Daily News*, October 7, 1997.
5. Quoted in Jenny Hontz, "'Simpsons': No Dough, New 'D'Oh,'" *Variety*, March 19, 1998.
6. Fleming, "'Simpsons' Gang Sees D'Oh."
7. Japan Probe, www.japanprobe.com/?p=2698.
8. Fleming, "'Simpsons' Gang Sees 'D'Oh.'"
9. Weinraub, "Negotiations Are Stalled for Voice Actors in 'The Simpsons.'"
10. Ibid.
11. Siri Agrell, "No More D'Oh Without Hefty Raise, Says Simpsons Cast," *National Post (Canada)*, April 2, 2004.
12. Weinraub, "Negotiations Are Stalled for Voice Actors in 'The Simpsons.'"
13. Ibid.
14. Bernard Weinraub, "'The Simpsons' Reach a Deal with Fox," *New York Times*, May 1, 2004.
15. Nellie Andreeva, "'Simpson' Voice Actors Reach Deal," *Hollywood Reporter*, June 2, 2008.

16. Nellie Andreeva, "Dough! Cast Gets a Raise," *Hollywood Reporter*, June 3, 2008.
17. Ibid.
18. "Bart the Murderer," *The Simpsons: The Complete Third Season*, Vol. 1, supplementary commentary by Al Jean, DVD, 2003.
19. "A Streetcar Named Marge," *The Simpsons: The Complete Fourth Season*, Vol. 1, supplementary commentary by Mike Reiss, DVD, 2004.
20. Quoted in Mike Reiss, "A Backstage Tour of *The Simpsons* with Mike Reiss," 92nd Street Y. Tribeca, New York, April 24, 2009.
21. Quoted in Michele Orecklin, "¡Ay Caramba!" *Time*, April 22, 2002.
22. Quoted in David Scheff, "*Playboy* Interview: Matt Groening," *Playboy*, June 1, 2007.

16: THE GUEST STARS
1. "Rosebud," *The Simpsons: The Complete Fifth Season*, Vol. 1, supplementary commentary by David Mirkin, DVD, 2004.
2. Andrew Miller, "Homerphobic—The Simpsons Voice-Over Curse," *Spy*, December 1993–March 1994.
3. Quoted in "Phil Hartman, Wife Die in Apparent Murder-Suicide," CNN.com, May 28, 1998, www.cnn.com/SHOWBIZ/TV/9805/28/hartman/.
4. "Stark Raving Dad," *The Simpsons: The Complete Third Season*, Vol. 1, supplementary commentary by James L. Brooks, DVD, 2001.
5. Ibid.
6. Quoted in David Sheff, "*Playboy* Interview: Matt Groening," *Playboy*, June 1, 2007.
7. Conan O'Brien, "A Bob Hope Clause Means Without Him, All Bets Are Off," *New York Times*, May 24, 1998.

17: ON AND ON
1. "List of Week's TV Ratings," Associated Press, September 18, 1995–May 20, 1996.
2. "Prime-time Nielsen Ratings," Associated Press, November 3, 2000–May 22, 2009.
3. "Prime-time TV Rankings," *Los Angeles Times*, October 8, 2008–April 1, 2009.
4. Quoted in Caroline Bellinger, "Simpsons Still Calling the Toon 15 Years On," *Daily Telegraph* (Sydney), April 1, 2004.
5. Adam Buckman, "Time to Put 'The Simpsons' to Everlasting Rest," *New York Times*, September 11, 2005.
6. Ben Wasserstein, "The Last (Great) Season of 'The Simpsons,'" *New York*, September 11, 2006.
7. Andrea Chang, "Rolling in D'Oh!," *Daily Northwestern*, November 4, 2004.
8. Terry Gross, "Matt Groening Discusses 'The Simpsons,'" *Fresh Air*, NPR, December 29, 2004.
9. Lawrence Van Gelder, "China Restricts Mickey and Homer," *New York Times*, August 14, 2006.
10. Quoted in "Life in Heaven," Newsweek.com, January 25, 2001, www.newsweek.com/id/153648?tid=relatedcl.
11. Dan Snierson, "Homer's Odyssey," *Entertainment Weekly*, July 27, 2007.
12. Ibid.
13. Nick Curtis, "The Simpsons' Big Screen Test," *Evening Standard* (London), July 12, 2007.

14. Todd McCarthy, "Spanglish," *Variety*, December 9, 2004.
15. Gail Schiller, "Doh! Simpsons Limits Tie-in Partners," *The Hollywood Reporter*, July 6, 2007.
16. Quoted in Will Harris, "A Chat with Alf Clausen," Bullz-Eye.com, September 26, 2007, www.bullz-eye.com/television/interviews/2007/alf_clausen.htm.
17. Snierson, "Homer's Odyssey."

18: UNDER THE INFLUENCE OF DUFF
 1. Quoted in "Archbishop's Views Have Often Sparked Controversy," Agence France-Presse, February 9, 2008.
 2. Yasmine El-Rashidi, "D'oh! Bart and Homer Now Badr and Omar," *Globe and Mail*, (Toronto), October 17, 2005.
 3. Chris Ayres, "Simpsons Producers 'Have a Cow' as Bart Lends His Voice to Scientology," *Times* (London), January 30, 2009.

Dramatis Personae

JOHN ALBERTI: A professor of English at Northern Kentucky University, Alberti has written on popular music, television, and the movies, including his book *Text Messaging: Reading and Writing About Popular Culture.* He is the editor of *Leaving Springfield:* The Simpsons *and the Possibility of Oppositional Culture*, a book of critical essays on *The Simpsons*. He also has a band called the Bitter Pills.

GARTH ANCIER: Former president of entertainment at Fox Broadcasting, currently president of BBC Worldwide America. Ancier was the top exec at Fox Broadcasting in the mid-1980s, running the network day to day and ultimately in charge of programming and buying shows. Ancier is credited with changing television by placing shows like *Married . . . with Children* and *The Simpsons* on the air.

RICHARD APPEL: A former prosecutor and *Lampoon* veteran, Appel joined *The Simpsons* as a story editor (the entry-level writing position) in 1995, under David Mirkin, and was named co–executive producer before he left in 1999. Appel's credits include *The Bernie Mac Show, Family Guy*, and *American Dad*.

WESLEY ARCHER: Former *Simpsons* animator and director. Archer, who studied animation at CalArts, is one of the original directors, hired by Gabor Csupo (along with David Silverman and Bill Kopp), to animate *The Simpsons* shorts for *The Tracey Ullman Show*. Archer directed twenty six episodes of *The Simpsons* and became the supervising director at *King of the Hill* in 1996.

HANK AZARIA: A phenomenally talented voice and improv actor, Azaria joined *The Simpsons* in 1989 to lend his voice to characters like Chief Wiggum, Apu, Moe, and Comic Book Guy (there are more than 160 to date). Azaria's acting career has placed him on such TV shows as *Friends, Mad About You*, and *Huff*, and films including *The Birdcage* and *Quiz Show*. He has won four Emmys for his voice-over work on *The Simpsons*.

DON BARROZO: Current *Simpsons* film editor. Barrozo has been with *The Simpsons* from the very first episode. It's his job to place the sound tracks into the episodes when they come back from Korea, allowing the director of an episode to see it for the first time with both the visuals and sound. "It's the closest thing to instant gratification that you can get in animation," he says.

JERRY BELSON: Partnered with Garry Marshall in the 1960s when they wrote for *The Dick Van Dyke Show*, Belson was part of a crew of writers and producers that included James L. Brooks, Marshall, Allan Burns, and Albert Brooks. He went on to write episodes of *The Odd Couple, I Spy, The Tracey Ullman Show*, and *The Drew Carey Show*, as well as the films *Fun with Dick and Jane, Barefoot in the Park, Smile*, and *Close Encounters of the Third Kind*. Belson was James L. Brooks's best friend until the early nineties. He died of complications from cancer in 2006.

BRAD BIRD: Former *Simpsons* executive consultant, he was essentially the supervising director at Gracie. When the first Simpsons episode came back as a disaster, Brad Bird was brought in, and he stayed with the show until 1997. Bird has gone on to become one of the predominant names in animation, directing the cult hit *The Iron Giant* and helping to make Pixar the juggernaut it is with *The Incredibles* and *Ratatouille*.

ALBERT BROOKS: Five-time *Simpsons* guest voice and a giant of comedy. Brooks's films include *Broadcast News* (for which he received an Oscar nomination), *Finding Nemo, The Simpsons Movie*, and the hilarious *Taxi Driver*. Originally a radio and then stand-up comic, he went on to write and direct short films for the first episodes of *Saturday Night Live*, later writing and directing *Lost in America, Modern Romance*, and *Defending Your Life*, as well as appearing in those films, and the ones above.

JACOB BURCH: An administrator for NoHomers.net, Burch is one of the chief operators of the largest *Simpsons* discussion site on the web.

KENT BUTTERWORTH: Former *Simpsons* animator, Butterworth directed the infamous "first episode," which resulted in the first season being delayed and Butterworth being fired. Butterworth worked in Ralph Bakshi's studio, animating *Mighty Mouse* and Dr. Seuss specials before being hired away by Klasky-Csupo.

MICHAEL CARRINGTON: A *Simpsons* spec script written by Carrington and his partner, Gary Apple, eventually got them an episode, "Homer's Triple Bypass." Carrington has gone on to write and produce many sitcoms, including *The Jamie Foxx Show, Sinbad, Martin*, and *That's So Raven*.

NANCY CARTWRIGHT: Voice of Bart Simpson, Nelson, Ralph, and others. Cartwright, the Church of Scientology's largest donor in 2007, came to Los Angeles from Ohio in the early eighties to pursue a career in voice acting, a pursuit she had been involved with since high school and encouraged by her mentor, Dawes Butler, the voice of Yogi Bear. After some minor roles in cartoons, she found her place as the voice of Bart, winning a Best Voice-Over Emmy in 1992, and improvising Bart's catchphrase, "Eat my shorts!" She has appeared in several sitcoms and films, and has authored a book, *My Life as a Ten-Year-Old Boy*.

DONICK CARY: Cary wrote for *Just Shoot Me* and the *Late Show with David Letterman*, coming to *The Simpsons* in 1996 (under Bill Oakley and Josh Weinstein). Cary wrote key episodes, including "Thirty Minutes Over Tokyo," before leaving the series in 1999. He is the creator and executive producer of *Lil' Bush* on Comedy Central.

DAN CASTELLANETA: Voice of Homer Simpson, Grandpa Simpson, Krusty the Clown, and others. An improv actor from Chicago's Second City, Castellaneta has provided much more than Homer's voice; his formidable voice and acting talents have helped create one of the most iconic characters in the American pantheon. He's taken home three Emmys for his voice work on the *Simpsons* and has appeared in films and in sitcoms like *Arrested Development*, *Entourage*, *Everybody Loves Raymond*, *Frasier*, *Friends*, and *Murphy Brown*.

ROB COHEN: A production assistant, Cohen was transferred over to *The Simpsons* full-time when *Ullman* was canceled in 1990, eventually writing the episode "Flaming Moe's." Cohen's younger brother, Joel, is now a writer/producer on the show. When I interviewed him during the writers' strike of 2008, Cohen was looking for his Mr. Spock ears to attend a *Star Trek*–themed writers' event.

JENNIFER CRITTENDEN: An intern on *Letterman* in the early nineties, Crittenden won a spot in the Young Writers Program at Fox in 1993, observing *The Simpsons* writing team for nearly six months. At the next story conference, she submitted material, was assigned a story, and was put on staff for Seasons 6 and 7.

GABOR CSUPO: Executive animation producer, *The Simpsons* (1989–92), and co-owner of Klasky-Csupo Animation, which has animated *Duckman*, *Rugrats*, and *The Wild Thornberrys*. Csupo escaped from Hungary in the seventies with several of his animator friends, setting up shop in Los Angeles in 1980. In 1987, his company won the bid to animate *The Simpsons* shorts on *Ullman*.

BARRY DILLER: Along with Rupert Murdoch, Diller invented the Fox Network and reinvented television. Starting in the William Morris mailroom, Diller went on to become chairman and CEO of Paramount in 1976, when he was thirty-four. In 1985, he was scooped up by Rupert Murdoch to help with Fox Broadcasting Company. He is currently CEO of IAC/InterActiveCorp., the owner of the Home Shopping Network, Ticketmaster, CollegeHumor.com, and Lavalife.

LARRY DOYLE: Former *Simpsons* writer/producer (1998–2001). Doyle came to the show from *New York* magazine, where he was an editor. His work is regularly published in the *New Yorker*, *Esquire*, and *GQ*, and he is the author of the bestselling *I Love You, Beth Cooper*, which has been adapted for the screen.

CHARLEEN EASTON: A writer and producer of TV shows including *What About Joan?* and *Kim Possible*, Easton was David Mirkin's assistant on *The Edge*, *Get a Life*, and *The Simpsons*. She and her husband, David Richardson—a former *Simpsons* writer she met on the show—remain close friends with Mirkin.

KEN ESTIN: Estin was a writer on *Taxi* under Jim Brooks and the show's creators, Glen Charles, Les Charles, and James Burrows. With Heide Perlman and Jerry Belson, Estin was a cocreator and executive producer of *The Tracey Ullman Show* in 1986.

HARVEY FIERSTEIN: Brooklyn-born Harvey Fierstein is one of two people (the other is Tommy Tune) ever to have won four Tony awards in four separate categories. He is internationally recognized as an icon of the stage and film and an important activist and cultural voice on gay issues. Onstage, he has appeared in *Torch Song Trilogy* and *La Cage Aux Folles*, both of which he wrote, and *A Catered Affair*, *Fiddler on the Roof*, and *Hairspray*.

BRENT FORRESTER: A writer on Judd Apatow's critically acclaimed *The Ben Stiller Show* before being nabbed by David Mirkin to work on *The Simpsons* in 1994, Forrester wrote scripts like "Homerpalooza" before moving on to write for HBO's *Mr. Show*. Since 1998, Forrester has taken chief writing roles on *King of the Hill* and the American version of *The Office*. His next screenplay will be produced by Apatow.

RICKY GERVAIS: Since he exploded onto the BBC as David Brendt in *The Office*, which he created, Gervais's brand of discomfort-turned-hilarity has produced an American version of *The Office*, *Extras* on HBO, and won him three Golden Globes, two Emmys, seven BAFTAs, and a Peabody. He has appeared in films, written a series of children's books (*Flanimals*), and hosted radio shows and podcasts. A champion of animal rights, Gervais has publicly demanded that the British government replace the bear fur in the hats worn by the Royal Guards, taken from Canadian black bears, with synthetic.

CHARLIE GOLDSTEIN: Former executive vice president in charge of production for Fox Television. When *The Simpsons* was being established as a series, Goldstein was one of the go-betweens for Fox and Gracie Films. It was his job to watch over the production of the series for Fox Television, which was paying for *The Simpsons*.

JONATHAN GRAY: A professor of communications and media studies at Fordham University. Gray's thesis for his PhD (from the University of London) became his first book, *Watching the Simpsons: Television, Parody, and Intertextuality*. When we spoke, Gray had just returned from collecting data about media consumption in Malawi, where, he said, Dolly Parton is huge (he met several children named Jolene).

DEBORAH GROENING: Deborah dated Matt Groening while they were both at the *LA Reader* in the early 1980s, becoming the driving force behind the cottage industry of mugs, calendars, and other products that the couple built around *Life in Hell*. The couple were married in 1987, and divorced in 1999.

MATT GROENING: The alternative cartoonist whose *Life in Hell* strips in *The LA Reader* (eventually syndicated in more than two hundred newspapers) caught the attention of James L. Brooks in 1987. Brooks was looking for someone to draw cartoons to fill in time between sketches on *The Tracey Ullman Show*. Groening came up with a family based on his own, named *The Simpsons*.

SHERRY GUNTHER: Gunther took over from Margot Pipkin in 1990 as Klasky-Csupo's animation producer on *The Simpsons*. She ran up against producers at Gracie Films and the execs at Fox; it was ultimately Gabor Csupo's refusal to replace Gunther that led to his animation company's loss of the show.

AL JEAN: With his writing partner, Mike Reiss, Jean worked on *The National Lampoon*, *The Tonight Show*, *It's Garry Shandling's Show*, and *Alf* before joining the original writing room at *The Simpsons* in 1989. Jean ran the show with Reiss for its third and fourth seasons, and then on his own from 2001 to the present. He was an executive producer on *The Simpsons Movie*.

HARRIS KATLEMAN: President of Fox Television from 1980 to 1992. He oversaw the production of such shows as *M*A*S*H*, *LA Law*, *Doogie Howser, M.D.*, *Dynasty*, and *The Simpsons*.

JULIE KAVNER: Voice of Marge Simpson, Patty, and Selma. Havner's history with Jim Brooks goes back to the series *Rhoda*, where she played Brenda Morgenstern to much acclaim (and an Emmy). Her success prompted Brooks to ask her to join the cast of *The Tracey Ullman Show*, where she took on the voice of Marge and a host of other live-action roles. A Los Angeles native and former stand-up, Kavner has appeared in seven of Woody Allen's films, *Dr. Dolittle*, and *Click*, as well as several comedic roles on TV shows like *Taxi*, *Lou Grant*, and *Tracey Takes On . . .* She has been nominated for ten Emmys (winning twice) and four Golden Globes.

ROB KENNEALLY: Kenneally was twenty-six and VP of development at Fox Television (the studio) when Barry Diller coaxed him to Fox Broadcasting to oversee programming in 1987. Kenneally went on to become president of television at Rysher Entertainment, producing shows like *Oz* and *Sex and the City*. He now works in the television department at Creative Artists Agency and is a reserve deputy with the LA County Sheriff's Department.

JAY KOGEN: The son of Arnie Kogen, a writer for *MAD* magazine, Jay reconnected with his friend Mark Wallace Wolodarsky on *It's Garry Shandling's Show* in 1986 and the two began writing together. In 1987, Kogen was hired as a young writer on *The Tracey Ullman Show* before being drafted by Sam Simon to work on the first season of *The Simpsons*. After he left in 1992, Kogen, who has won five Emmys, wrote for *Newsradio*, *Malcolm in the Middle*, *Everybody Loves Raymond*, and *Frasier*, which he ran.

BOB KUSHELL: Former *Simpsons* writer/producer. Originally a scribe on the HBO series *Dream On*, Kushell was a writer on *The Simpsons* for two seasons under show runner David Mirkin. Kushell went on to co-executive-produce *3rd Rock from the Sun* and, more recently, *Samantha Who?*, with Christina Applegate. If you look up Kushell's name on YouTube and Hulu, you will find some very funny videos.

STAN LEE: There is no person more important to the world of comics than Stan Lee. Born in 1922, he cocreated *X-Men*, *The Fantastic Four*, *Spider-Man*, *Captain America*, and *The Incredible Hulk* on his way to becoming chairman and president of Marvel. Lee made his mark on the medium with his complex characters, by giving writers and designers conspicuous credit for their work and by influencing a reformation of the Comics Code Authority. In 2008, he was awarded the National Medal of Arts.

JANE LEVINE: Levine was the publisher of the *LA Reader* from 1977 to 1984, serving as a mentor to Matt Groening's future wife, Deborah. Levine went on to work on the business side of the *Chicago Reader*, retiring from publishing in 2004. She cheerfully credits Craigslist with the death of free weeklies.

COLIN A.B.V. LEWIS: Lewis was a PA on *Ullman*, but Sam Simon brought him over to *The Simpsons* when *Ullman* went down in 1990. Lewis was worked in ADR, helping to record the voices.

TIM LONG: Long worked at *Spy* magazine in the early nineties and wrote for *Politically Incorrect* and *Late Night with David Letterman* before arriving at *The Simpsons* in 1998. While not a showrunner, he has been credited as an executive producer and one of the head writers (he is now a consulting producer).

SETH MACFARLANE: Creator of *Family Guy* and *American Dad*. Despite its cancellation (twice) in the early 2000s, *Family Guy* returned to the airwaves in 2005 and has become a billion-dollar franchise. MacFarlane, who has two Emmys and an honorary doctorate from the Rhode Island School of Design, recently signed a contract with Fox, making him the highest paid writer/producer in TV history.

TOM MARTIN: Former *Simpsons* writer/producer. A stand-up comedian with a few TV writing credits, Martin interviewed for *The Simpsons* in 1999 and hit it off with Mike Scully, staying on staff until 2001. Martin has since written for *Nikki*, *The Showbiz Show with David Spade*, *Clone High*, and *Still Standing*.

MICHAEL MENDEL: Former *Simpsons* associate producer and postproduction coordinator, Mendel reluctantly moved from *Ullman* to *The Simpsons* when it got its own series. Mendel was essentially a line producer—he worked between Gracie Films and Fox Network to make sure everything came in on time and on budget. Mendel left the show in 1992 and returned for the fifth through tenth seasons.

GEORGE MEYER: One of the members of the original writers room. Though Meyer had written for *The Harvard Lampoon* and *Late Night with David Letterman*, he came to Sam Simon's attention with a small comedy zine he was publishing out of his apartment in Boulder, Colorado. Credited with providing the series with its signature voice, Meyer is legendary among comedy writers. A committed environmentalist, he lives with his wife and daughter out west, but not in L.A.

RUPERT MURDOCH: The CEO of News Corp and by far its largest shareholder. Rupert Murdoch's holdings include the newspapers the *Times* of London and the *New York Post* and the television networks Fox and Sky One in Britain. He is ultimately the man to blame for *The Simpsons*, *American Idol*, and Bill O'Reilly.

BILL OAKLEY: A former editor in chief of the *Harvard Lampoon*, Oakley served seven years in *The Simpsons*' writing room, two of them as showrunner, with his writing partner,

Josh Weinstein. Afterward, he and Weinstein created the animated series *Mission Hill* and worked on Matt Groening's *Futurama*. They are currently developing projects, including the sitcom *Business Class*.

CONAN O'BRIEN: To be as famous as Conan O'Brien, one *Simpsons* writer told me, you would have to shoot a president. One of television's best-known personalities, the host of his own groundbreaking late-night talk show since 1994, *Late Night with Conan O'Brien*, Conan took over *The Tonight Show* from Jay Leno in 2009.

JOUNI PAAKKINEN: Unofficially, the biggest *Simpsons* fan on the planet. An early contributor to the alt.tv.simpsons newsgroup, the Finnish Paakkinen maintains the Simpsons Archive on the Internet, which has 1.5 million page views every month and 50 maintainers, and is a veritable library of *Simpsons* info. His book about *The Simpsons* is available in Finland.

GAVIN PALONE: A major figure on the business side of comedy, Palone represented many *Simpsons* writers, including Jay Kogen, Wallace Wolodarsky, Al Jean, Mike Reiss, George Meyer and, most significantly, Conan O'Brien. Eventually, Palone stopped making money only for other people; he has gone on to executive-produce series created by his clients, including *Curb Your Enthusiasm* and *Gilmore Girls*.

GARY PANTER: A member of the late-seventies music scene in LA, Panter defined punk art style with his drawings for *Slash* magazine and numerous album covers. His cartoons have been published in The *New Yorker*, *Time*, and *Rolling Stone*, and he has won two Emmys for his set design work on *Pee-wee's Playhouse*. In 2006, Panter, along with Will Eisner, Jack Kirby, Harvey Kurtzman, and Robert Crumb, was acknowledged as one of the Masters of American Comics by the Jewish Museum in New York City.

DARIA PARIS: Sam Simon's assistant during his days at *The Simpsons* and then afterward as president of Gracie TV. Paris is animated as Barney's redheaded date in the Christmas special premiere episode. After *The Simpsons* she went on to be Brett Butler's assistant and then a production coordinator on *Two Guys, a Girl and a Pizza Place*.

ROBERT PINSKY: The poet laureate of the United States from 1997 to 2000, Pinsky has published nine collections of his poetry and edited several anthologies. As poet laureate he started the Favorite Poem Project, which fosters the reading and sharing of poetry among thousands of young Americans. Pinsky is a professor at Boston University and the recipient of a Guggenheim Fellowship and the PEN award for poetry. His translation of Dante's *Inferno* has been critically lauded and is widely read throughout the English-speaking world.

MARGOT PIPKIN: The first animation producer for *The Simpsons* when it was still shorts on *Ullman*. It was her job at Klasky-Csupo to produce the bumpers, and eventually the series, as well as balance the animation budget. Pipkin who was pregnant with her son—left after the first season.

POLLY PLATT: With her partner and then-spouse, Peter Bogdanovich, Platt began her career in Hollywood under the guidance of Roger Corman. She wrote the film *Pretty*

Baby and was a production designer on *Paper Moon*, *A Star Is Born*, and *The Last Picture Show*, and was nominated for an Academy Award for Art Direction for *Terms of Endearment*. While she had no official title at his company, Jim Brooks described her as the "mother" of Gracie Films.

DOMINIC POLCINO: Hired by Klasky-Csupo to draw the second season, Polcino worked on character layouts and storyboards before being made a full director in 1994. He has been with Film Roman ever since the show moved, and is currently directing *Family Guy* episodes, like the famous *Star Wars* parody, *Blue Harvest*. His adult comic, *Lovesick Fool*, is available at www.shadycomics.com.

GYORGYI POLUCE: Former *Simpsons* color designer and the genius behind *The Simpsons* color scheme. Poluce had worked with Csupo at a Hungarian film studio, where she had colored a cartoon called *Hugo the Hippo* (an animated musical about hippos and Zanzibar, narrated by Burl Ives; Marie Osmond was also involved with the project).

DAVID RICHARDSON: Richardson had been writing for *Empty Nest* when the people at Gracie read his work and asked the young writer to join David Mirkin's writing room. Richardson worked on *The Simpsons* for a year before moving on to Gracie's ill-fated series *Phenom*. Afterward, he wrote for *The John Larroquette Show* and was co–executive producer of *Ed* and *Malcolm in the Middle*.

BRIAN ROBERTS: An editor and postproduction coordinator on *The Simpsons* from the early days at *Ullman* until he left the show in 1992 (the voice actors recorded him a rap song when he left), Roberts wrote one of the early episodes, "Brush with Greatness." He went on to a successful career directing sitcoms and other programs, including *The George Carlin Show*, *The Drew Carey Show*, *Lizzie McGuire*, *Everybody Loves Raymond*, and most recently *Little Mosque on the Prairie* (in Canada).

PHIL ROMAN: In 1948, when Roman was eighteen, he was inspired by the film *Bambi* to move to LA from his hometown of Fresno, enlisting in the only art school he could find that taught animation. After the Korean War and a stint with Disney, Roman worked with Ralph Bakshi and animated Charlie Brown TV specials. In 1984, he founded Film Roman, animating Saturday morning cartoons and eventually prime-time series like *The Simpsons*, *King of the Hill*, and *Family Guy*. He currently runs Phil Roman Animation, an independent studio.

GARY ROSS: Ross and his cowriter, Anne Spielberg, submitted their script for *Big* to Gracie Films, which James L. Brooks had set up to be a welcoming environment for writers in the feature film business. Ross and Spielberg were nominated for the Academy Award for Best Original Screenplay in 1988.

DOUGLAS RUSHKOFF: A humor writer and media expert. Rushkoff's books include *The GenX Reader* and the graphic novel series *Testament*. Rushkoff does commentaries on NPR's *All Things Considered* and was involved with the documentaries *The Merchants of Cool* and *The Persuaders* on PBS. He is a lecturer at NYU, where he runs the Narrative Lab, and his website is www.rushkoff.com.

BILL SAVAGE: A television, media, and pop culture expert, Savage is a member of the faculty of Northwestern University's English Department, where he lectures on twentieth-century American literature and popular culture topics such as baseball and animation. His essay "So Television's Responsible!" was included in *Leaving Springfield: The Simpsons and the Possibility of Oppositional Culture.*

HARRY SHEARER: Voice of Mr. Burns, Principal Skinner, Ned Flanders, and others. One of the industry's most varied and prolific talents, Shearer has worked in the performing arts since 1950: acting, singing, playing music, writing, directing, and working in radio. He was first cast on the *Jack Benny Program* when he was seven years old and has gone on to act in films as varied as *Abbott and Costello Go to Mars, Serpico, This Is Spinal Tap,* and *A Mighty Wind.* He's written music for films like *Waiting for Guffman*; has appeared on TV shows like *Saturday Night Live* and *Dawson's Creek*; and has hosted a weekly radio program, *Le Show*, since 1983, first on NPR and now on Sirius/XM. He has won three Emmys and two Grammys.

SAM SIMON: The third leg of the tripod responsible for *The Simpsons* (Groening and Brooks being the other two). Simon was a veteran TV writer and producer, with *Taxi, Cheers,* and *The Tracey Ullman Show* on his résumé when James L. Brooks asked him to run *The Simpsons.* Simon and Matt Groening fought over creative differences and, eventually, financial issues. The president of Gracie Films Television, Simon left the company acrimoniously in 1993. He now runs the Sam Simon Foundation, which rehabilitates abused and abandoned dogs and trains them to help the disabled.

YEARDLEY SMITH: Voice of Lisa Simpson. Raised in Washington, D.C., Smith (her first name is pronounced "yard-lee") used her acting talent and unique squeaky voice to land her small roles on and off Broadway, as well as on TV (*Brothers*) and in film (*Heaven Help Us*) in the mid-eighties. For Lisa, whom she has voiced since the shorts, Smith won the voiceover Emmy in 1992. She's since appeared in films like *As Good as It Gets* and sitcoms like *Dharma and Greg*, has written and starred in a one-woman show off-off-Broadway, and has authored a children's book.

ART SPIEGELMAN: Art Spiegelman, a regular contributor to *The New Yorker*, is the first cartoonist to win a Pulitzer Prize Special Award for Letters. His comics, detailing his father's experiences in Nazi Germany and then Auschwitz, *Maus* and *Maus II*, are considered among the great achievements in the genre. He knew Matt Groening through their mutual friend Gary Panter as "Gary's punk rock friend."

ANNE SPIELBERG: One of the writers who, in the eighties, worked with Jim Brooks and Gracie Films to produce films where the writer's role in developing the script was considered paramount. *Big*, which she cowrote with Gary Ross, was nominated for the Academy Award for Best Original Screenplay in 1988. Her brother Steven is also involved in the film business in some way.

MATT STONE: The cocreator of *South Park* (with Trey Parker), which premiered in 1997 and is currently in its fourteenth season, doing for Comedy Central what *The Simpsons* had done for Fox. When Fox and Stone's *South Park* film was nominated for an Oscar in

2000, he and Parker arrived on the red carpet wearing dresses popularized by Gwyneth Paltrow and Jennifer Lopez. Stone and Parker later said they had been on acid.

JENNIFER TILLY: An actress who has starred in more than sixty films (including Woody Allen's *Bullets Over Broadway*, for which she received an Oscar nomination), Tilly was married to the Simpsons cocreator and original head writer Sam Simon from 1984 to 1991. She has voiced characters in *Stuart Little*, *Monsters, Inc.*, and *Family Guy*. Still close with Simon, Tilly has gone on to become a poker champion.

CHRIS TURNER: A Canadian journalist, Turner is the author of *Planet Simpson*, a deeply insightful look into the cultural significance of the series. He is also the author of *The Geography of Hope: A Tour of the World We Need*. He lives with his wife and daughter in Calgary, Alberta.

STEVEN TYLER: Lead singer of Aerosmith, who have been touring since 1970, when they formed in Boston. With more gold and platinum albums than any other group, four Grammys, places in the Rock and Roll Hall of Fame and on *Rolling Stone*'s "100 Greatest Artists of All Time" list, they are, quite simply, America's greatest rock-and-roll band.

JAMES VOWELL: In 1978, Vowell founded the *LA Reader*, a civic-minded, left-leaning publication focusing on Los Angeles's subcultures. He hired *Simpsons* creator Matt Groening in 1979, first as a freelance writer, then as his assistant editor, publishing *Life in Hell* in April 1980 (Vowell also published cartoons by *Eraserhead* auteur David Lynch). In 1996, the *LA Reader* was sold to New Times Media, which closed the paper.

JOSH WEINSTEIN: A graduate of Stanford, where he ran their comedy newspaper, *The Stanford Chaparral*, with his partner Bill Oakley, Josh was one of the first writers added to the original room. They were showrunners at *The Simpsons* for seasons seven and eight, and consulting producers at *Futurama* in 2001 and 2002, after attempting their own animated sitcom, *Mission Hill*.

TOM WERNER: One half of Casey-Werner productions, the company behind *The Cosby Show*, *Roseanne*, *3rd Rock from the Sun*, *That 70's Show*, among others, Werner may be the only producer of sitcoms more successful than James L. Brooks. He currently lives in Boston, where he owns that city's baseball team, the Red Sox. He also helped Oprah start the Oxygen network.

ERIC WIRTANEN: A founder of the website NoHomers.net, where *Simpsons* episodes are rated, discussed, and gone over with a fine-tooth comb. Wirtanen had a fansite while he was in college in the late nineties—the most popular section of which was *Simpsons*-related—which he eventually migrated to NoHomers in 2001.

TOM WOLFE: One of the most significant authors, journalists, and critics of the last century, Wolfe has written *The Electric Kool-Aid Acid Test*, *The Right Stuff*, and *Bonfire of the Vanities*, among many other books. Known for his signature white suits, Wolfe is one of the founders of the New Journalism, and coined that term, along with "radical chic," the "Me Decade," and "Masters of the Universe" (when referring to bankers).

WALLACE WOLODARSKY: Wolodarsky and writing partner Jay Kogen worked on *The Tracey Ullman Show* before being hired as writers when *The Simpsons* got its own series. He and Kogen were the first writers hired on *The Simpsons*, leaving during Season 4. Most recently, he wrote the screenplays for *Monsters vs Aliens* and *The Rocker*, and played a supporting role in Wes Anderson's *The Darjeeling Limited*.

Acknowledgments

If the following acknowledgments seem long for a book, it's because this is my first and I had a great deal of help. *The Simpsons* history grew out of a story I wrote as a twenty-six-year-old associate at *Vanity Fair*, a good place to start.

I owe a Canada-size debt to Graydon Carter, who hired me and let me write for his magazine. One could not ask for a better break; I hope I honored it.

To Bruce Handy—a phenomenal boss, editor, and friend—who assigned me *The Simpsons* piece and backed me at every turn. Much respect and love to Wayne Lawson, the über mensch of Condé Nast who knew my mother when she was a "slip of a girl." Big thanks to Doug Stumpf for the early education and support, and to Punch Hutton, for her guidance and humor. As well, to Aimee Bell and Susan White, *Vanity Fair*'s sappers; their generosity made a world of difference.

To the brilliant and funny David Harris: *You're* the treasure. And to Michael Roberts, who let me hang out in his office, and once even told me he liked what I was wearing. I can't mention *VF* without thanking Chris Garrett, whose help was essential and who could have an excellent second career as a circus master.

I want to thank Anne Fulenweider, for her remarkable patience, and for making my year when she asked me to write a Hall of Fame entry back in 2004; the very funny and very gracious Matt Tyrnauer; Peter Devine, whose candor and curiosity made every day a little more interesting; the very zen Ian Bascetta; Bryan Burrough, my favorite Texan; Lizzie Hurlbut and Sarah Switzer, the most charming and fearsome duo since Remington Steele; Michael Hogan, for his understanding "Cheer up, Charlie."

The twenty-second floor was an amazing place to work, thanks in no small part to Marnie Hanel, Dana Brown, Darryl Bentley, Dina Deshan, Dori Amarito, Peter Newcomb, Jessica Flint, Abby Field, Matt Pressman, Jon Kelly, Ron Beiner, Chris Israel, and Rhoda Boone.

To David Kuhn, for whom I have great affection. Calling you an "agent" is like calling Lenin a "Marxist." If you are not the best, I am terrified to know who is. Thank you.

This book would be read very differently, or not at all, without the deft editing of Mitzi Angel at FSG and the keen eye of Denise Oswald—not sure what I did to deserve you.

To the indispensable Billy Kingsland and the incomparable Chantal Clarke—my hat goes off to both of you. Same to Jessi Cimafonte and Jessica Ferri. And to Kate Pastorek, whose research was key.

To those people in publishing without whom I'd be lost (even more so): Chris Bollen, Sarah Hochman, Ingrid Sischy, Nina Munk, Nathaniel Rich, Brian Coats, Carl Swanson, and Tom Wolfe.

And to names behind the acronyms: Amy Schiffman at PGI, Tiffany Ward at CAA, and Alex Galan at DAP.

To Simon Wilkinson and Jose Lourenco, my sometimes collaborators and stalwart supporters, for all their help and near constant mockery.

Love and thanks to Alison Pill for letting me be shameless and a million other smaller things. And to Sarah Wilkinson (roar, poof, dragon nuzzles).

To Henry Fletcher, Thobey Campion, Yasemin Emory, and Madeline Weeks, who all contributed in their own weird little ways; Amir and Annie, the smartest young couple I know; Sasha Suda, the Bohemian Queen of Bobst; Clara Bottoms and Laura Bickford— Lala land's hosts with the most; Noot Seear, who put a roof over my head, my king in mate, and taught my first and best lessons in NYC.

I would be remiss not to mention Damian Abraham, who shook me violently; Michael Fountain, who knows the correct spelling of Binscarth; Doug McGrath, who is too funny for words; Alex Cushman, Daniel, and the entire Macdonald clan; Dan Werb, Alison Lewis, Juliann Wilding, and Sarah Kennedy.

There's more: Angad Bhalla, John McSwain, James Lourenco, Jasmin Tuffaha, and all the residents of 2 Castle Frank.

To the dispensers of caffeine, food, and booze, the propellant for my katyushas; Enrique and the crew at Café Condesa—the best in the West (Village); Joshua et al. at Joe's; Sean at Rabbit Club; Harry and Dan at Max Fish.

I have saved my most profound thanks for my family:

My mother and father for their honesty, support, and all but common sense.

My sister Allie for her wisdom and understanding.

My brother, Chat, for being the single best audience on the planet.

My sister Anouk for her inspiration.

My favorite additives: Peter, Stephanie, Patrick, and Jodi.

—April 7, 2009

Index